Remembering *Annie Hall*

Remembering *Annie Hall*

Edited by
Jonathan Ellis and Ana María Sánchez-Arce

BLOOMSBURY ACADEMIC
NEW YORK • LONDON • OXFORD • NEW DELHI • SYDNEY

BLOOMSBURY ACADEMIC
Bloomsbury Publishing Inc
1385 Broadway, New York, NY 10018, USA
50 Bedford Square, London, WC1B 3DP, UK
29 Earlsfort Terrace, Dublin 2, Ireland

BLOOMSBURY, BLOOMSBURY ACADEMIC and the Diana logo are
trademarks of Bloomsbury Publishing Plc

First published in the United States of America 2023
Paperback edition published 2025

Copyright © Jonathan Ellis, Ana María Sánchez-Arce and contributors, 2023, 2025

For legal purposes the Acknowledgements on pp. xi–xii constitute an
extension of this copyright page.

Cover design: Eleanor Rose
Cover illustration by Annabel Hewitson and Eleanor Rose

All rights reserved. No part of this publication may be reproduced or transmitted
in any form or by any means, electronic or mechanical, including photocopying,
recording, or any information storage or retrieval system, without prior
permission in writing from the publishers.

Bloomsbury Publishing Inc does not have any control over, or responsibility for, any
third-party websites referred to or in this book. All internet addresses given in this
book were correct at the time of going to press. The author and publisher regret any
inconvenience caused if addresses have changed or sites have ceased to exist,
but can accept no responsibility for any such changes.

A catalog record for this book is available from the Library of Congress.

ISBN:	HB:	978-1-5013-5849-4
	PB:	979-8-7651-0604-4
	ePDF:	978-1-5013-5847-0
	eBook:	978-1-5013-5848-7

Typeset by Integra Software Services Pvt. Ltd.

To find out more about our authors and books visit www.bloomsbury.com
and sign up for our newsletters.

Contents

List of figures — vii
Contributors — ix
Acknowledgements — xi

Introduction: After the fall
Jonathan Ellis and Ana María Sánchez-Arce — 1

1. *Annie Hall* and the invention of film studies
   Annette Kuhn — 19
2. The story of Woody and Diane: Stars and hit patterns in the New Hollywood
   Peter Krämer — 39
3. 'Not a morose type': The Windsor font and *Annie Hall*
   J. T. Welsch — 57
4. *Annie Hall* as a memory-film
   Sue Vice — 77
5. I love speaking to you: Narcissism in *Annie Hall*
   Reidar Due — 95
6. Narrative transformations of joke-work in *Annie Hall*
   Ruth D. Johnston — 113
7. The mechanical bride: On not-knowing in and after *Annie Hall*
   Sarah Kennedy — 133
8. 'I'm not haunted by *Annie Hall*. I'm happy to be Annie Hall': The tangled relationship between Annie and Diane
   Julie Lobalzo Wright — 151
9. The Spanish Annie Hall: Pedro Almodóvar's *Mujeres al borde de un ataque de nervios*
   Ana María Sánchez-Arce — 169
10. 'Don't look back': The relationship between Richard Linklater's *Before …* trilogy and *Annie Hall*
    Jonathan Ellis — 191

11 Dancing and falling: *Annie Hall*'s influence on *Frances Ha*
    Jessica Hannington   209
12 'The sadness of goodbye in a funny movie': Desiree Akhavan's
    Appropriate Behavior and the melancholic legacy of *Annie Hall*
    in contemporary US film and television break-up narratives
    Hannah Hamad   227

Index   246

Figures

1.1	*Annie Hall*'s opening sequence shot: Alvy and Rob walking through New York	29
1.2	Alvy leaves the frame for the last time	30
1.3	A street shot from *News from Home* (1977)	32
3.1	The opening titles of *Annie Hall* (1977)	58
3.2	The opening titles of *Hannah and Her Sisters* (1986)	65
3.3	The opening titles of *The Godfather* (1972)	73
6.1	Annie dressed as Charlie Chaplin's Tramp	126
6.2	Alvy's birthday gift to Annie: a red see-through body suit	127
8.1	Annie's internal monologue ('lah-di-dah, lah-di-dah, la, la … yeah')	158
8.2	Diane Keaton as J. C. Wiatt in *Baby Boom* (1987)	163
9.1	Pepa dons one of her skirt suits (designed by José María Cossío) as she disposes of Iván's things; Iván is in a phone booth calling her	170
9.2	Spanish poster for *Annie Hall* (1977)	182
10.1	Celine and Jesse falling in love in a record store: *Before Sunrise* (1995)	197
10.2	Looking sideways: *Before Midnight* (2013)	198
11.1	In the dance studio: *Frances Ha* (2012)	214
11.2	Lev's photographic studio	220
11.3	Annie's lobster photos	220
11.4	Frances running home	223
12.1	In one of the many *Annie Hall*-esque flashback vignettes that structure the film's depiction of the doomed relationship of Shirin (Desiree Akhavan) and Maxine (Rebecca Henderson), Shirin's parents occupy the space between them in the frame, representing the barrier created by their ignorance of her bisexuality	236
12.2	Shirin's riposte 'You're ruining my twenties' to Maxine's accusation 'You are ruining my birthday' is her final quip of their relationship before they agree to break up, and is illustrative of the film's depiction of 'the sadness of goodbye in a funny movie'	239

Contributors

Reidar Due is Associate Professor in European Cinema and French Literature at Magdalen College, Oxford University. He is the author of *Deleuze* and *Love in Motion: Erotic Relationships in Film*. His current research is concerned with the interface between ethics and aesthetics.

Jonathan Ellis is Reader in American Literature at the University of Sheffield. He is the author and editor of several books on Elizabeth Bishop. Non-fiction work has appeared in *The Letters Page*, *The Manchester Review* and *The Tangerine*. He is currently finishing a book on letter writing.

Hannah Hamad is Senior Lecturer in Media and Communication in the School of Journalism, Media and Culture at Cardiff University. She is the author of *Postfeminism and Paternity in Contemporary US Film: Framing Fatherhood* and *Film, Feminism and Rape Culture in the Yorkshire Ripper Years*. She is a member of the editorial collective of *Soundings: A Journal of Politics and Culture*.

Jessica Hannington's PhD was titled '"Only Woody Allen Gets To Do That?": The Influence of *Annie Hall* on Contemporary American Cinema'. Her research interests include dance, contemporary cinema and intersectional theories such as disability studies, queer theory and race theory. This is her first academic publication.

Ruth D. Johnston is Professor of Film and Screen Studies, Pace University, New York. Related publications include 'Ethnic and Discursive Drag in Woody Allen's *Zelig*' and 'Technologically Produced Forms of Drag in *Singin' in the Rain* and *Radio Days*'. Current research interests include media archaeology, aerial vision and Kracauer's theory of the mass ornament.

Sarah Kennedy is College Associate Professor and Fellow in English at Downing College, University of Cambridge. She works on modern and contemporary poetry, fiction, film and the visual arts. She is the author of *T. S. Eliot and the Dynamic Imagination* and has published essays on Elizabeth Bishop, Judith Wright, T. S. Eliot, Wallace Stevens, Barbara Hepworth and Elisabeth Frink. Her essay on Eliot and Stevens won the John Serio Award 2019.

Peter Krämer is Senior Research Fellow in Cinema and TV in the Leicester Media School at De Montfort University. He also is a Senior Fellow in the School of Art, Media and American Studies at the University of East Anglia and a regular guest lecturer at several other universities in the UK, Germany and the Czech Republic. He is the author or editor of twelve books, mainly about Hollywood cinema.

Annette Kuhn is Emeritus Professor in Film Studies at Queen Mary University of London and a Fellow of the British Academy. Publications include *Family Secrets: Acts of Memory and Imagination*; *An Everyday Magic: Cinema and Cultural Memory*; *Little Madnesses: Winnicott, Transitional Phenomena and Cultural Experience*; and, with Guy Westwell, *Oxford Dictionary of Film Studies*.

Julie Lobalzo Wright is Assistant Professor in Film and Television Studies at the University of Warwick. She is the author of *Crossover Stardom: Popular Male Music Stars in American Cinema*, co-editor of *Musicals at the Margins: Genres, Boundaries, Canons*, and *Lasting Screen Stars: Images that Fade and Personas that Endure*, and has published widely on film stardom.

Ana María Sánchez-Arce is Reader in Contemporary and Postcolonial Literatures at Sheffield Hallam University. Publications include *The cinema of Pedro Almodóvar* and the edited collections *Identity and Form in Contemporary Literature* and *European Intertexts: Women's Writing in English in a European Context*, co-edited with Patsy Stoneman and Angela Leighton.

Sue Vice is Professor of English Literature at the University of Sheffield, where she teaches contemporary literature, film and Holocaust studies. Her publications include *Textual Deceptions: Literary Hoaxes and False Memoirs in the Contemporary Era*, the co-edited volume *Representing Perpetrators in Holocaust Literature and Film*, with Jenni Adams, and *Barry Hines: 'Kes', 'Threads' and Beyond*, with David Forrest. Her latest book is *Claude Lanzmann's 'Shoah' Outtakes: Holocaust Rescue and Resistance*.

J. T. Welsch is Senior Lecturer in Literature and Creative Industries at the University of York, where he is also Director of the Centre for Modern Studies and Co-director of Thin Ice Press. His most recent books are *The Selling and Self-Regulation of Contemporary Poetry* and the anthology *Wretched Strangers: Borders Movement Homes*, co-edited with Ágnes Lehóczky.

Acknowledgements

The origins of this book lie in a one-day conference held at the University of Sheffield to mark the fortieth anniversary of *Annie Hall*'s release. The conference was generously supported by a British Association for American Studies/US Embassy Small Grant and the University of Sheffield's Arts and Humanities Post Graduate Forum. The co-organizers of the conference, Jonathan Ellis and Jessica Hannington, would in particular like to acknowledge the assistance of Rachel Hughes and Sophie Maxwell for chairing panels and keeping participants to time on the day. Thanks, too, to School of English graduate Emily Cuthbert for designing a wonderful poster.

The commissioning, drafting and revising of work for this book has taken place during an extraordinary time of disorder and loss for everybody. If a global pandemic had not arrived, the book would almost certainly have been finished at least a year earlier. Industrial action on an annual basis to defend our constantly eroding pay and pensions has also slowed down our activity, as it must. Our commissioning editor at Bloomsbury, Katie Gallof, has been both patient and supportive throughout this process, especially in regard to our requests for extensions. The contributors have also accepted these delays with grace and understanding.

Jonathan would like to thank the School of English at the University of Sheffield for granting him research leave to complete the editing of this book. Undergraduate students at Hull, Reading and Sheffield have kept me on my toes since I first began teaching *Annie Hall* in 2001. A special shout-out to the first-year students at Sheffield who took Lit181 Introduction to Cinema in 2011. I could have kept talking about films with you forever. My Mum had awful taste in films, but was never afraid to cry at a Hollywood Ending. My Nan had better taste, but always fell asleep halfway through every Saturday afternoon film. Thanks, both, for filling my childhood with magical images. My brother has probably never seen a single Woody Allen film, but he does at least share my love for Indiana Jones and James Bond. Thanks as ever to all my friends who have kept me sane over the past few years, whether you enjoy accompanying me to the cinema or not. Joe Bray kept me company on the golf course. Maddy Callaghan let me complain about the parts of our job that don't matter and reminded me of the parts that do. Stuart Green has accompanied me to every new *Star Wars* film over the last few years. Deryn Rees-Jones is my best epistolary friend. Without Amber Regis I may never have seen *Wild Mountain Thyme*. Without Amy Ryall I certainly would never have watched *The Holiday*. Last but not least, a decibel-busting shout-out to my weekly film night companions: Ana María and Pablo (you'll be old enough for *Annie Hall* soon!).

Ana María would like to thank the Humanities Research Centre at Sheffield Hallam University for a partial sabbatical to complete the editing of this book and Jonathan Ellis for suggesting working on this collection together. I am grateful for many great conversations with Jessica Hannington about films, the trouble with an auteurist approach to the films of Woody Allen, and women in academia more generally. Colleagues at the Sheffield Hallam University cluster on Popular Culture as a Catalyst for Social Change, particularly Anja Louis, Esther Johnson and Amy Wigelsworth, have kept me going over the last, very challenging year with wonderful events and research plotting. Colleagues in the Humanities Department (you know who you are!) have been sources of support when things were tough. Many thanks to Harriet Earle for walks, cross-stitching gifts and comic-lending. Doug Hamilton patiently worked through all the university red tape so I could obtain copies of research materials from the Spanish film archive after Brexit (not an easy task!). Kathy Parsons, generously answering a stranger's call for help, searched through piles of *Elle* magazine issues to find the article I could not find. Lisa and Chris Hopkins have cheered on and mentored me. My parents first introduced me to films, and even though the films of Woody Allen (always dubbed on Spanish TV) were dismissed as 'not very funny' and 'weird', I owe them my extensive yet haphazard knowledge of Spanish and American film and television. Finally, thank you to Jonathan and Pablo: may our serendipitous film watching continue!

Jonathan and Ana María would like to dedicate this book to Neil Sinyard, film critic extraordinaire, but, more importantly, the best of friends and kindest of mentors.

Introduction: After the fall

Jonathan Ellis and Ana María Sánchez-Arce

This is a book about *Annie Hall*, not Woody Allen. It is not the first book to focus on the film. That distinction goes to Peter Cowie, who in 1996 published a short book on *Annie Hall* as part of the British Film Institute's Film Classics series. Rereading Cowie's study today, one is struck by the confidence with which he interprets *Annie Hall* not just as a film primarily by Allen but also about Allen. For Cowie, *Annie Hall* is a watershed moment for Allen's career and for 1970s American cinema more generally. 'Allen's films concern themselves with emotional politics', he asserts: 'Allen's genius extrapolates from the general to the particular' (28). It is 'Woody Allen's adoration of New York' that we notice in the film: 'Allen's camera [that] lingers on the Upper East Side' (19). Marshall Brickman and Gordon Willis, among others, are given very little credit for any of these formal or thematic traits. Even Diane Keaton, the actor playing one of the film's two main characters, is sidelined in Cowie's account: 'Although her special beauty and downtrodden wife would become familiar to *Godfather* audiences, it was Woody Allen who shaped forever her eccentric comedienne image in the 70s' (16). Cowie's comment sounds more like an example of film reviewing written in the 1970s than a piece of film analysis about the 1970s. Given the tone of what he says about Keaton, it is perhaps not surprising that his approach is dated in other ways too. An auteur-centred interpretation of the film goes hand in hand with reading it as autobiographical: '*Annie Hall* exerts a perennial appeal because of Allen's willingness – even eagerness – to share his most intimate experiences with us' (50). 'The distinction between Woody Allen and Alvy Singer becomes increasingly difficult for the audience to sustain, and soon we abandon ourselves to the comfortable intimacy of the situation' (24).

Do 'we abandon ourselves' to the film in this way? Did 'we' ever? Such statements make uncomfortable reading nowadays in the aftermath of Dylan Farrow's repeated accusations about Allen's conduct as a father and in the wake of HBO's 2021 documentary mini-series *Allen v. Farrow*, but it is important to remember that such statements were already uncomfortable to read in 1996, when the book was published, just four years after Allen's relationship with Soon-Yi Previn became public and an acrimonious custody battle with Mia Farrow began. Cowie makes two, very brief references to these events in his book, on both occasions entirely glossing over the nature of both what Allen admitted to (an affair with Soon-Yi Previn, the adopted daughter of his then-partner, Mia Farrow) and what he denied (molesting his adopted daughter, Dylan Farrow). Neither Soon-Yi Previn nor Dylan Farrow are mentioned by name in the book. Indeed, the events appear important for Cowie *only* in terms of the effect they may have had on younger cinephiles, not the people affected: 'Film buffs seeing the film in the late 90s may think more spontaneously of Allen's embarrassing court appearances after his break-up with Mia Farrow' (1996, 51). This is at best euphemistic, at worst an awful example of looking the other way. 'Most filmgoers remember *Annie Hall* with a smile and a chuckle' (10), he opens his close reading of the film. The chapters in this book remember the film differently.

Our book about *Annie Hall*, not Woody Allen, is a book about all the filmmakers involved in creating the film. It covers the production of the film and its early reception. It is a book about the influences on *Annie Hall* and the influence of *Annie Hall* on other films. It is a book in which Woody Allen is one of the people involved in creating the film, not the only person. It is a book in which Woody Allen's reputation, cinematic and personal, is debated rather than simply stated. Not every film critic or spectator will accept or endorse this position. When approaching contributors to write for this book, we received several articulate and principled refusals to take part. For example, we were asked why we were not amplifying the work of female, LGBTQ and indigenous filmmakers, especially those who document and decry abuses of power. In our consideration of female and queer filmmakers in the latter half of the book, we hope to have addressed at least one element of this criticism. Other potential contributors cited Allen's crass comments surrounding Harvey Weinstein in 2017 when, after initially appearing to make light of Weinstein's behaviour, Allen was forced to clarify what he actually thought of him. 'When I said I felt sad for Harvey Weinstein', Allen pointed out, 'I thought it was clear the meaning was because he is a sad, sick man'. This half-hearted apology did more harm than good and lost us another contributor to the book. They could no longer proceed with any writing related to his work. It was not their job to 'save' Woody Allen via a feminist narrative on Keaton (much as they believed her authorship to be essential to the characterization of Annie). It is not within our remit to 'save' Woody Allen either.

This book does not aim to gloss over or ignore the criticisms of Allen's cinema (and life). Indeed, we hope the book provides a robust assessment of what the film does well and where it might do better, not just in terms of its representation of romance and sexuality but also in relation to class, gender and race. In 2013, Joanna E. Rapf noted that 'the majority of scholars writing on Woody Allen are men' (273). This arguably accounts for the framing of films directed by Allen within an auteur framework that ignores other subject positions in the film and its reception. Martin R. Hall's edited collection, *Women in the Work of Woody Allen* (2022), goes some way to address this imbalance with an equal number of male and female contributors. This volume does likewise, consciously setting out to privilege previously understudied perspectives not just as a nod to diversity but as a central guiding principle to our thinking about the film.

Criticism of *Annie Hall* in relation to these topics is nothing new, though one has to go looking to find it. In 1986, Pauline Kael used her review of *Hannah and Her Sisters* (1986) to complain about both Allen's audience ('It's about people that members of the press can identify with; it's what they imagine themselves to be ... that's what the press is applauding – the romance of gentrification') and the preciousness of his filming technique ('the picture is all tasteful touches. He uses style to blot out the rest of New York City'; 43–4). A year after Kael's broadside, Neil Sinyard also refused to be swept along by uncritical appreciation of *Annie Hall*, noting that 'the shift in Woody Allen's persona from being an embodiment of urban anxiety to being an authority on it is not without its suspicions of smug superiority' (1987, 49). Sinyard was equally unconvinced by readings of Allen as a 'feminist' filmmaker: 'Woody Allen has never seemed very progressive in his attitude to women in his movies. He adores them, but does he really respect them? He loves their emotional generosity, but does he occasionally condescend to their intelligence?' (85). Two decades later, Renée R. Curry was just as repulsed by the edited nature of Allen's Manhattan, particularly in relation to race. 'The Allen template for centering whiteness on a city landscape has been problematic throughout his career' (2013, 286), she states, referring to Allen's depictions of Barcelona, London and New York City. 'It is difficult', she concludes, 'to imagine that the intellectual circles of Manhattan in the later 1970s would not have included significant numbers of peoples of color frequenting galleries, fundraisers, and foreign films. Allen has whitewashed Manhattan and significantly diminished the population of its peoples of color'

(287). The different experiences of the co-editors emphasizes this. While one of us initially felt included in Allen's world, the other felt repulsed. While one of us found Allen's jokes funny, the other was left cold.

Criticism of this kind has multiplied and sharpened in the last few years as authors have returned to the films for evidence of behaviour they believe Allen has been found guilty of in real life. In her 2017 essay for *The Paris Review*, Claire Dederer provocatively asks what to do with 'the Art of Monstrous Men': 'The awful thing disrupts the great work; we can't watch or listen or read the great work without remembering the awful thing.' To answer this conundrum, Dederer worked her way through Allen's back catalogue in an effort to process and understand her feelings about Allen's art now. Watching *Annie Hall* again 'was pretty undramatic'. In addition to still finding it funny, Dederer cherished the feelings it generated: 'To watch *Annie Hall* is to feel, for just a moment, that one belongs to humanity. Watching, you feel almost mugged by that sense of belonging.' Revisiting *Manhattan* was less straightforward. 'Allen is fascinated with moral shading, except when it comes to this particular issue – the issue of middle-aged men fucking teenage girls.' She identifies neither with Isaac nor with Tracy but with the grown-up women in the film who are 'brittle and all too aware of death'. Dederer does not know what to do with her conflicted feelings about the film. She admits to her reading of the film being 'disrupted' by her knowledge of Allen's relationship with Soon-Yi Previn, but wonders whether it would have been 'upsetting' anyway. Our experience of *Manhattan* and similar stories in Allen's work is that they have always been uncomfortable to watch.

There is no way of answering Dederer's question definitively. Some critics have always had misgivings about Allen's cinema, including *Annie Hall*, as we have already seen. Before 1992, such critics were in the minority, drowned out by those determined to see Allen above all as a cinematic genius. After this point, particularly since the publication of Dylan Farrow's open letter to the *New York Times* in 2014 and op-ed piece in *The Los Angeles Times* in 2017, it is impossible to consider Allen's work as a filmmaker without first coming to terms with Allen's reputation as a sexual predator. As Sam B. Girgus observes, thinking about his own grandchildren in the acknowledgements to his 2002 monograph about Allen's work: 'As they grow up, they never will know about Woody Allen and his work without also being aware of and connecting him to the controversy and family scandal that erupted around him in the early 1990s' (xii). To his credit, Girgus draws attention to the extent to which Allen himself contributed to this confusion of art and life much as he continuously denies this to be the case. 'In contrast to Chaplin', Girgus observes,

> Allen invariably plays himself, thinly disguising himself as various film characters who are themselves fictionalized versions of Allen's own manufactured identity as Woody Allen. In the case of Chaplin, the mask of The Tramp established some protection for his career in the midst of scandals involving young women. For Allen, no such cover exists. In Allen's case, the fusion of the public and private selves helped him achieve success, but as it turned out, the same merger of the public and private in life and work increased his vulnerability to painful exposure concerning his private life. He has not been able to inoculate his public image against an association with his private behavior.
>
> (1)

Allen, in other words, is at least partly to blame for our identification of the life with the work. Unlike Chaplin, there is no mask for him to hide behind. This is even more the case in a film like *Annie Hall*, in which both Allen and Keaton play versions of themselves, or at least characters close to their screen personas. As allegations about his past behaviour have been aired, repeated and repackaged with increasing detail and ferocity, more and more critics have felt emboldened to attack Allen via not just the accusations of others but also via the films he has created. *Annie Hall* has not escaped the fall-out.

That fall-out has been dramatic. As recently as 2015, *Annie Hall* was voted the funniest screenplay ever by the Writers Guild of America. Commenting on the Guild's decision, Lowell Peterson, executive director of Writers Guild of America East, said: 'I think it's a combination of Woody's unique sensibility and his commitment to drama as well as to joke. *Annie Hall* is the complete screenplay in that sense; it is that sublime intersection between compelling characters, dramatic conflict and great jokes.' The Guild's decision to name *Annie Hall* the overall winner was not as neutral seeming as these comments perhaps suggest. In November 2013, Dylan Farrow, in a feature article on Mia Farrow in *Vanity Fair*, went on record for the first time about Allen's alleged abuse of her in August 1992. On 1 February 2014, she also penned an open letter on a *New York Times* blog. Dylan Farrow's brother and Allen's son Moses Farrow defended Allen and refuted Dylan's allegations in an interview with *People* later that week. On 9 February, Allen denied the allegations personally in the Opinion section of the *New York Times*. When asked by *The Guardian* a year after these events whether their choice was a controversial one, Peterson surprisingly said,

'No': 'Our members voted entirely on the quality of the scripts and I think that many writers, maybe most writers, prefer to focus on that. When they are voting on these screenplays, they tend to put to the side the weaknesses, transgressions or allegations about individual artists' personal lives and make purely artistic judgments.'

In October 2017, when the #MeToo hashtag went viral in response to articles regarding allegations of sexual harassment and rape against Harvey Weinstein, accusations about Allen's conduct were raised again. The author who broke the Weinstein story for *The New Yorker* was Ronan Farrow, Allen and Farrow's biological child, and a vocal supporter of his sister, Dylan. In her op-ed piece for the *Los Angeles Times* in December 2017, Dylan Farrow asked, 'Why has the #MeToo revolution spared Woody Allen?' She directed much of her anger at the A-List actors who continued to work with Allen:

> It isn't just power that allows men accused of sexual abuse to keep their careers and their secrets. It is also our collective choice to see simple situations as complicated and obvious conclusions as a matter of 'who can say'? The system worked for Harvey Weinstein for decades. It works for Woody Allen still.

In the aftermath of Dylan Farrow's piece, many actors who had previously worked with Allen, including Colin Firth, Greta Gerwig and Timothée Chalamet, made statements in support of her or donated their salaries from his films to charity. In 2019, Amazon backed out of a $68 million four-film deal. In 2020, Hachette Book Group's Grand Central Publishing imprint pulled out a deal to publish Allen's memoir, *Apropos of Nothing*.[1] In 2021, the HBO four-part documentary mini-series *Allen v. Farrow* was aired.

Remembering Annie Hall was conceived at the time of *Annie Hall*'s fortieth anniversary, after Dylan Farrow's 2014 open letter in the *New York Times* but before the October 2017 publication of Ronan Farrow's *New Yorker* article, in the gap, in other words, between the time Hollywood still believed in Woody Allen and the time when he, like Harvey Weinstein, became persona non grata. Our aim is not to defend or explain Allen's behaviour but to consider the influences on a film Allen helped make in 1977, a film that has gone on to influence countless other filmmakers since then. Interpretations of what Allen did and did not do or did and did not say inevitably play a part in contributors' readings of Allen's work. 'Purely artistic judgements' (to cite executive Guild director Lowell Peterson's words) are, in our view, impossible.

One response to this might be to refuse to teach or write on films that feature the contributions of alleged or proven abusers. That is the position of film critics like Rebecca Harrison, who, in her chapter 'Fuck the Canon (or, How Do You Solve a Problem Like Von Trier?): Teaching, Screening and Writing about Cinema in the Age of #MeToo', questions the amount of time spent by academics on 'problematizing': 'That's a whole lot of energy expended telling your students or viewers about how awful that man is or was when what you really want to discuss is mise en scène, or the horror genre, or sound design.' Our response would be to caution against such either/or proposals, tempting as they might seem in theory. Why can't we discuss the 'awful' man *and* the mise en scène, or, better still, what about discussing the relationship between the 'awful' man and the mise en scène? Pure art (like the pure artist) is always an illusion. Having said this, forgetting the filmmaker is arguably easier than forgetting the film. Can we really pretend *Annie Hall* does not exist – that nobody remembers it?[2]

Remembering Annie Hall makes a significant contribution to the field of American cinema and debates about canon formation, film history and film influence in relation to representations of gender, sexuality, disability and race. It responds to arguments in academia and in wider society made in the wake of the #MeToo movement regarding the position of filmmakers like Allen and the treatment of films associated with them. By acknowledging the need to work through the complex and contradictory feelings that arise in re-evaluating (formerly) canonical works, contributors to this book look for ethically sensitive ways to respond to the challenge of looking back while at the same time looking forward. As such, the collection offers new readings, not just of *Annie Hall* but also of how to analyse any film. In so doing, it contributes to the erosion of patriarchal principles of canon formation, encouraging us to think of new ways of conceptualizing film history and intertextuality in cinema. The book addresses both the context of *Annie Hall*'s production and release in the late-1970s and its reputation today, offering dynamic and original perspectives on one of American cinema's most influential films, even as its director's status is under renewed scrutiny. Indeed, we think the book will participate in this scrutiny too.

Annette Kuhn was at the UK premiere of *Annie Hall* at the Lothian Road ABC in Edinburgh on Sunday 21 August 1977. In her opening chapter to this book, she recalls her own relationship with the film and with film studies more generally over the last half-century. In doing so, she looks at how film scholars might have read *Annie Hall* in 1977 via key critical categories at the time, specifically narration, authorship and genre, and how the film and its contexts might be re-appraised today via new concepts such as embodied spectatorship and revisionist film history. In the second half of her chapter, she analyses Chantal Akerman's 1977 film *News from Home*, another film screened at the Edinburgh International Film Festival that year, 'as a kind of intertext for *Annie Hall*'.

The focus of Kuhn's chapter, the contexts for *Annie Hall*'s production and reception in 1977 and the extent to which these have changed today are shared by other contributors to this book. Her closing questions importantly address the repeated accusations about Allen's own conduct and the impact that this has had not just on the reputation of the film but even on the willingness of spectators to admit having seen it:

> To what extent will basic aspects of cinema memory (when and where the film was first seen and so on) be admissible to recollection in the face of knowledge of its director's catastrophic fall from grace, especially when seen in light of the current #MeToo movement? Will women's and men's memories of *Annie Hall* admit reference to an innocent enjoyment of the film, and/or acknowledge a more complicated relationship, or even refuse any engagement with it? What might be the tone of such responses?

These questions are at the heart of this book. Relatively few people now admit 'innocent enjoyment of the film', if 'enjoyment' was ever the dominant emotion occasioned by seeing it. In the case of the contributors here, we are undoubtedly in the middle of 'a more complicated relationship' with *Annie Hall*, a relationship that still involves conversation, debate and disagreement. It is our judgement that the film can and should be seen and that the feelings and thoughts occasioned by it, whether positive, negative or somewhere in between, might be productively published, shared and discussed. Our title, *Remembering Annie Hall*, is not, in other words, a front for or safer version of a collection more accurately titled *Remembering Woody Allen* but a reflection of the film's important place in the cinema history of the past, present and future. Our focus is on a film, not a particular filmmaker, significant as one of those filmmakers may be in the marketing of the film and its subsequent reputation.

As the author of several books and essays on cultural memory in relation to cinema and photography, Kuhn helps situate *Annie Hall* as a 'memory-text' and in relation to memory studies. Sue Vice does likewise in her chapter on *Annie Hall* as a film 'all about memory … In extra-diegetic terms *Annie Hall*'s memorious state includes the implicit recall of its own textual history as part of the final form. The film has in turn become a memory-object, with a global influence on romantic comedy and self-representation'. Interpreting the film as a 'memory-text' or 'memory-object' does not close off awkward encounters, in Kuhn's and Vice's chapters or elsewhere in the book, with the film's other contexts, not least as an (auto) biographical film that might be related to Allen's own life story and/or to the life story of Allen's close friend and former girlfriend, Diane Keaton. Peter Krämer takes up this story, or rather the story of Allen and Keaton as film stars in the 1970s, in the second chapter of the book. Readers might be surprised to learn of Allen's film star status among college students (he was ranked tenth in a 1978 survey). They will be less surprised to read a summary of contemporary reviews of *Annie Hall* from 1977, the majority of which discussed the film via auteur theory as the transparently autobiographical creation of a single person. As Krämer points out,

> In this and other reviews the attention paid to the great auteur sidelined the title character and erased the actress, who was also its real-life inspiration, altogether ... When reviewers made an effort to discuss Annie Hall as a character at all, they tended to reduce her to the archetype of the lovable kook, completely ignoring the fact that Annie changes substantially during the story.

Such partial readings of the film stand in contrast to the popularity of the film among female spectators. Annie/Keaton was quickly becoming a fashion icon in summer 1977. In 1978, *Variety* reported that the film studio had even licensed an Annie Hall fashion line. Krämer's chapter concludes with the film's success at the 1978 Academy Awards, where it received Oscars for Best Picture, Director and Actress (Allen was nominated for Best Actor, but did not win). In her chapter, Julie Lobalzo Wright explains what happened next, providing an overview of Keaton's career in terms of her lifelong association with the film and spectators' continual desire 'to see her as Annie'. Informed by star studies, Lobalzo Wright examines the pre-history of the 'Annie-type' in 1930s screwball comedies and its contemporary iteration in the figure of the Manic Pixie Dream Girl. Her attention to Keaton's performance in *Annie Hall* and other romantic comedies after this ('the mumbling, the darting eye, and the nervous giggle') suggests that 'the character type is recognized more so than the star actress'.

Reading Keaton 'as Annie' is not the same as pretending the film is told from her perspective. Kuhn makes the important point that 'the story is told by the character Alvy, and all the events are presented as it were through that character's consciousness or point of view', before parenthetically recognizing that '*Annie Hall* is not a woman's picture ... however much we may love the

Diane Keaton character'. The contributors to this book concur with the first half of this statement; there is significant disagreement over the extent to which Annie is a character we should either identify with or love.

Disagreements about Annie's status as a feminist icon are particularly to the fore in Ana María Sánchez-Arce's chapter on Pedro Almodóvar's 1988 film, *Mujeres al borde de un ataque de nervios/Women on the Verge of a Nervous Breakdown*. Sánchez-Arce compares the impact of *Mujeres …* on Almodóvar's international reputation to the impact of *Annie Hall* on Allen's a decade earlier, noting that in both cases the films draw for their popular appeal on their respective stars' images. The chapter cites Susan Sontag's criticism of Almodóvar's costume choices for Pepa ('Here's this guy who's supposed to be a new breeze from Spain, iconoclastic and irreverent, reproducing this musty, old-fashioned image of women in high heels with their rears sticking out') and the director's furious response in the film's pressbook ('I respect the imitator of Barbie dolls as much as the woman who dresses like Charlie Chaplin, such as Sontag's compatriot Annie Hall') to address wider questions about the correlation (or misalignment) between costume and identity in film. An attention to embodied form, in dress, gesture and movement, is a concern of several contributors to the book. Sánchez-Arce also demonstrates the international dimension of Allen's reputation and the surprising ways in which the influence of *Annie Hall* is felt in a different national cinema. One could easily imagine an entire book on *Annie Hall*'s influence on French or Italian cinema, for example.

Another way in which Kuhn's chapter prepares the ground for other contributors is in her consideration of genre. In her breakdown of the plot, Kuhn reveals the narrative to be 'a mix of classical and non-classical elements'. There are 'at least four versions of the same story … the memory/association version; the romantic comedy version; the fantasy play version; and the "kicking around old times" version. … *Annie Hall* is an expression of the classic romantic comedy, then, and at the same time undercuts it with a self-conscious and rueful caricature of the expectations associated with that genre'. Critics of the film hardly ever acknowledge this fact, foregrounding one or two versions of the story over its messy totality. This might be one reason for the film's initial popularity on release and its enduring (if increasingly unacknowledged) influence: an astonishing ability to be all things to all people. Bearing in mind Kuhn's comments, perhaps we need to see the film less as a coherent romantic, or indeed anti-romantic, comedy, and more of a film that is simultaneously both and neither. Chapters that acknowledge the imprint of *Annie Hall* on films as diverse as *Mujeres al borde de un ataque de nervios* (1988), *Frances Ha* (2012) and *Appropriate Behavior* (2014) certainly suggest this to be so. Is *Annie Hall* a portmanteau film in disguise? A film, in other words, that tells several kinds of love story, many contradictory, not just one.

There is, of course, much repetition in *Annie Hall*, not just of lines and scenes but also of love affairs and relationships. Does Alvy know any more about why his relationship with Annie went wrong at the end of the film than at the beginning? Do we? In Alvy's conversation with Annie on the flight home from California, he compares their dying relationship to a shark: 'It has to constantly move forward or it dies. And I think what we got on our hands is a dying shark.' Alvy typically refuses to take blame for the failure of their relationship. His shark analogy is made in response to Annie's admission that she does not think '*our* relationship is working [our emphasis]'. While Annie accepts shared responsibility for their affair's failure, Alvy disassociates himself from what has happened and instead blames 'it'. In so doing, he becomes an observer of the relationship rather than an active partner, just as in the film's formal presentation he often steps outside of the film world to comment on actions that have just taken place as if he were a director of somebody else's story rather than his own. Every romantic relationship in the film is a form of ménage à trois: Alvy and/or Annie, plus the spectator. If we cannot intervene to change the course of events or take sides, we are undoubtedly given more than enough evidence to do so. Alvy and to a lesser extent Annie both have multiple confidants and friends in the film, but the person in whom they confide most frequently and intimately is us. 'If the film text were an analysand', Kuhn points out, 'we might say that it (the text) presents symptoms of obsession or neurosis'. Many contributors analyse the text in explicit or implicit psychoanalytical terms, from Reidar Due's chapter on narcissism and Ruth D. Johnston's focus on joke-work to Jonathan Ellis and Jessica Hannington's concern with nostalgia. Sue Vice's chapter on *Annie Hall* as a 'memory-film' rather than a romantic comedy also considers the contrast between 'a broadly achronistically presented narrative' and the tone of 'romantic nostalgia' that characterizes the courtship scenes of the film's mid-section.

It is difficult, if not impossible, to consider *Annie Hall* without engaging with Freud at some point. Reidar Due, following Paul Ricoeur's analysis of Freud, looks at 'the breaking points in Freud's texts, moments where the underlying philosophical stakes of psychoanalysis come to the surface'. Due applies this methodology of unearthing textual cracks to his reading of *Annie Hall*. He believes that 'the aesthetic charm' of the film resides in an unresolved tension between 'comic cynicism and romantic innocence'. Expanding on the ideas of Stanley Cavell on moral subjectivity, Due suggests that Annie and Alvy 'meet and separate at the site of a shared attitude towards life, as they appear concerned with themselves, yet not quite at peace with themselves. One could say that they fall in love because of their shared narcissism'. Due is equally interested in why Alvy and Annie fall *out* of love and whether either character can step outside of their own subjectivity. His concluding remarks suggest he has more faith in Annie to do this than in Alvy. Due, like other contributors to the book, is attracted to the film's ellipses and omissions, not just scenes that were filmed but then cut from the final version but also scenes that are implied or perhaps not even mentioned. 'It is a merit of *Annie Hall*', he states, 'that in spite of aligning itself so thoroughly with the authority of its protagonist, the film nevertheless grants enough independence to the character of Annie for us to prolong the story within our own reflection and think through what the film does not directly show'.

As much as *Annie Hall* invites us to remember what we have seen, it somehow also invites us to imagine what is not there at the same time. In Ruth D. Johnston's chapter on joke-work, she brings Freud and Homi Bhabha together to consider 'the joke's ethical dimension, which takes into account the hearer'. Johnston draws attention to the representation of Jewish women in the film and the frequency with which they are subjected to culturally stereotyping, even or especially when Alvy makes a joke about doing so. She offers a close reading of appearances by and references to Alvy's first wife, Allison Portchnik, as an example of the film's 'structural exclusion of the Jewish woman'. 'Her absence facilitates the forging of a relation between the teller and listener and produces a gender/ethnic imbalance into the joke-work that requires attending to the performative effects of the not-shown, the un- or under-narrated, the un-narratable'. What is 'un-narratable' in *Annie Hall*, and why, once we recognize it, do we feel such an impulse to narrate it?

Sarah Kennedy's chapter, suggestively subtitled 'On not-knowing in and after *Annie Hall*', provides several possible answers. It is the book's pivot-point, bringing together the concerns of the chapters in the first half of the book that focus on the history and reception of *Annie Hall* with those in the second half that look at the influence of *Annie Hall* on contemporary culture. Kennedy's association of the construction of *Annie Hall* with the fantastical machines made popular by American cartoonist Rube Goldberg, for example, chimes with Johnston's interest in canned laughter. Her comparison of Allen's revolving cast of female bodies to an 'assembly line' is picked up in Jonathan Ellis's sense that in 'Allen's films, there are one or two unique people at best; everybody else is making up the numbers'. Like other contributors to the book, Kennedy has faith in *Annie Hall*'s ability to outlive its ostensible creator. She characterizes Allen as 'not a magician, but a technician, a monstrous inventor', contrasting the control Allen exerts as actor-director-screenwriter with the quirks and unpredictability of the film he eventually released. '*Annie Hall* is so effective as a film in part because it retains a consciousness quite beyond that of its maker, of the uncontainability of the desires (and minds) it seeks to order and record – it knows that machines, too, run riot.' Kennedy responds to that which cannot be controlled or predicted by the film's patriarchal machinery. She suggests that 'Keaton's hybrid persona surpasses the material that was written for/about it just as Keaton surprised Allen by having a strong personality and original convictions'. Kennedy's answer to the question regarding what is 'un-narratable' in *Annie Hall* and why, once we recognize it, we feel such an impulse to narrate it, is to highlight the uncontainability of desire: our desire for an insight into Annie's inner life and for a different conclusion to her story, one not dependent on Alvy's fetishization of Annie as a Not-Knowing-Girl. The final four chapters in the book, from Ana María Sánchez-Arce's chapter on Pedro Almodóvar's cinema to Hannah Hamad's concluding piece on contemporary US film and television break-up narratives via Ellis's focus on the *Before …* trilogy and Hannington's close analysis of *Frances Ha*, celebrate films that give contemporary Annie Halls a fuller backstory and a less predictable future. They leave less to the spectator's imagination.

Freud is by no means the only intellectual figure to have a prominent role in evaluations of the film's philosophy. In one of the first scenes of the film, Alvy famously conjures up the Canadian philosopher and media theorist Marshall McLuhan from behind a film poster to humiliate the so-called academic expert who has been oversharing his interpretation of McLuhan's work with the rest of the cinema queue. 'You know nothing of my work', McLuhan tells him. 'How you ever got to teach a course in anything is totally amazing.' Alvy, as ever, gets the scene's final line: 'Boy, if life were only like this!' Alvy's anti-intellectualism in this scene is challenged by his actions and discourse elsewhere in the film, his promotion of adult learning, for example, or his constant recommendation and/or rejection of books to Annie. Sue Vice's reading of Alvy and Annie's very first meeting makes the important point that Alvy is not 'so different from the pretentious man in the film queue'. Name recognition for McLuhan is not what it once was. As J. T. Welsch observes: 'For many viewers, Marshall McLuhan might be better known for his *Annie Hall* cameo than his once-influential theories of media.' What were these theories? Welsch cites the distinction McLuhan draws between 'hot' and 'cool' media in his 1964 book, *Understanding Media*, in order to consider the role of typography in Allen's cinema, specifically the Windsor font often identified with Allen, the font that makes its first appearance in *Annie Hall*. Welsch's chapter uncovers unexpected origin stories for both the Windsor font and its appearance in Allen's film. He also analyses the analogous association of both the font and the film with a 'nostalgic style'. Windsor's blend of 'classical and whimsical features' is a perfect match for 'Allen's own blend of arthouse and commercial aspirations'.

Jonathan Ellis's chapter begins nostalgically, reflecting on his own cinematic encounter with *Annie Hall* via Richard Linklater's 1995 film, *Before Sunrise*. In so doing, he considers the influence of a film he had not encountered at that point and the frequency with which, following Linda Hutcheon's formulation, we often see the 'original' text after watching the 'adaptation' (2006, xiii). For Hutcheon, we need to give up 'the authority of any notion of priority. Multiple versions exist laterally, not vertically' (xiii). Given Allen's reputation nowadays and the impact that this has clearly had on access to and screening of his back catalogue, filmgoers are unlikely to have the chance to see *Annie Hall* at the cinema. Although Allen continues to make and release films annually, relatively few of these new works are given a cinematic release, at least in the UK or the United States. Courses on which Allen's films are taught, including *Annie Hall*, are also less numerous than they once were. This, too, is a consequence of the fall-out from the events discussed earlier. The likelihood of coming across an old or new film by Woody Allen is, in other words, increasingly rare. Allen's back catalogue has not been censored – you can still borrow or rent the films from the library, purchase DVD copies online and stream them on various services – so much as quietly ignored or forgotten about. The Allen brand is clearly damaged goods, and corporations, including cinemas, movie studios and streaming services, are keeping their distance from it. Cinemagoers who grew up with Allen's work and may have seen *Annie Hall* on its release may be nostalgic for their first impressions of the film and personal associations with it. Those who began following Allen's work after 1992 do not have access to such feelings.[3] From that year on, a film directed by Woody Allen had extra-cinematic baggage attached to it. Ellis interestingly considers nostalgia to be an important theme in *Annie Hall* and an important part of its legacy for contemporary filmmakers like Linklater. He interprets the conclusion of *Annie Hall* as 'an important questioning of nostalgia, of dwelling on memories that are simply that, memories. Allen does not prevent us looking back on the film we have just seen – the flashback structure of the film is to some extent the very essence of nostalgia – but he does prevent us remaining there'. Ellis considers Linklater's refusal to look back, what American non-fiction writer Sarah Manguso has termed 'ongoingness', as an extension of this process. He finds a concrete example of this in Linklater's use of the long take and the sideways glance, both formal techniques that place the spectator in the space between characters.

Jessica Hannington's chapter also examines the vexed legacy of *Annie Hall* on contemporary cinema. Taking inspiration from Jack Halberstam's *The Queer Art of Failure*, she examines *Frances Ha* (2012) as a film that 'dances and stumbles away from Allen's influence, creating a new space for itself amongst the plethora of films by Allen, and one that has a decidedly less androcentric focus'. Like Ellis, Hannington is fascinated by how contemporary filmmakers conceptualize the gaze. She offers a close reading of Frances's work as a dancer and choreographer. Frances, unlike Annie, has control of both her body and how it is seen. 'We see the transformative power of looking when it is held by the subject as well as the object, as Frances can adjust her body to how she wants it to be viewed. It is not the gaze that transforms Frances into art, but rather Frances's art that is transformed by her own gaze'. Hannington is careful not to romanticize every element of *Frances Ha*, however. In the conclusion to her chapter, she notes the 'film's notable lack of people of colour', wondering why the filmmakers 'repeat the white middle-class New York featured in Allen's films'. Is it, she wonders, nostalgia for nostalgia?

Hannington's concerns about the compulsory heteronormativity and uniform whiteness of *Annie Hall* are addressed by the final chapter in the book, where Hannah Hamad provides an overview of a cluster of tonally and narratively cognate films from the mid-2010s about failed romance and relationship breakdowns. Hamad analyses the reception of Desiree Akhavan's *Appropriate Behavior* (2014) as a self-styled 'gay *Annie Hall*' (the phrase was first used by the director) to consider 'the persistence of a problem often faced by women filmmakers. This is a problem whereby their work struggles to be seen or understood on its own terms, independently of comparison with a canonised male filmmaker'. This is 'all the more noteworthy in this case', notes Hamad, 'given that the filmmaker in question is a queer, minority ethnic woman of colour'. Akhavan has rightly objected to her work being limited by such comparisons. 'I don't see many male counterparts written about in the same way, as being the new Woody Allen.' Such comparisons would probably harm rather than help a woman director's career today. 'Being the new Woody Allen' is not the compliment it once was. Indeed, the phrase nowadays sounds more like an accusation or insult. Akhavan's point about film criticism still holds, of course. How can women filmmakers be read on their own terms, not somebody else's? Inviting comparison of one's work to a canonical male auteur is one means of getting your film a foot in the door. After that, the film can hopefully make its own way in the world.

Hamad's conclusion is echoed in spirit if not in words by all of the contributors to this book. After admitting that Akhavan was 'complicit' in encouraging these comparisons, she then defends such packaging of her work as 'a strategy of survival.' We do not need to condemn or indeed defend Woody Allen to recognize that *Annie Hall* need not be the first or only film we remember when writing about contemporary romantic comedies. A healthy film culture must have more than one cinematic touchstone in mind when writing about contemporary cinema. Just as nearly every film is the product of a team of people not just one person, so all films are a response to literally hundreds of influences, some conscious, others not. This is not the same as pretending *Annie Hall* no longer exists. It is impossible to ignore or undo its influence. 'I do not advocate the erasure of anything or anyone from film history', Hamad declares. 'We should remember *Annie Hall*, but I also think we should move on.'

Before the process of moving on can begin, we encourage you to look back.

Notes

1 The memoir was picked up and published within weeks by Arcade Publishing.
2 Jason Lee addresses many of these questions and the complicated background to them in his 2022 essay, 'Too Much, Too Young? Woody Allen's Life, Work and Women in the #MeToo Era.'
3 The decision to dedicate a special issue of the film journal *Post Script* to 'Woody Allen after 1990' was a tacit admission of this reality.

Works cited

Allen, Woody. 2014. 'Woody Allen Speaks Out', *The New York Times*, 9 February. https://www.nytimes.com/2014/02/09/opinion/sunday/woody-allen-speaks-out.html

Barraclough, Leo. 2017. 'Woody Allen Clarifies Harvey Weinstein Comments', *Variety*, 15 October. https://variety.com/2017/film/news/woody-allen-harvey-weinstein-1202590319/

Cowie, Peter. 1996. *Annie Hall*. London: British Film Institute.

Curry, Renée R. 2013. 'Woody Allen's Grand Scheme: The Whitening of Manhattan, London, and Barcelona', in *A Companion to Woody Allen*, ed. Peter J. Bailey and Sam B. Girgus, 277–93. West Sussex, UK: John Wiley & Sons, Inc.

Dederer, Claire. 2017. 'What Do We Do with the Art of Monstrous Men?' *The Paris Review*, 20 November. https://www.theparisreview.org/blog/2017/11/20/art-monstrous-men/

Ellis-Peterson, Hannah. 2015. 'Woody Allen's *Annie Hall* Voted Funniest Screenplay Ever Written', *The Guardian*, 12 November. https://www.theguardian.com/film/2015/nov/12/woody-allens-annie-hall-voted-funniest-screenplay-ever-written

Farrow, Dylan. 2014. 'An Open Letter from Dylan Farrow', *The New York Times*, 1 February. https://archive.nytimes.com/kristof.blogs.nytimes.com/2014/02/01/an-open-letter-from-dylan-farrow/

Farrow, Dylan. 2017. 'Why Has the #MeToo Revolution Spared Woody Allen?', *Los Angeles Times*, 7 December. https://www.latimes.com/opinion/op-ed/la-oe-farrow-woody-allen-me-too-20171207-story.html

Farrow, Ronan. 2017. 'From Aggressive Overtures to Sexual Assault: Harvey Weinstein's Accusers Tell Their Stories', *The New Yorker*, 23 October. https://www.newyorker.com/news/news-desk/from-aggressive-overtures-to-sexual-assault-harvey-weinsteins-accusers-tell-their-stories

Girgus, Sam B. 2002. *The Films of Woody Allen* (2nd edition). Cambridge: Cambridge University Press.

Harrison, Rebecca. 2018. 'Fuck the Canon (or, How Do You Solve a Problem like Von Trier?): Teaching, Screening and Writing about Cinema in the Age of #MeToo', *MAI: Feminism & Visual Culture*, 2 November. https://maifeminism.com/fuck-the-canon-or-how-do-you-solve-a-problem-like-von-trier-teaching-screening-and-writing-about-cinema-in-the-age-of-metoo/

Hutcheon, Linda. 2006. *A Theory of Adaptation*. New York: Routledge.

Kael, Pauline. 1996. '*Hannah and Her Sisters*', in *Perspectives on Woody Allen*, ed. Renée R. Curry, 41–4. New York: G. K. Hall & Co.

Lee, Jason. 2022. 'Too Much, Too Young? Woody Allen's Life, Work and Women in the #MeToo Era', in *Women in the Work of Woody Allen*, ed. Martin R. Hall, 205–24. Amsterdam: Amsterdam University Press.

Orth, Maureen. 2013. 'Momma Mia!' *Vanity Fair*, 23 October. https://www.vanityfair.com/style/2013/11/mia-farrow-frank-sinatra-ronan-farrow

Rapf, Joanna E. 2013. '"It's Complicated, Really": Women in the Films of Woody Allen', in *A Companion to Woody Allen*, ed. Peter J. Bailey and Sam B. Girgus, 257–76. West Sussex, UK: John Wiley & Sons, Inc.

Royal, Derek Parker, ed. 2012. 'Woody Allen after 1990'. Special issue of *Post Script*, vol. 31, no. 2.

Sinyard, Neil. 1987. *The Films of Woody Allen*. New York: Exeter Books.

1

Annie Hall and the invention of film studies

Annette Kuhn

The eagerly anticipated UK premiere of *Annie Hall* took place at the 1977 Edinburgh International Film Festival (EIFF77), where it featured as the opening gala screening, enjoyed by a packed audience in the huge main auditorium of the Lothian Road ABC. At this time, the EIFF was playing a part in creating film studies as a distinctive area of scholarly enquiry, with the 1977 Festival hosting a thread of screenings, talks and discussions, billed as a 'special event', on the theme 'History/Production/Memory'. These ran alongside the main Festival programme and sought to 'provide critical and theoretical work to accompany the events of the Festival as well as the Festival's practice in general' (Edinburgh International Film Festival 1977). There was no programmed engagement with the films in the broader Festival programming strand, but I was certainly not alone in taking part in the Festival's critical-theoretical 'special event' and also attending the screening of *Annie Hall*. This chapter will effect an encounter between the film *Annie Hall* and the EIFF's engagement with film criticism and theory – an encounter that did not take place at the time but which is illuminating, in retrospect, to imagine.

Reading *Annie Hall* in 1977

EIFF77's 'History/Production/Memory' event took place during a period of intense, and somewhat politicized, activity around the idea of 'film culture'. At the time, film studies barely existed as an academic discipline and film theory in particular was something of an ideological battleground. In recent years, the 'invention' of film studies has become a topic of scholarly enquiry in its own right (Bolas 2009; Grieveson and Wasson 2008; Polan 2007); and, venturing onto the terrain of the *disciplinary inquiry*, I shall consider first of all how *Annie Hall* might have been – and might still be – elucidated in terms of key critical categories available within the discipline in the 1970s: narration, authorship, genre. Second, I shall look at how the film and its contexts might be reappraised through the prism of some prevalent concerns within film studies today – new understandings of the cinematic experience, and innovative approaches to film history (MacDonald 2016).

While films and cinema had been objects of serious critical attention from the earliest years of the medium, a new surge in this kind of interest appears to have taken place within and around the film society movement of the years following the Second World War, an interest which fostered ventures in 'film appreciation', and cultivated cinephilia – a loving fascination with, and depth of knowledge of, films. An early focus principally on art cinema evolved into attention to Hollywood and to popular forms of cinema more generally, and a move to bring the teaching of popular culture into schools and further education. Alongside a number of institutional initiatives in the UK during the 1960s and 1970s, the EIFF, somewhat controversially, took up an active role in promoting and supporting the serious study of films of all kinds, maintaining 'not only a dialogue with film theory, but … also a primary platform for its dissemination' (Kuhn 2019; Stanfield 2008, 63). Paradoxically perhaps, cinephilia remained an aspect of, and indeed an important impulse behind, this concern with 'film culture'. Film studies,

> founded in the main by radicals of the 1960s generation, in some respects combined a commitment to taking popular culture seriously with a vanguardist stance towards creating new knowledge, developing a rigorous approach towards theorizing and tempering their cinephilia with a critical stance vis-à-vis the forms, styles and themes of Hollywood cinema.
>
> (Kuhn 2019; Kuhn and Westwell 2020, 209–10)

Between 1969 and 1975, the EIFF published six 'little books' in conjunction with retrospectives and talks focused on certain Hollywood directors – Raoul Walsh, Sam Fuller and Jacques Tourneur among them – promoting and provoking debates on the nature of authorship in cinema (Betz 2008). This approach to film analysis and criticism focuses on the ways in which the personal influence, individual sensibility and artistic vision of a film's director might be identified across their work. After 1975, the Festival dropped this theme from its events programme, exploring instead more overtly theoretical questions; and in 1976 and 1977, the 'little books' gave way to essays on various critical, theoretical and historical themes published in edited collections under the title *Edinburgh*

Magazine (Betz 2008; Mulvey and Wollen 2008). More broadly at this point, a central concern for film studies becomes to expose, through the act of reading or interpretation, subtexts in films – here mainly Hollywood films of the studio years – appropriating approaches and methods associated with ideological criticism, structuralism, semiotics and psychoanalysis. At the 1976 EIFF, the 'film culture' event took psychoanalysis and cinema as its central theme, and that year's *Edinburgh Magazine* featured essays on, among others, Jacques Lacan, Christian Metz and Julia Kristeva, and the relevance of their thinking to understanding meaning production in films and cinema (Hardy 1976).

In 1977, the year of the 'History/Production/Memory' event, the EIFF programme booklet prominently featured an announcement of the gala screening of *Annie Hall* on the Festival's opening night, Sunday 21 August. On the following afternoon, the first of the 'History/Production/Memory' screenings took place. *Moi, Pierre Riviere/I, Pierre Riviere* (France, 1965), directed by René Allio and scripted by writers associated with the journal *Cahiers du cinéma*, is based on Michel Foucault's dossier of the case of a Normandy peasant who in 1835 murdered his mother, sister and brother (Foucault 1978). It was accompanied by screenings of some short workers' and labour movement films made in Britain in the 1930s. The *Edinburgh Magazine* included extracts from *Cahiers du cinéma* on film and popular memory inspired by the journal's involvement with *Moi, Pierre Riviere*, alongside articles on cinema, and film history and historiography (Johnston 1977). Other screenings mounted in conjunction with the 1977 event included four episodes from the Ken Loach/Tony Garnett television serial *Days of Hope* (BBC TV, 1975), *Velikii put/The Great Way* (Esfir Shub, USSR, 1927) and four films made at the GPO Film Unit during the 1930s. The main Festival programme in that year featured a strand of films by female directors, with screenings inter alia of US director Joan Micklin Silver's 1977 feature *Between the Lines*; *Riddles of the Sphinx* (Laura Mulvey and Peter Wollen, UK, 1977); and a programme of shorts by filmmakers based in the UK and North America headlined 'Women's Cinema'. Also screened as part of this strand was Chantal Akerman's *News from Home* (Belgium/France/West Germany, 1977). Akerman's film, as I shall explain, may be regarded as a kind of intertext for *Annie Hall*.

Annie Hall's first UK outing, then, took place at a time and place of energetic activity around 'film culture', film studies and, in particular, around film theory. However, I recall no discussion of *Annie Hall* at the 'History/Production/Memory' event, nor did I give this absence any thought at the time. Did the two really exist in separate worlds? In retrospect, I would contend that the worlds of

Annie Hall and of 'History/Production/Memory' were parallel, perhaps, rather than discrete, and that a look at *Annie Hall* forty or more years on offers an opportunity to bring the two together. What happens if we put into a single frame the film *Annie Hall* and the ideas about 'film culture' and film theory circulating in and around the Edinburgh International Film Festival at the time of its release? And what happens if we venture further and look at the film in relation to the discipline of film studies as it exists today?

The principal critical concepts available in film studies at the time of *Annie Hall*'s release included questions of authorship, of plot and narrative, of narration and address, and of genre. What light is shed when these concepts are brought to bear upon a reading of *Annie Hall*? What questions or issues do they bring to the fore – about the film itself, about the serious study of films and about cinema more generally?

Authorship

The 'film culture' debates around the directors' retrospectives at the EIFF between 1969 and 1975 took an increasingly critical approach to the very idea of authorship in cinema, eventually allowing it to be acknowledged more or less exclusively in terms of *auteur-structuralism*, which

> no longer considered the director as the intentional creator of meaning: instead the director was deemed nothing more than a name given to a body of work identified by a common signature [so that] the real-life figures Sam Fuller, Howard Hawks, or Alfred Hitchcock should not be methodologically confused with 'Fuller' or 'Hawks' or 'Hitchcock' – the recurrent structures appearing in the films signed by these directors and given their name only after the fact.
>
> (Kuhn and Westwell 2020, 29)

This qualification sets strict limits to claims of authorial intentionality and allows for unintended, perhaps unconscious, meanings in film texts to be identified and decoded. In relation to *Annie Hall* these would be designated 'Woody Allen', the quotation marks emphasizing the distinction between the film as a set of 'structural configurations' as against a creation attributable to the person of the director. As far as authorship in *Annie Hall* is concerned, we might consider asking questions about the character Alvy Singer, as well as about Woody Allen and 'Woody Allen'. I shall come back to this question.

Plot, narrative and narration

In literary theory, these terms refer to a story or sequence of events (whether fictitious or true) and the order and manner in which they are recounted. In film studies, they relate also to the distinctive qualities of storytelling in cinema and films as against those in other platforms or media through which stories are told. Across media, narratives are very commonly organized around a basic enigma-resolution structure: at the beginning something happens that disrupts the world of the narrative, whose task then becomes to work the story through to its resolution, or closure.

With *Annie Hall*, as with any other film, in analysing the workings of narrative, it is rewarding to begin with a breakdown of the plot. This activity is highly revealing, and – a finding in itself – it is by no means a straightforward exercise in this case, because the plot of *Annie Hall* does not have a beginning, a middle and an end in the usual order (Table 1.1). That is, the plot is clearly not typical of the 'classical Hollywood narrative' with its characteristic linear enigma-resolution structure. What motivates the narrative? What is the aim of the plot, and what issues does it set itself up to resolve? This is laid out explicitly, or so it seems, in the Prologue: the character Alvy Singer sets himself the task of

Table 1.1 *Annie Hall* plot segmentation.

A	1. Prologue
B	2-5. Alvy's childhood
C	The romance 1: the memory/association version 6. Alvy and Rob, New York 7-9. Cinemagoing with Annie 10-16. Previous relationships; sex problems
D	The romance 2: the romcom version 17-21. 'Meet cute' and early progress 22-30. Difficulties begin (inc *visit to Midwest* to meet Annie's parents) 31-49. 'Love fades'; break-up (inc *Christmas in LA*)
E	Epilogue 50-52. 'I miss Annie'; Lobster joke reprise fails 53-55. *Alvy in LA*; Annie rejects him. The fantasy play (the romance version 3) 56-57. Coda: 'Kicking around old times' (the romance version 4). 'I need the eggs'

understanding what went wrong in his relationship with Annie Hall. Is there a resolution? Does Alvy, and does the viewer, come to any conclusion about this by the end of the film?

Alvy's question implies that what follows will be an exploration (by him) of certain aspects of his own past. But the plot engages several distinct pasts, and these are not always clearly delineated from each other, nor even from the 'present tense' of the film, whatever that is. At the same time, the plot does feature some very classical elements: this is especially true of segment D, on which more below. What a breakdown of *Annie Hall*'s plot reveals is that the narrative is a mix of classical and non-classical elements, and indeed some critics have asked whether the film's plot is modernist (Schatz 1982). What does the mix of classical and non-classical elements do to how we think about *Annie Hall*'s plot?

It is impossible, however, to separate the plot structure of *Annie Hall* from the way the film's story is told – its *narration*. The element of narrative voice, narrative viewpoint or address in fact remains consistent – or rather, consistently inconsistent – throughout the film. The story is told by the character Alvy, and all the events are presented as it were through that character's consciousness or point of view (*Annie Hall* is not a woman's picture, then, however much we may love the Diane Keaton character). But who is Alvy? In the famous moment in the Prologue when the comedian performing a stand-up routine direct to camera morphs into a fictional character ('Annie and I broke up'), there is a slippage: between the personae of an apparently real-life comedian (whom we will probably recognize as Woody Allen) and the fictional character, Alvy Singer. Such distanciating moments recur several times through the film.

Nonetheless, the narrative viewpoint remains consistently 'with' the central male character. This does not make the narration stable, however. Another significant point revealed by the plot breakdown is that Alvy's enquiry into the failure of his relationship with Annie takes the form of at least four versions of the same story: what I have called in turn the memory/association version, the romantic comedy version, the fantasy play version and the 'kicking around old times' version. These accounts are in varying degrees fragmented and repetitious. If the film text were an analysand, we might say that it (the text) presents symptoms of obsession or neurosis (the film was of course billed as a 'nervous romance'). In the first version of Alvy's story (segment C in the plot breakdown), there is a particularly marked jumping around in time, and what we see are events, or rather memories of events, that are linked in the telling more by association than by any causal narrative logic. This version works very similarly to a mode of expression that I have called elsewhere a 'memory text', in that it embodies similar qualities of fragmentation, vignettishness, repetition, jumping around in time and so on (Kuhn 2000).

In essence, then, Alvy's quest is not worked through or resolved through the narration: it is simply worked over and over in rehashed versions of the same events and situations. The film's story – its content as well as its mode of narration – is reminiscent of Freud's famously incomplete case study of his hysteric patient 'Dora' (Freud 1977). Freud's write-up of the case is full of repetitions, and over the years after it was first published, he continued to revisit the essay, adding footnotes and fresh interpretations. Freud's problem was that 'Dora' had got away from him, just as Annie has got away from Alvy. The story (which in both cases is about what 'went wrong' in a relationship) cannot come to a satisfactory conclusion. It cannot be told in a straightforward way. To put it another way, as Marilyn Fabe notes, as traces of lived experience, memories can be (and here have been) rearranged (Fabe 2014, 190). Alvy's closing 'eggs' quip suggests that the same thing will keep on happening. The 'neurotic' narration in *Annie Hall,* alongside the self-presentation of the 'narrator', clearly invites an attribution of the text's 'symptoms' to the character, Alvy – or, perhaps better, conflates the two. Whichever, a symptomatic reading of the film text, as propounded within an emergent discipline of film studies at the time *Annie Hall* was released, offers an illuminating interpretation.

Genre

Questions around genre have long been a staple of film studies, and serious study of certain Hollywood genres, such as the Western and the gangster film, was important in the shift of focus that took place in the 1960s and 1970s from 'film appreciation' towards the scholarly study of films and cinema, where work on genre divides into two main strands: first, and more prominently, the study of individual film genres, and second, enquiries into genre seen as a system of expectations and conventions that circulates between film industry, film texts and cinemagoers. The former approach involves classifying films according to repetitions of iconography, mise en scène, plot themes, situations, characters and so on, with films sometimes also grouped in terms of characteristic modes of expression or reception (e.g. the 'weepie' or the thriller). The romantic comedy is a subgenre of the comedy film: it invites the response of laughter, and romance is integral and interdependent with comedic elements:

> In the romantic comedy the formal characteristics of the comedy film – a lightness of tone and a narrative resolution governed by harmony, reconciliation and happiness – shape the telling of a 'boy-meets-girl' story in which a (more often than not) white, heterosexual, middle-class, couple successfully overcome a series of obstacles to their romantic union/marriage.
>
> (Kuhn and Westwell 2020, 410)

In his study of the Hollywood romantic comedy, Leger Grindon looks at the defining features of the genre and traces their evolution or transformation over time. The romantic comedy's basic plot structure, he argues, follows the sequence: unfulfilled desire, the meeting ('meet cute'), fun together, obstacles arise, the journey, new conflicts, the choice, the crisis, epiphany and resolution (Grindon 2011, 9–11). He emphasizes that 'a work may select from, vary, or add to this narrative pattern, but still operate within the conventions of the genre' (11). Grindon's book includes a chapter on *Annie Hall*, a film which is at once illuminating and challenging when considered in terms of genre, and which Grindon characterizes as marking a 'seismic shift in the shape of the romantic comedy genre' (150). It has already been noted that the story of the Alvy-Annie romance is told at least four times over in the film. One of these versions (segment D of the plot breakdown) is narrated very much in the Hollywood romantic comedy mode as laid out in Grindon's schema. Another – the third, 'wish-fulfilment', version (segment E) – then sends up the expectations of 'happy ever after' held out by the romcom version. *Annie Hall* is an expression of the classic romantic comedy, then – and at the same time undercuts it with a self-conscious and rueful caricature of the expectations associated with that genre.

Nonetheless, it *is* worth reminding ourselves that comedy in all its forms is 'permitted' – and indeed in some variants is even expected – to incorporate departures from the norm of the classical narrative – particularly in that verbal and visual gags routinely interrupt, or even disrupt, the flow of the plot, bringing a quality of self-reflexivity to the narration. This, in other words, is one of the genre's conventions. Therefore, such moments in a romantic comedy should not necessarily be regarded as subversive. Looked at in generic terms, then, should *Annie Hall* be regarded as transgressive, or conventional, or both? In approaching this question, it is well to attend to the film's prominent intertextual elements. These are at their most evident in expressions of cinephilia and 'quotations' from films: allusions to the art cinema canon (Ingmar Bergman's *Ansikte mot ansikte/Face to Face* (Sweden, 1976) and *Le chagrin et la pitié/The Sorrow and the Pity* (Marcel Ophuls, Switzerland/West Germany, 1969)), as well as to Disney's *Snow White and the Seven Dwarfs* (US, 1937), a formally and technically innovative film in its time and a major feature of childhood memory for Allen's/Alvy's generation. Though less explicit, expressions of intertextuality are also discernible in the film's adoption of elements of cinematic style, approaches to acting and performance, and modes of narration that may be regarded as more characteristic of European art cinema than of the Hollywood romantic comedy (Fabe 2014; Schatz 1982).

Reading *Annie Hall* today

In 1977, therefore, *Annie Hall* would undoubtedly have repaid analysis drawing on concepts and methods that were available at the time within film studies. Indeed, it still repays such attention. The discipline has evolved considerably since the 1970s, however; and as we remember *Annie Hall,* it is worthwhile to consider how the film might respond to a re-appraisal in light of current concerns within film studies – concerns such as a broadening understanding of the nature of the cinematic experience (via concepts such as embodied spectatorship and filmic space) as well as extended conceptualizations of, and new methodological approaches in, film history (including 'revisionist' film history and questions around cinema memory). Approaching *Annie Hall* through the prism of these current concerns stands to refresh, renew, recreate and also – as I shall suggest – complicate the film for later generations of film lovers and film scholars.

The cinematic experience

The term *embodied spectatorship* signals a shift in attention away from looking as the sole component of viewers' engagement with films, and draws on notions of *haptic visuality,*

> [a] sense of physical touching or being touched engendered by an organization of the film image in which [the image's] material presence is foregrounded and which evokes close engagement with surface detail and texture. This mode of engagement can take various forms: for example, the viewer may be invited to

contemplate the image itself rather than, say, being pulled into a narrative flow; and/or the viewer may become immersed in, or pulled into, the images on the screen and the sensations they produce. In psychology, haptic perception combines the tactile (the sense of touch), the kinaesthetic (relating to an inner sense of movement), and the proprioceptive (relating to a sense of the body's position achieved via responses to stimuli from inside the body) …. Work on haptic visuality and embodied spectatorship is part of a more general critique of the centrality of vision in film theory that is advanced by proponents of the view that film engages more of the senses than merely vision.

(Kuhn and Westwell 2020, 236)

The kinaesthetic and proprioceptive aspects of embodied spectatorship are most obviously at work in engagements with – or immersion in – films and viewing contexts where the viewer experiences inner sensations of moving, or being moved, through space – hurled along, say, or sucked into an abyss – or simply feels drawn into the film's spaces. Here, then, it can be productive when analysing a film also to consider how *filmic space* is organized. This may involve looking at the relationship between the different spaces and places set out within (and beyond) the film frame; at how these are expressed through camera movement, shot scale, shot duration, framing, composition and so on; and at how they are articulated through editing. As with the plot breakdown, a systematic exercise such as this can generate insights into the specific qualities of the cinematic experience that may be evoked by a particular film.

Looking at *Annie Hall* in this way brings to light some striking features of the film's organization of both narrative space (setting, place) and filmic space. Commentators have noted the prominence of New York City as a setting in many of Woody Allen's films (Cowie 1996), and indeed story action in *Annie Hall* moves beyond New York City on only three occasions, each of which is clearly constructed as very much 'other' from Alvy's standpoint; and each of which presages, precipitates or confirms failure in his relationship with Annie. The romcom version of Alvy's story (segment D in the plot breakdown) includes scenes set in the Midwest (Alvy meets Annie's parents) and in California (Alvy spends Christmas away from New York). In the Epilogue (segment E), Alvy follows Annie to Los Angeles to try and get her back, but is firmly rejected. While these shifts of *place* are clearly significant in terms of the film's plotline, examination of aspects of the organization of *filmic space* in *Annie Hall* may reveal yet more. How, say, is the opposition New York *versus* Not New York figured through framing, shot scale, editing and other formal or expressive elements? How does the film organize kinesis: that is to say, how does the framing and timing of movement in and through its spaces work, and how does this solicit embodied forms of viewer engagement?

In *Annie Hall,* average shot length (ASL) is relatively high, an observation that sits alongside the observation that the film is closer in style to European art cinema than to Hollywood. And indeed, *Annie Hall* certainly features some unusually long takes. In particular, some scenes shot in the streets of New York City combine noticeably long takes with considerable redundancy in terms of plot. For example, the first version of the Alvy-Annie romance story (segment C in the plot breakdown) opens with a single take lasting 75 seconds (Figure 1.1). This *sequence shot* shows Alvy and his friend Rob walking side-by-side alongside a busy New York street. As the shot opens, the pair is just about visible in the far distance, but their conversation is audible. In fact, at this point Alvy is doing all the talking. As they move towards camera, the characters fill more and more of the frame, and at some 55 seconds in, the camera starts tracking back, keeping the characters, who are still walking, in medium two-shot. The conversation turns to California: Rob says he wants to escape New York to live there, but Alvy hates the idea. The sequence closes as Alvy tells Rob that he is on his way to meet Annie, and the two men move out of frame. The opening seconds of this sequence shot function in the same way as an establishing shot would in a film in the classical style: they set the scene in terms of place or location. But in comparison with the classical style, they do so with some redundancy, with foregrounded emphasis on the setting and its distinctive, recognizably New York, features – buildings, people,

Figure 1.1 *Annie Hall*'s opening sequence shot: Alvy and Rob walking through New York.

traffic, ambient noise. At the same time, however, the shot eventually does the very classical job of establishing character and moving the plot along: the discussion about California and its otherness for Alvy pays off in later scenes; and Alvy's observation that he is late for his rendezvous with Annie brings the story back to the central theme (and 'enigma'), the Alvy–Annie relationship.

Annie Hall's bittersweet closing sequence shot consists of a one-minute take with static camera, shot from inside a café: a distanced viewpoint on Alvy and Annie, who are seen mid-frame and in long shot, standing close together on the busy street outside. They have met by chance in Manhattan and, in the fourth retelling of the romance story (Segment E), have been 'kicking around old times'. Their conversation is inaudible, the characters onscreen dwarfed by their surroundings. On the soundtrack, Annie sings her signature tune, 'Seems like old times', and in voice over Alvy talks about this being their final meeting. Just short of halfway into the shot, Annie walks away, exiting frame left. Four lanes of traffic begin to move towards camera when the traffic light changes. Alvy turns and exits frame right (Figure 1.2): in voice-over, on the subject of relationships and their difficulties, he recalls an old joke: 'I need the eggs.'

In *Annie Hall*, New York City figures as a topic in its own right as well as a setting for the narrative. In these moments, certainly, *Annie Hall* becomes a film about New York, and New York figures as a character in a troubled relationship. In both these respects – the centrality of New York City as setting, topic, and also as protagonist in a relationship – *Annie Hall* has much in common with a very different film showcased at EIFF77, the Belgian filmmaker Chantal Akerman's *News from Home*:

Figure 1.2 Alvy leaves the frame for the last time.

> *News from Home* is a film about New York. The images are of New York. The soundtrack is partly composed of letters my mother sent me from Brussels. They're love letters. My mother was asking me when I'd come back.
>
> (Edinburgh International Film Festival 1977, 19)

Akerman spent some years in New York City in the early 1970s, becoming acquainted with the North American experimental and avant-garde film scene before returning to Europe. In 1976 she went back to the city and shot *News from Home*. The film, in many respects a love letter to New York, is almost 90 minutes in running time, with an ASL of around 90 seconds. It is composed of shots of streets, subways and other city spaces, and includes some extremely long takes, with audio of the city's sounds along with Akerman's voice over, reading from letters she received from her mother whilst she was away from home.

I saw *News from Home* for the first time at EIFF77, and did not see it again until many years later. (Akerman's *Jeanne Dielman, 23 Quai du Commerce, 1080 Bruxelles*, which has since become a feminist classic, had been screened at the previous year's Festival.) I have no specific memory of this my first viewing of *News from Home*, but do recall my excitement at its *hommage* to Michael Snow (of *Wavelength* fame): I was a member of the London Filmmakers' Co-operative at the time and had become well acquainted with the Canadian filmmaker's *oeuvre*. Latterly, I have also been inspired by the film's mother-daughter dynamic, a theme that was to become central in much of Akerman's subsequent work. Over the years, I have carried around in my imagination quite specific remembered sounds and images from *News from Home*; and on re-viewing *Annie Hall* recently after several decades, was struck by some intriguing points of comparison between the two films in terms of their respective sensibilities around, and filmic renderings of, the city's public spaces. In both films, different as they are, New York City figures as both setting and topic; and in both, the New York *versus* Not New York tension is in different ways absolutely central. Both films also solicit an embodied engagement with the spaces of New York City, *News from Home* pervasively and *Annie Hall*, as I have suggested, intermittently but conspicuously.

A 46-second shot in *News from Home* offers a telling counterpoint to the two sequences from *Annie Hall* discussed above. The view, from a static camera, is of a busy intersection in New York City, with traffic flowing in several directions. Random groups of pedestrians walk towards camera, while others walk away from it, as all approach the cross street and wait for the 'walk' light to show. On the soundtrack the ambient noise of the New York traffic almost drowns out the voiced-over words from the mother's letters from home – letters from 'Not New York'. Four men cross the street and walk towards the camera (Figure 1.3); they separate into pairs and exit frame on either side of it. Here, as throughout *News from Home*, the viewer is given time to contemplate a statically framed image: an image, however, whose edges enclose a great deal of (unstaged) action. The experience is one of distanced observation – perhaps a stranger's or a foreigner's view: the viewer observes the busy action within the frame, while other senses are engaged, perhaps in a less detached manner, by the overwhelming (also unstaged) sounds of traffic, and activated by the effort to hear the (staged) low-key monotone of the letters from home, repetitive and demanding in their tone and content. The images and sounds of the city command temporally extended attention. The city is multifarious, unending. The letters from home – the mother's desires and demands – are ever-present, even intrusive: in this moment, they don't stand a chance. If *Annie Hall* tries (and arguably fails) to understand the collapse of a romantic relationship by telling the same story over and over, *News from Home* stages the tensions of a mother–daughter relationship through its very sounds and images. In each case the city – New York City – is a rival, over

Figure 1.3 A street shot from *News from Home* (1977).

against, respectively, the lover and the mother, for the affections of the 'narrator': it is the true object of desire.

Annie Hall, film history and cinema memory

Today, the historical study of films and cinema is a lively and very productive area within film studies, where *revisionist film history* has come to assume a key role. This approach took off in the mid-1980s, and currently embraces an influential body of work styling itself *New Cinema History*:

> An international trend in research in film and cinema history that treats cinema as a social, economic, and cultural institution and centres on the circulation and consumption, rather than on the content, of films. Its roots are twofold. First, its concerns can be traced back to post-1970s debates on, and calls for, inquiries into contemporary and historical social audiences – calls, that is, to look at real-life cinemagoers as opposed to the theoretical spectators implied in the film text. Second, it is a successor to the revisionist film history that came to the fore in the 1980s, with its call for methodological rigour in research methods and deployment of historical source materials.
>
> (Kuhn and Westwell 2020, 332)

In all its variants, revisionist film history departs significantly in its objectives, source materials and methods from historical studies that look, say, at the relationships between themes and contents of films and broader social and/or historical issues, trends and events. Since its focus tends to be cinema-institutional issues such as the production, distribution and above all the exhibition and consumption of films, revisionist approaches, by definition, also involve a shift of attention away from the film text as a starting point for investigation.

How might *Annie Hall* fare within revisionist film history? It would be perfectly in accord with the objectives of the revisionist approach to conduct a case study of *Annie Hall,* researching the history of the film's 'circulation and consumption', for instance. A well-designed study of *Annie Hall*'s reception by reviewers, critics and other commentators could certainly prove rewarding; and particularly so, given the vicissitudes suffered by the director's reputation. Serious allegations concerning Woody Allen's private life began to enter the public domain in the early 1990s, and those who review and comment on his films are well aware of these, as is the wider public. A reception study, undertaken longitudinally and tracing any changes in quantity, focus and tone of commentaries on *Annie Hall* published over the years since its initial release, and especially since Allen's fall from grace, could offer illuminating insights into changing audience responses to films and their directors.

As well as looking at reviews and the like, a rounded picture of *Annie Hall*'s reception would usefully call for some audience research. This might range from looking at industry statistics on box-office takings, which are readily available and may be taken as a measure of the film's popularity with audiences; through to enquiries among persons who have seen the film. While widely regarded as the best-loved of Woody Allen's films, *Annie Hall* does not appear to elicit among cinemagoers the extent, intensity and longevity of attachment enjoyed by, say, *Star Wars* – a film which was also released in 1977 but which, unlike *Annie Hall*, has become the subject of a considerable film studies literature centred around fandom and cult cinema (Elovaara 2013; Hills 2002). This may or may not be a consequence of the vicissitudes of Allen's reputation, which have undoubtedly rendered his work a problematic area of enquiry within film studies, notwithstanding the depersonalizing aspirations of auteur-structuralism, in which the work assumes primacy in interpretation and analysis over against the person of its creator. At the same time, this very challenge may offer an opportunity. Taking on board the current state of Allen's reputation, and in relation to a film that came out four decades ago, an alternative approach to a historical reception study of *Annie Hall* might draw on another methodological development within film history: memory work with cinemagoers. Research in this area indicates that, in discursive terms, *cinema memory* – people's recollections of their past cinemagoing – displays idiosyncratic discursive characteristics that mark it out as a highly distinctive subset of broader cultural or collective memory (Kuhn 2011).

What might be expected of a programme of memory work conducted with filmgoers who, like me, saw *Annie Hall* on its first release? Research on cinema memory suggests that the circumstances in which a film was viewed will be more prevalent in people's recollections than details of the film itself. Will this be true of *Annie Hall*? If so, we might expect emphasis to be on where (especially in relation to people's personal geographies), when, and with whom, the film was seen and on what was going on elsewhere in the filmgoer's life at the time (peer group activities, or courtship, say, or perhaps even a relationship breakdown). Such an enquiry would likely also elicit some anecdotes or amusing stories about memorable incidents associated with seeing the film in question.

With *Annie Hall*, however, it would be particularly enlightening to see whether, and how, memories of actually seeing the film overlap with a broader current of cultural memory, or tap into a set of associations to the film that may not be tied specifically to having actually seen it. Among the observed discursive qualities of cinema memory is a 'past/present register', which 'often takes the form of an apparently detached observation, and is always firmly rooted in the present, the moment of narration [of the memory]' (Kuhn 2002, 10). An illuminating instance of this phenomenon arises in a historical reception study involving depth interviews of British cinemagoers of the 1930s, carried out in the 1990s, in which a number of interviewees talked about British films and stars of the interwar years. The films of singer, dancer and actress Jessie Matthews (perhaps the best-known being *Evergreen* (Victor Saville, 1934)) did well at the box office and were popular at the time with British filmgoers; yet there is no unqualified praise of Matthews in these recollections. In retrospect, for these 1930s cinemagoers the 'problem' with Jessie Matthews was twofold. Aside from frequent allusions to the fakeness of her over-elocuted 'posh' accent – and by association a sense of phoneyness surrounding the star herself ('Jessie Matthews … epitomised to me all that was class-ridden …. Now I've since discovered that Jessie Matthews was a kind of low-grade Cockney'), a very public scandal associated with her marriage to the performer Sonnie Hale ('She was a bit of a husband-stealer') is neither forgotten nor forgiven in people's recollections of the star sixty years on. Memories of Matthews's films, or acknowledgement of her talents, appear to have been overtaken by 'common knowledge' about Matthews as a person and about a scandal in her life (Kuhn 2009, 184–8).

On *Annie Hall*'s release, speculation abounded about the extent to which the film was autobiographical. Does Alvy's account of his early life relate in any way at all to Woody Allen's childhood? Does the Alvy-Annie relationship have any echoes of that between Allen and his co-star, Diane Keaton? Keaton and Allen had previously worked together on a number of projects and had been romantically involved for a while. And so, given the nature of cinema memory, the actual and the fictional relationships are likely to become conflated in recollections of the film. However, all this stands to pale into significance beside the scandal surrounding Allen that emerged more than a decade after *Annie Hall*'s release. This is a difficult and controversial issue, but it is of some interest as far as film history and historiography are concerned. How exactly might memory be discursively framed in such an extreme instance of the 'past/present register'? To what extent will basic aspects of cinema memory (when and where the film was first seen, and so on) be admissible to recollection in the face of knowledge of its director's catastrophic fall from grace, especially when seen in light of the current #MeToo movement (Boyle 2019)? Will women's and men's memories of *Annie Hall* admit reference to an innocent enjoyment of the film, and/or acknowledge a more complicated relationship, or even refuse any engagement with it? What might be the tone of such responses? Such an enquiry could add a great deal to our understanding of the workings of cinema memory and its instrumentality within cultural memory. It is waiting to be done.

Works cited

Betz, Mark. 2008. 'Little Books', in *Inventing Film Studies*, ed. Lee Grieveson and Haidee Wasson, 319–49. Durham, NC: Duke University Press.

Bolas, Terry. 2009. *Screen Education: From Film Appreciation to Media Studies*. Bristol: Intellect.

Boyle, Karen. 2019. *#MeToo, Weinstein and Feminism*. Cham: Palgrave Macmillan.

Cowie, Peter. 1996. *Annie Hall*. London: British Film Institute.

Edinburgh International Film Festival. 1977. *31st Edinburgh International Film Festival*. Edinburgh: Edinburgh International Film Festival.

Elovaara, Mika, ed. 2013. *Star Wars*. Fan Phenomena, Bristol: Intellect.

Fabe, Marilyn. 2014. 'Film and Postmodernism: Woody Allen's *Annie Hall*', in *Closely Watched Films: An Introduction to the Art of Narrative Film Technique*, 173–190. Berkeley, CA: University of California Press.

Foucault, Michel, ed. 1978. *I, Pierre Riviere, Having Slaughtered My Mother, My Sister and My Brother*. Harmondsworth: Penguin.

Freud, Sigmund. 1977. 'Fragment of an Analysis of a Case of Hysteria (1905[1901])', in *Pelican Freud Library, Volume 8: Case Histories 1*, 44–164. Harmondsworth: Penguin.

Grieveson, Lee and Haidee Wasson, eds. 2008. *Inventing Film Studies*. Durham, NC: Duke University Press.

Grindon, Leger. 2011. *The Hollywood Romantic Comedy: Conventions, History, Controversies*. Malden, MA: Wiley-Blackwell.

Hardy, Phil, ed. 1976. *Edinburgh '76 Magazine: Number 1: Psycho-Analysis/Cinema/Avant-Garde*. Edinburgh: Edinburgh Film Festival.

Hills, Matt. 2002. *Fan Cultures*. London: Routledge.

Johnston, Claire, ed. 1977. *Edinburgh '77 Magazine: Number 2: History/Production/Memory*. Edinburgh: Edinburgh Film Festival.

Kuhn, Annette. 2000. 'A Journey through Memory', in *Memory and Methodology*, ed. Susannah Radstone, 179–196. Oxford: Berg.

Kuhn, Annette. 2002. *An Everyday Magic: Cinema and Cultural Memory*. London: Bloomsbury.

Kuhn, Annette. 2009. 'Film Stars in 1930s Britain: A Case Study in Modernity and Femininity', in *Stellar Encounters: Stardom in Popular European Cinema*, ed. Tytti Soila. New Barnet: John Libbey.

Kuhn, Annette. 2011. 'What to Do with Cinema Memory', in *Explorations in New Cinema History: Approaches and Case Studies*, ed. Richard Maltby, Daniel Biltereyst and Philippe Meers, 25–39. Malden, MA: Wiley-Blackwell.

Kuhn, Annette. 2019. 'What Is Film Studies?' British Academy blog. https://www.thebritishacademy.ac.uk/blog/what-is-film-studies (accessed May 2019).

Kuhn, Annette and Guy Westwell. 2020. *A Dictionary of Film Studies* (2nd edition). Oxford: Oxford University Press.

MacDonald, Richard Lowell. 2016. *The Appreciation of Film: The Postwar Film Society Movement and Film Culture in Britain*. Exeter: Exeter University Press.

Mulvey, Laura and Peter Wollen. 2008. 'From Cinephilia to Film Studies', in *Inventing Film Studies*, ed. Lee Grieveson and Haidee Wasson, 217–32. Durham, NC: Duke University Press.

Polan, Dana. 2007. *Scenes of Instruction: The Beginnings of the U.S. Study of Film*. Berkeley, CA: University of California Press.

Schatz, Thomas. 1982. '*Annie Hall* and the Issue of Modernism', *Literature/Film Quarterly* 10: 180–7.

Stanfield, Peter. 2008. 'Notes Towards a History of the Edinburgh International Film Festival', *Film International* 6: 62–71.

2

The story of Woody and Diane: Stars and hit patterns in the New Hollywood

Peter Krämer

In November 1977, the film journal *Take One* published a long article entitled 'Looking for Diane Keaton' by its associate editor James Monaco (1977, 26–8). The piece dealt with the somewhat reluctant superstardom of the actress who had only recently, and quite suddenly, been exposed to the 'deafening roar of media attention'. According to the article's first sentence, '[t]he trouble began for Diane Keaton in late August', when (arts and entertainment) journalists returning from their holidays were 'scrounging for the lead fall story', and the actress was seen to qualify best:

> *Annie Hall*, one of the surprise hits of the spring, was still making money; the film (and its star) had set a new hip style for late 1970s bas couture, and Keaton, starring in the upcoming *Looking for Mr. Goodbar*, was about to emerge from the shadow of her mentor, friend and sometime lover Woody Allen.

With its many references to real people and their actual experiences, *Annie Hall* focused attention on the life and personality of Diane Keaton: 'it was, after all, an emotional biography of the Diane Woody knew.'

Despite huge demand, Keaton only gave one interview to promote the October release of the film adaptation of Judith Rossner's controversial 1975 bestseller *Looking for Mr. Goodbar* about a school teacher who picks up men in singles bars and is murdered by one of them in the end, and this interview earned her a *Time* magazine cover story at the end of September. According to Monaco, it was hard to imagine a 'more effective career move' than releasing *Annie Hall* (in April) and *Looking for Mr. Goodbar* so close to each other: 'What the two films did, in effect, was to announce: "here's an attractive, appealing woman who's a good-natured role model (*Annie*), and she can act in tough, dramatic roles (*Goodbar*)."'

Monaco noted that 'Keaton is now, at this moment, actually bankable. Her name in a package will insure that a film is made'. This was remarkable because in the preceding years there had been only two 'truly bankable female stars': Barbra Streisand and Liza Minnelli. However, referring to two high-profile 'women's buddy films' released in autumn 1977 – *Julia* and *The Turning Point* – Monaco pointed out that 'the balance between men and women in the Hollywood fantasy version of our world' might be changing. The four female leads of these two films – Jane Fonda, Vanessa Redgrave, Anne Bancroft and Shirley MacLaine – had 'reached (or passed) the age of forty'. While, '[f]or the longest time, that birthday [had] marked the end of a star actress's career', the success of these two films could bring about fundamental change. Monaco also pointed to the rise of a host of younger actresses on the verge of the kind of breakthrough Diane Keaton (who was born in 1946) had just achieved.

Yet, the writer expressed doubts about Keaton's career, noting that she was 'about to start her fifth Woody Allen movie [which turned out to be *Interiors*]. She has made only six without him and had a leading role in only three of those'. Negotiations for a promising non-Allen project, an adaptation of Johanna Davis's 1973 novel *Life Signs* with 'a strong role, and a rather political one', for Keaton, had broken down in August, reportedly mainly due to her salary demands. Given her reluctance to play the 'publicity game' and the 'precious few really interesting roles for women that come up every year', Keaton might not be able to sustain her current status and revert back to being largely perceived as an appendage to writer-director-actor Woody Allen, whose status as one of Hollywood's top directors and top stars was consolidated by the critical and commercial success of *Annie Hall*.

In this chapter, I take a closer look at the success of *Annie Hall*, before situating the film in the context of Allen's career. Starting with an analysis of the marketing and reviews of *Annie Hall*, I then discuss the film's place in Keaton's career, and in wider currents in Hollywood cinema to do with female stars and female audiences.

The success of *Annie Hall* and the shape of Woody Allen's career

By the time James Monaco published *American Film Now*, his magisterial 1979 volume on contemporary Hollywood cinema, *Annie Hall* had already taken its central place in Woody Allen's filmography – 'it marks a quantum jump for him as a filmmaker', in Monaco's words (1979, 244) – and also in the American canon more generally. In 1978 Monaco had organized a survey of 'twenty of the world's best film critics' concerning the best American films released between 1 January 1968 and 31 December 1977, and *Annie Hall* came in third place, jointly with *Petulia* (1968) (412, 415). *Time* magazine included *Annie Hall* on its list of the ten best American films of the 1970s (Steinberg 1980, 179). In 1992, it was selected by the National Film Preservation Board as one of the all-time classics of American cinema, and in the American Film Institute's list of the 100 best American movies ever it was ranked 31st in 1997 and 35th in 2007.

Although it was not immediately clear that *Annie Hall* would come to be regarded as a classic, its initial critical reception was very positive indeed. It was chosen as one of the ten best films (American or non-American) of 1977 by the *New York Times* and *Time* magazine, while the National Board of Review listed it among the ten best English-language films of the year; both the National Society of Film Critics and the New York Film Critics declared it to be the best picture of 1977 (Steinberg 1980, 175, 179, 264, 270, 284). In addition, the film won numerous awards for its direction, for example from the New York Film Critics and the Directors Guild of America, and also for its screenplay (co-written by Woody Allen and Marshall Brickman), for example from the National Society of Film Critics, the New York Film Critics, the Los Angeles Film Critics Association and the Writers Guild of America; and for Keaton (more about this below). Perhaps most impressively, *Annie Hall* dominated the Oscars, with an almost clean sweep of the main categories: Best Picture, Director, Actress and Original Screenplay (Allen was nominated for Best Actor, but did not win).

The film was also a substantial commercial hit. In *Variety*'s end-of-year US chart for 1977, *Annie Hall* came in at number 26, with rentals (i.e. the money the distributor receives from cinemas, usually about half of their revenues from ticket sales) of $12 million (*Variety* 1978a, 21), but as the film continued earning money in subsequent years (its rental income rising to $19 million), it eventually ranked thirteenth among all films released in 1977.[1] In the light of the fact that 167 films were released by national distributors in the United States in 1977 (84 by the major studios Columbia, Fox, Paramount, Universal, Warner Bros. and United Artists [which also handled MGM's productions]), this is an impressive achievement (Cook 2000, 492).

From today's perspective, when Woody Allen has long been operating as a kind of American arthouse filmmaker whose work is in commercial terms negligible (rare moderate hits such as *Midnight in Paris* [2011] notwithstanding), the box office success of *Annie Hall* is astonishing. A different picture emerges when we look at Allen's career before *Annie Hall*. Let's start with his output as a performer.

After several years in which Allen had toured the United States as a stand-up comedian (also releasing records featuring his routines from 1964 onwards) and appeared on numerous prime-time and late night television shows,[2] he had a supporting role in the big-budget ensemble comedy *What's New, Pussycat?* (1965), for which he had also written the script (his first one). His next appearance in a major Hollywood movie came in the even more expensive James Bond parody *Casino Royale* (1967).[3] With rentals of $8.5 million, *What's New, Pussycat?* was the eighth highest grossing film of 1965 in the United States, while rentals of $10.2 million put *Casino Royale* at number 13 in 1967.

Leaving supporting roles behind, from 1969 onwards Allen starred in a series of medium budget, and mostly quite profitable, productions,[4] the majority of which could, like the above films, be characterised as 'zany' or 'wacky' comedies[5] and also often had parodistic elements. *Take the Money and Run* (1969) – a mixture of fictional biopic and mockumentary about an incompetent criminal – earned $3 million in rentals and just made it into the top 50 for its year of release. *Bananas* – a film, once again with mockumentary elements, about an accidental revolutionary – did better, earning $3.5 million in rentals and being ranked 33rd in 1971.

Allen starred in two films in 1972: *Everything You Always Wanted to Know About Sex (But Were Afraid to Ask),* which consists of a series of sketches answering questions from a bestselling sex advice book, and the romantic comedy and *Casablanca* homage *Play It Again, Sam*, an adaptation of Allen's 1969 Broadway play. The former was at number 11 in the 1972 chart with rentals of $8.8 million, the latter at number 24 with $5.8 million. *Sleeper*, a futuristic slapstick comedy, was at number 19 in 1973 with $8.3 million in rentals. In 1975, *Love and Death*, a parodistic historical drama, was at number 33 with $7.4 million in rentals. Finally, *The Front* (1976), a drama about the Hollywood blacklist, like *Take the Money and Run*, barely made it into the top 50 for its year of release with rentals of $5 million.

Thus, after appearing as a supporting actor in two big hits in the mid-1960s, from 1969 to 1976 Allen was the star of seven films, all but two of which made it into the top 35 for their year of release; three were among the top 25. His next star turn after *Annie Hall* came in 1979 in the romantic comedy *Manhattan*, which earned $17.6 million and was ranked 23rd in the annual US rentals chart.

In terms of box office success, then, *Annie Hall* is fairly consistent with the performance of Allen's pre-1980 star vehicles.

While Allen did not star in really big hit movies, he was regarded as one of Hollywood's major stars. Every year Quigley Publications asked American film exhibitors about the stars they considered the biggest box office attractions; these were not necessarily the actors appearing in the biggest hits but those who exhibitors thought were actually responsible for a film's success. Woody Allen was included in Quigley's top 10 every year from 1975 to 1979.[6] Furthermore, in a late 1978 survey of college students concerning their favourite movie stars, Allen was ranked 10th (Steinberg 1980, 182–3).

He did not retain his status as a major movie star in the 1980s. The box office revenues of his star vehicles collapsed. For example, the follow-up to *Manhattan*, *Stardust Memories* (1980) – a bleak comedy about a filmmaker at a turning point in his life – earned rentals of only $4.1 million in the United States (Fox 1996, 277–8).[7] Yet, concurrent with overall commercial failure (interrupted by the occasional moderate hit such as *Hannah and Her Sisters* [1986]), throughout the 1980s Allen consolidated his status as a highly acclaimed writer-director. This is indicated by Academy Award nominations and wins for his films.

Before *Annie Hall*, none of his star vehicles (all but two of which he also [co-]wrote and directed)[8] had received any Oscar nominations, nor did *Don't Drink the Water* (1969), a film based on Allen's first ever stage play which ran on Broadway in 1966/67. *What's New, Pussycat?* did receive a nomination, but it was for 'Best Song' rather than for anything Allen contributed. As we have seen, *Annie Hall* received five nominations with four wins. *Manhattan* received two nominations (Best Screenplay for Woody Allen and Marshall Brickman, and Best Supporting Actress for Mariel Hemingway). *Interiors* (1978), the first film Allen wrote and directed without starring in it and his first serious drama, received five nominations, including Best Director, Best Original Screenplay, Best Actress and Best Supporting Actress. While there were no nominations for *Stardust Memories*, throughout the following years and, indeed, decades, the films Allen wrote and directed, both those he starred in and those he did not, have received numerous Oscar nominations, mostly in the writing, acting and directing categories, including several wins.

Thus, starting with *Annie Hall*, Woody Allen's films became central to how the Hollywood community, through the Academy of Motion Picture Arts and Sciences, presented itself to the world in the Oscar ceremony. By contrast, in commercial terms, after *Annie Hall* and *Manhattan* Allen's output became increasingly marginal. As *none* of his post-1977 films were as celebrated, nor as highly ranked in US box office charts, as *Annie Hall*, this production was not only a turning point in Allen's filmmaking career but also, arguably, its high point.

Annie Hall and Diane Keaton's career in the 1970s

Annie Hall's title focused attention, in all of the film's marketing, on Diane Keaton and the character she played. The trailer starts with three scenes featuring her together with Allen/Alvy, representing the imminent end of their relationship (a conversation on a plane in which Alvy says that their relationship is no longer moving forward and therefore, like a shark, has to die), the very beginning (a conversation in the street shortly after they have met for the first time at a tennis match) and an important development in the middle (Annie moving into the flat of a somewhat reluctant Alvy). This is followed by several scenes without Annie, mostly showing Alvy interacting with other characters, including three women, but at the end the trailer returns to the central couple, showing them both before and after having sex.

While Allen/Alvy is constantly making jokes, the trailer has a very measured pace, introducing each scene with an austere title card (white lettering against a black background) carrying the name of one of the actors (which is also spoken by a male voiceover) and featuring soft piano music. Towards the end of the trailer, the voiceover completes its listing of the actors' names by adding 'in the new Woody Allen film' and then, accompanying title cards with the film's title, twice says 'Annie Hall'. One of these title cards carries the film's tagline 'A nervous romance', while another displays Allen's credits as both co-writer and director.

The trailer, then, emphasizes Allen's authorship and the absolute centrality of his character and of Allen/Alvy's jokey dialogue in the film, but it also suggests that the film brings together an ensemble of (more or less) prominent performers, and examines Alvy's relationships with several women, most importantly with the title character. The tagline encapsulates the fact that the film's central romance is full of tension and comic relief, and might not have a happy ending.

The film's poster displays a list of actors' names (all with the same size lettering) on the right-hand side, while on the left there is a picture of the two leads standing by, and looking at, each other. With his hands in his trouser pockets, Allen is slightly turned away from the camera while Keaton is slightly turned towards it, so that her smile is visible.[9] Underneath this picture the film's title is presented in large print, and beneath the title, in smaller print, 'A nervous romance'. Unlike in the trailer, here the tagline, in conjunction with the picture, does not suggest the ultimate failure of the relationship; the two lovers may well overcome their nervousness, and the Allen character may also learn to deal with the detachment that his posture and the placement of his hands indicate, so that perhaps the relationship can be made to work.

Difficult romantic relationships (including marriages), played for laughs or drama or both, had been at the centre of Keaton's film career before *Annie Hall*.[10] Her three supporting roles in *Lovers and Other Strangers* (1970), *The Godfather* (1972) and *The Godfather, Part II* (1974) – the first of these films a moderate hit in the United States, the third a major hit and the second one of the biggest hits of all time – all revolved around unhappy marriages. In 1976, she had major roles in two box office flops, the comedy of remarriage *I Will, I Will ... For Now* and the historical crime comedy *Harry and Walter Go to New York* in which she teams up with two small-time crooks who compete for her affection until she goes off with a big shot criminal.

Both of Keaton's 1976 releases (and also *Lovers and Other Strangers*) belonged to the same type of comedy – telling stories with strong parodistic or satirical elements about rather dysfunctional romantic relationships – as the first three films in which she appeared with Woody Allen. Like *Harry and Walter Go to New York*, *Love and Death* situates its story in a comically distorted version of the past, while *Sleeper* presents a comic vision of the future. In all three films Keaton's character is associated with radical politics, which are mostly being made fun of.

Most importantly, just as in *Love and Other Strangers*[11] and *I Will, I Will ... For Now*,[12] divorce features prominently in *Play It Again, Sam*, in which Allen's character, post-divorce, falls for, and has sex with, the wife of his best friend (played by Keaton), but, making good use of his obsession with *Casablanca*, manages to renounce this adulterous relationship in the end. In *Sleeper* the protagonist's unsatisfactory marriage has been terminated by his being cryogenically frozen; awaking 200 years in the future, he eventually develops a more fulfilling relationship with Keaton's character. In *Love and Death* Allen's character manages to marry his beloved cousin twice removed (Keaton) after many trials and tribulations, only to be talked by his wife into attempting to assassinate Napoleon, which leads to his execution.

There was a strong sense that Keaton became ever more central to Allen's films. For example, while *Variety*'s review of *Sleeper* noted that in this film 'Diane Keaton once again plays [Allen's] foil', the paper's review of *Love and Death* saw the two performers as equals, highlighting 'the terrific synergism of the two stars' (Elley 2000, 510, 781).

In many ways, then, Keaton's whole previous film career – with *The Godfather* films adding a strong sense of seriousness to her otherwise primarily comic performances – had prepared her for the role she played in *Annie Hall* and for her centrality to the marketing of the film. Some of the publicity surrounding her in 1975 and 1976 can also, in retrospect, be seen as setting her up perfectly for her role as Annie Hall. For example, an article in *People* magazine, published in August 1975 (Lax 1975, 42–4), highlighted her close association with Allen, her perennial lack of confidence and the fact that she was seeing a psychoanalyst, while also pointing out that, not least with the *Godfather* movies, she was developing a career away from Allen and that, in any case, she was a great comedienne and also a singer, who performed in clubs. She and Allen were described as former lovers who were now best friends. Last but not least, 'her fashion-model looks aside, Diane prefers to plotz around in men's clothes'. Her portrait in this article could well serve as a kind of blueprint both for her character in and for the story of *Annie Hall* – which suggests that Annie Hall was indeed closely based on Keaton, or at least on her public image.

The publicity surrounding the release of *Annie Hall* also foregrounded similarities between actress and character. Thus, a United Artists press release initially focused on Allen, but then turned to Keaton, introducing her as '[a]n accomplished dramatic actress, a radiant song stylist, and a deft comedienne', before discussing her work as a singer in clubs and on television shows, concluding with the announcement that as a 'special treat' in *Annie Hall* 'Diane sings two songs' (United Artists 1977). The press release also pointed out that Keaton had been 'selected to play one of the most coveted women's roles in recent films', namely the lead in *Looking for Mr. Goodbar*, suggesting that she might finally be successful on her own as a movie actress, breaking away from Allen, much like Annie does with regard to Alvy.

Two articles in New York papers from April 1977, both based on interviews with Keaton, were centrally concerned with her relationship to the character of Annie Hall (as well as the other characters she had played in Allen's films). One of these stated: 'Although she concedes that the title character in Allen's new film is based partly on her, she staunchly maintains that the stormy, hilarious relationship it depicts is fiction' (Gold 1977, 31). The second article observed: 'In person, Miss Keaton seems very much like the kooky comedy characters she has played in four Woody Allen films', with the actress once again speaking about similarities and differences between film and reality (Klemesrud 1977, 1, 13). The overall gist of the article, which is entitled 'Diane Keaton: From Mr. Allen to "Mr. Goodbar"', is that the actress is about to transcend her close association with the filmmaker through her involvement with *Looking for Mr. Goodbar*, described like *Annie Hall* as 'potentially a "blockbuster."' While it is not stated explicitly, there is certainly the implication that *Looking for Mr. Goodbar* might do for Keaton what singing does for Annie Hall, namely to allow her to establish herself apart from Allen.

Interestingly, reviewers of *Annie Hall*, who by and large wrote extremely positively about the film,[13] did not examine such parallels very much, because they were focused on discussing the film in terms of Allen's authorship, artistic development and autobiographical reflections. Several reviews did not even mention Keaton's name (e.g. Rich 1977, 22; Kissell 1977, 72; Sterritt 1977, 20), or mentioned it only in passing (e.g. Crist 1977, 38). One of the reviewers that never mentioned Keaton (Rich 1977, 22) wrote about the film's 'rich emotional texture [which] sets it triumphantly apart from the rest of [Allen's] work', and described it as 'a sorrowful love story, a celebration of its New York City setting, an idiosyncratic satire of American culture and social mores, and an affectionate tribute to some of the greats [of cinema]' (Ingmar Bergman and *Scenes from a Marriage* [1973] being referred to in several reviews). According to this review the film also is 'a slightly fictionalized portrait of the life, times and psyche of Woody Allen himself' which 'seems to have been ripped, painfully, from its creator's heart'. In this and other reviews the attention paid to the great auteur sidelined the title character and erased the actress, who was also its real-life inspiration, altogether.

Some reviews acknowledged that the film is not just about Allen but about a relationship between two people. Thus, Richard Schickel (1977, 70) wrote: 'What really interests Allen is the lady of the title'. But both he and other reviewers did not seem to share Allen's interest in that character (or the actress playing her), because they had little to say about her. Janet Maslin (1977, 78) described Keaton/Annie as 'a fine comic foil for Allen, and an even better romantic one'. When she adds that '[f]or the first time, he seems capable of inviting genuine identification from his viewers', the implication is that viewers identify with Allen/Alvy, rather than Keaton/Annie. Indeed, while mentioning that Keaton, Allen's 'still-close but former girl-friend', was the inspiration for Annie, this is only important for Maslin insofar as such inspiration 'enabled Allen to progress from the realm of simple self-representation to that of the artfully shaped self-portrait'; the idea that the film is also a portrait of Annie Hall, arguably shaped as much by Keaton as by Allen, is lost.

When reviewers made an effort to discuss Annie Hall as a character at all, they tended to reduce her to the archetype of the lovable kook, completely ignoring the fact that Annie changes substantially during the story (much more so than Alvy; arguably it is Annie who matures while Alvy remains stuck in a rut). Thus, Maslin (1977, 78) described Annie as a 'compleat flibbertigibbet, a creature so endearingly scatterbrained that she makes Allen seem serene by comparison'. Similarly, Keaton's performance was reduced to what were claimed to be natural attributes rather than acting choices. According to Kathleen Carroll (1977, 85), '[w]ith her special brand of flighty charm, her glowing good looks and her innate shyness, Keaton is a completely beguiling Annie'. Judith Crist (1977, 38) only once referred to Keaton in her review, calling her 'that uniquely beautiful comedienne', while, according to Penelope Gilliatt (1977, 136), she is 'one of the most dazzlingly and beguilingly funny girls in movies in years'. These female critics did pay more attention to Annie/Keaton than their male counterparts, but still ignored the actress's work and the character's development.

In many ways, then, *Annie Hall*'s critical reception sidelined the title character and the lead actress. Yet, at the same time, reviewers foregrounded two generic features which had long been associated with films addressed to, and preferred by, women: romantic love and a strong sense of loss (especially in so-called melodramas or weepies), both providing an opportunity for the audience to be deeply moved, perhaps even to tears (cp. Krämer 1999, 98–112). According to Kathleen Carroll (1977, 85), the Alvy-Annie scenes 'are filled with such warmth and genuine affection that one inevitably feels a deep sense of loss at the movie's end'; in fact, the film is 'so tinged with sadness it tends to encourage actual weeping'. Penelope Gilliatt (1977, 136) described the film as 'a love story told with piercing sweetness and grief', while Andrew Sarris (1977, 45) referred to it as a 'cinematic valentine': 'The pairing is so ridiculously impossible that it becomes indescribably moving.'

This emphasis on love and loss in reviews of *Annie Hall*, together with the centrality of Annie/Keaton in the film's marketing and story, suggests that a good proportion of the film's audience was made up of women. This would seem to be confirmed by the fact that Annie/Keaton became a fashion icon. In July 1977, an article in the *New York Times* (Nemy 1977, 34), with the title 'The Hall-Mark of the Annie Look', focused on the clothes Keaton wore in the film (as well as, reportedly, in her private life, although the film's costume designer Ruth Morley is also credited): 'a curious mixture of raffish tomboy and femininity'. The article featured pictures of women wearing similar clothes: 'The Annie Hall look is now popping up on the streets with amazing frequency.' In May 1978, *Variety* (1978b, 2) reported that United Artists had licensed an Annie Hall fashion line.

By then, Keaton had appeared in another hit movie, *Looking for Mr. Goodbar*, which had a mixed critical reception, including a lot of praise for Keaton. The film did not appear on any of the best of the year lists or receive many awards (it was nominated for the Best Supporting Actress and Best Cinematography Oscars). However, *Looking for Mr. Goodbar* probably helped Diane Keaton win numerous accolades for *Annie Hall*, with critics and Academy voters taking both of her 1977 roles into account when selecting her. In addition to the Best Actress Oscar, Keaton won the Best Actress award from the National Society of Film Critics and the New York Film Critics and also, strangely, the award for Best *Supporting* Actress from the National Board of Review (Steinberg 1980, 264, 270, 284). She was joint winner (with Marsha Mason) of the Golden Globe for Best Actress in a Musical/Comedy (297).

Because Keaton was widely held to be a key factor in the box office success of *Annie Hall*, she made it into Quigley's top 10 in 1977; she was at number 9 with Allen at number 6. In 1978 she was ranked seventh, just one place behind Allen; this was due to the success of *Looking for Mr. Goodbar*, which was at number 18 in the annual chart for 1977 with rentals of $16.9 million (by contrast, *Interiors*, in which Keaton was featured as part of an ensemble cast, made only $4.6 million in rentals and did not make it into the top 50 for 1978). As the film was released late in 1977, its success counted towards the 1978 Quigley rankings. In fact, *Annie Hall*'s success must also still have resonated in 1978 because otherwise Allen's ranking is inexplicable.

Despite the box office performance of *Manhattan* (at number 23 for 1979 with rentals of $17.6 million), Keaton did not make it into Quigley's top 10 in 1979, presumably because she was not regarded as one of the film's main draws; Allen, on the other hand, was ranked 4th. She never returned to Quigley's top 10, despite her Oscar-nominated co-lead role in Warren Beatty's romantic historical epic *Reds*, which was a substantial hit in 1981.[14] That she had indeed briefly been at the very top in 1977/8 was confirmed by the previously mentioned survey of college students about their favourite movie stars carried out late in 1978, in which she came in sixth place, ahead of Allen at number 10 (Steinberg 1980, 183).

Allen, Keaton and the New Hollywood

The careers of Woody Allen and Diane Keaton discussed in this chapter, in particular the key role played by *Annie Hall* within them, are indicative of broader developments in American film culture. Following on from his early career in the 1950s as a joke writer for newspaper columnists and television comedians, across the 1960s and 1970s Allen became a successful performer on the stage (in clubs and theatres), on prime-time and late-night television and in the movies, while also releasing records with his stand-up routines, publishing pieces in large circulation magazines (later to be collected in books), writing successful Broadway plays and working as a writer-director on usually profitable medium-budget movies. Thus, he had been a mainstream entertainer for decades before, in the wake of *Annie Hall*, *Interiors*, *Manhattan* and *Stardust Memories*, he turned into a, by and large, commercially marginal but critically acclaimed American art filmmaker, who acted in most of his own films and also occasionally starred in films made by others.

Born in 1935, Allen belonged to the interwar generation of directors, writers, executives, producers and stars, many of whom developed a career outside Hollywood before making studio films that had a transformative impact on American film culture, mostly from the mid-1960s onwards (Krämer 2005, 67, 81–7). This transformation has long been referred to as the 'Hollywood Renaissance' or the emergence of a 'New Hollywood' (Krämer 1998, 295–301), and while the late 1960s and early to mid-1970s have been celebrated as perhaps, in terms of style, form and content, the most innovative and richest period in American film history, these years also saw the lowest cinema attendance levels ever, with a particularly narrow focus on young, educated, urban cinemagoers and on male movie preferences (Krämer 2005, 58–65; Krämer and Tzioumakis 2018, xiii–xxvii).

The Hollywood (management and creative) elite had always been largely male, yet until the late 1960s this elite had considered females as the most important audience segment (Krämer 1999, 96), and catered to the known preferences of this segment with lead roles for female stars and with musicals, costume pictures, romantic comedies and (melo)dramas, most of them addressed to an all-inclusive family audience. Hence the biggest hits at the US box office in the mid-1960s were the romantic historical epics *Cleopatra* (number 1 in 1963), *Doctor Zhivago* (number 2 in 1965) and *Hawaii* (number 1 in 1966), as well as the musicals *My Fair Lady* (number 1 in 1965), *Mary Poppins* (number 2 in

1966) and *The Sound of Music* (number 1 in 1965). These films also received numerous Oscar nominations, with *My Fair Lady* and *The Sound of Music* each winning for both Best Picture and Best Director. Quigley's top 10 were headed by a woman (Doris Day, Elisabeth Taylor or Julie Andrews) in all but one of the years from 1960 to 1967.

After 1967, women were not only removed from the top spot but hardly featured in Quigley's top 10 at all. Whereas from 1960 to 1967, there had been on average three women in the top 10, in 1968, 1969 and 1972 it was two per year, and in 1970–1 and 1973–6 it was one; the only woman who was ranked in more than one year was Barbra Streisand (with six appearances in the top 10 from 1968 to 1976). In this context, Diane Keaton's listing in 1977, together with Streisand, and in 1978, together with Streisand and Jane Fonda, was remarkable.

Indeed, as James Monaco had speculated in the *Take One* article from November 1977 discussed at the beginning of this chapter, female stars, both older (like Fonda) and younger (like Keaton), were making a major, if only temporary, comeback at the box office in the late 1970s. In 1979 and 1980, there were, as in 1978, three women in Quigley's top 10, and in 1981 four. Afterwards the number of women in the top 10 returned to the low level of the years 1968–76. Apart from Streisand, only Fonda managed more than two listings in Quigley's top 10 during the 1970s and 1980s. Thus, Keaton's two appearances were quite typical for the careers of female stars at the time.

With reference to the two 'women's buddy films' *Julia* and *The Turning Point*, in November 1977 Monaco had also contemplated the possibility that Hollywood's high-profile releases might move away from their in places near-exclusive focus on male characters in the preceding years (star vehicles for Streisand had been the main exception to this male bias). Indeed, the biggest hits from 1968 to 1976 had included numerous male buddy films – ranging from *Midnight Cowboy* (number 3 in 1969) and *The French Connection* (number 3 in 1971) to *The Sting* (number 2 in 1973) and *One Flew Over the Cuckoo's Nest* (number 2 in 1975) – as well as many other films in which female characters were peripheral, for example *Patton* (number 4 in 1970) and *The Godfather* (number 1 in 1972). Furthermore, many of these and other hits from the period featured graphic violence and explicit sex, which, according to several surveys, tended to alienate older viewers and also females of all ages (Krämer 2005, 7, 49–55, 58–62). The main Oscar winners from these years included *Midnight Cowboy*, *Patton*, *The French Connection*, *The Godfather*, *The Sting*, *The Godfather, Part II* (the sixth biggest hit of 1974) and *One Flew over the Cuckoo's Nest*.

Following on from *Rocky* (the number 1 hit and main Oscar winner of 1976), which was as much a romantic and family drama as it was a boxing film, *Annie Hall* signalled a shift in the kinds of films rewarded by the Academy of Motion Picture Arts and Sciences. While two Vietnam dramas, which put a strong emphasis on the home front, dominated the Oscars for 1978 (*Deer Hunter* and the Jane Fonda vehicle *Coming Home*), the main winners in subsequent years included the tear-jerking family dramas *Kramer vs. Kramer* (1979), *Ordinary People* (1980) and *Terms of Endearment* (1983) as well as the romantic historical drama *Out of Africa* (1985). Some of these films gave top billing to their male leads (none more so than *Kramer vs. Kramer*), yet they clearly fit into genres generally preferred by women.

The same applies to many of the top hits from 1976 to 1983, including the family dramas *Kramer vs. Kramer* (number 1 in 1979), *On Golden Pond* (number 2 in 1981) and *Terms of Endearment* (number 2 in 1983); the musicals *A Star Is Born* (number 2 in 1976), *Saturday Night Fever* (number 3 in 1977), *Grease* (number 1 in 1978) and *Flashdance* (number 3 in 1983); the female ensemble comedy *Nine to Five* (number 2 in 1980); the romantic drama *An Officer and a Gentleman* (number 3 in 1982); and the romantic comedy *Tootsie* (number 2 in 1982).

We can get a sense of the actual audience composition of these films through surveys conducted by CinemaScore during the first three days of a film's release (cp. Kaminsky 1979, 3). These surveys determined the split between male and female cinemagoers and between those under twenty-five and those twenty-five or older. The audience share for each group indicates who was most attracted by the film's marketing. Across a large number of films, the average audience segmentation was as follows: 55 per cent male and 45 per cent female, 48 per cent under twenty-five, 52 per cent twenty-five and older (CinemaScore 1980).

Kramer vs. Kramer departed dramatically from these averages: 36 per cent male and 62 per cent female, 44 per cent under twenty-five and 55 per cent twenty-five and older. The results for *Nine to Five* were similar: 41 per cent male and 59 per cent female, 33 per cent under twenty-five and 67 per cent twenty-five and older; also for *Ordinary People*: 41 per cent, 59 per cent, 51 per cent, 49 per cent (CinemaScore 1981). The results for *On Golden Pond* were: 38 per cent male and 62 per cent female, 49 per cent under twenty-five and 51 per cent twenty-five and older (*Box Office* 1982: 80).

Importantly, *Manhattan* fit this demographic pattern, with above-average percentages for women and older people. The audience for *Manhattan* was

49 per cent male and 51 per cent female (as noted earlier, the averages across all films being 55 per cent and 45 per cent), 45 per cent under twenty-five and 55 per cent twenty-five and older (as compared to 48 per cent and 52 per cent). The figures for *Stardust Memories* were: 52 per cent male and 48 per cent female, 46 per cent under twenty-five and 54 per cent twenty-five and older. These results strongly suggest that by the late 1970s Woody Allen films had a larger-than-average following among women (especially those over twenty-five). Given the earlier discussion of the emphasis on Diane Keaton and romance in the marketing of *Annie Hall* as well as the foregrounding of romance and sentiment in the film's critical reception, I think we can assume that this bias towards (older) female cinemagoers already applied to *Annie Hall* (for which, unfortunately, there are no CinemaScore results).

Thus, *Annie Hall* is, in many ways, indicative of broader changes in American film culture, insofar as its success was part of a general shift away from Hollywood's exceptionally strong focus, during the late 1960s and early to mid-1970s, on male characters and stars, and on male movie preferences. From 1976/7 onwards, films fitting the genre preferences of women once again became, if only temporarily, more prominent in Hollywood's output, in US box office charts and at the Oscars, and female stars were back in greater numbers in Quigley's top 10. Having outlined this development, I should point out that it would require another chapter to try to *explain* it.

Notes

1 This is based on an unpublished chart compiled by Sheldon Hall from figures provided by Cohn (1993). Most chart rankings given in this chapter are taken from this source. However, for films released after 1979, I have used annual charts based on the actual box office gross (the money paid by cinemagoers for tickets); see https://www.boxofficemojo.com/year/1980/?grossesOption=totalGrosses (from this page other years can be accessed).

2 In addition to his film career starting in 1965, Allen continued to perform as a stand-up comedian on stage, television and records. He also starred in his second play on Broadway in 1969/70, wrote for magazines and published books. For overviews of Allen's career, see, for example, Evanier (2015), Meade (2001), Fox (1996) and Lax (1992).

3 Between his appearance in two major Hollywood productions, Allen made *What's Up, Tiger Lily?* (1966), a Japanese Bond-like movie which was re-edited and comically

dubbed. Allen, who was one of the writers and voice actors, was credited as an associate producer. In addition, he appeared in several newly shot scenes. The film does not appear to have been shown widely at the time, but has now become a cult classic.

4   On the budgets of Allen's films and their profitability, see Fox (1996, 276–8) and Balio (1987, 325, 328).
5   See *Variety* reviews excerpted in Elley (2000, 138, 943–4).
6   All Quigley rankings in this chapter are taken from https://en.wikipedia.org/wiki/Top_Ten_Money_Making_Stars_Poll#Poll_Results_by_Year; last accessed 1 July 2020.
7   *Stardust Memories* is at number 60 in the grosses chart for 1980.
8   The exceptions are *Play It Again, Sam*, which he wrote, adapting his second Broadway play from 1969, but did not direct, and *The Front*, which he neither wrote nor directed.
9   See http://www.impawards.com/1977/annie_hall.html.
10 It is worth pointing out that the amount of critical and biographical writing on Keaton is miniscule compared with the voluminous literature on Allen. In fact, most of the writing on Keaton appears in books on Allen. See, however, Moor (1989) and Keaton (2012).
11 Keaton plays the wife of the protagonist's brother who reluctantly appears at the protagonist's wedding and is then cajoled into discussing her marital problems with her mother-in-law. But there is no resolution to those problems in sight.
12 Keaton plays a divorcee who, having a secret relationship with her ex-husband's best friend, is being pursued by her ex-husband and eventually agrees to sign a contract which brings them back together on a temporary basis. After many turbulent, and farcical, events, she decides that it is best for her, her husband and her husband's best friend if they all go their separate ways romantically – but in the end she gives in to her husband's advances once more.
13 An important exception is John Simon, who judges *Annie Hall* to be 'painful in three separate ways: as unfunny comedy, poor moviemaking, and embarrassing self-revelation'. Unlike many reviewers, Simon also pays particular, albeit highly negative, attention to Keaton: 'Her work, if that is the word for it, always consists chiefly of a dithering, blithering, neurotic coming apart at the seams – an acting style that is really a nervous breakdown in slow motion' (1977, 74).
14 The film is at number 13 in the annual grosses chart.

Works cited

Balio, Tino. 1987. *United Artists: The Company That Changed the Film Industry*. Madison: University of Wisconsin Press.

Box Office. 1982. 'CinemaScore Card', February: 80.

Carroll, Kathleen. 1977. 'Love and Death II', *New York Daily News*, 21 April: 85.

CinemaScore. 1980. *1979 CinemaScore Audience Reaction Movie Almanac*, in the 'Surveys (1970–1979)' folder at the Margaret Herrick Library, Beverly Hills.

CinemaScore. 1981. *CinemaScore Audience Reaction Almanac Featuring 1980 Movies*, in the 'Surveys 1980–1984' folder at the Margaret Herrick Library, Beverly Hills.

Cohn, Lawrence. 1993. 'All-Time Film Rental Champs', *Variety*, 10 May: C76–C108.

Cook, David A. 2000. *Lost Illusions: American Cinema in the Shadow of Watergate and Vietnam, 1970–1979*. New York: Scribner's.

Crist, Judith. 1977. 'A Finer Mess', *Saturday Review*, 14 May: 38.

Elley, Derek, ed. 2000. *Variety Movie Guide 2000*. New York: Perigee.

Evanier, David. 2015. *Woody: The Biography*. New York: St. Martin's Press.

Fox, Julian. 1996. *Woody: Movies from Manhattan*. London: B. T. Batsford.

Gilliatt, Penelope. 1977. 'Woody at His Best Yet', *New Yorker*, 25 April: 136.

Gold, Sylvaine. 1977. *New York Post*, 16 April: 31; untitled clipping, *Annie Hall* clippings file, Performing Arts Research Center, New York Public Library at Lincoln Center.

Kaminsky, Ralph. 1979. 'CinemaScore: Could It Be a Prophet of Profit', *Box Office*, 20 August: 3.

Kissell, Howard. 1977. Review of *Annie Hall*, *Women's Wear Daily*, 18 April: 72.

Klemesrud, Judy. 1977. 'Diane Keaton: From Mr. Allen to "Mr. Goodbar"', *New York Times*, 17 April: 1, 13.

Krämer, Peter. 1998. 'Post-Classical Hollywood', in *The Oxford Guide to Film Studies*, ed. John Hill and Pamela Church Gibson, 289–309. Oxford: Oxford University Press.

Krämer, Peter. 1999. 'A Powerful Cinema-Going Force? Hollywood and Female Audiences since the 1960s', in *Identifying Hollywood's Audiences: Cultural Identity and the Movies*, ed. Melvyn Stokes and Richard Maltby, 98–112. London: BFI.

Krämer, Peter. 2005. *The New Hollywood: From Bonnie and Clyde to Star Wars*. London: Wallflower Press.

Krämer, Peter and Yannis Tzioumakis. 2018. 'Introduction', in *The Hollywood Renaissance: Revisiting American Cinema's Most Celebrated Era*, ed. Peter Krämer and Yannis Tzioumakis, xiii–xxvii. New York: Bloomsbury Academic.

Lax, Eric. 1975. 'Off the Screen: Out of the Woody (Allen) Work Emerges a Classically Insecure Comedienne, Diane Keaton', *People*, 18 August: 42–4.

Lax, Eric. 1992. *Woody Allen: A Biography*. London: Vintage.

Maslin, Janet. 1977. 'Woody's New Winner', *Newsweek*, 2 May: 78.

Meade, Marion. 2001. *The Unruly Life of Woody Allen*. London: Phoenix.

Monaco, James. 1977. 'Looking for Diane Keaton', *Take One*, November: 26–8.

Monaco, James. 1979. *American Film Now: The People, the Power, the Money, the Movies*. New York: Plume.

Moor, Jonathan. 1989. *Diane Keaton: The Story of the Real Annie Hall*. London: Robson Books.

Nemy, Enid. 1977. 'The Hall-Mark of the Annie Look', *New York Times*, 12 July: 34.
Rich, Frank. 1977. 'The Truth of the Matter Makes "Annie" the Greatest', *New York Post*, 2 April: 22.
Sarris, Andrew. 1977. 'Woody Allen's Funny Valentine', *Village Voice*, 25 April: 45.
Schickel, Richard. 1977. 'Woody Allen's Breakthrough Movie', *Time*, 25 April: 70.
Simon, John. 1977. 'Belated Juvenilia', *New York Magazine*, 2 May: 74.
Steinberg, Cobbett. 1980. *Film Facts*. New York: Facts on File.
Sterritt, David. 1977. 'Woody Allen's New One', *Christian Science Monitor*, 21 April: 20.
United Artists. 1977. United Artists Production Notes for *Annie Hall*, Annie Hall clippings file, Performing Arts Research Center, New York Public Library at Lincoln Center.
Variety. 1978a. 'Big Rental Films of 1977', 4 January: 21.
Variety. 1978b. '"Dreadful" Clothes Are In; Annie Hall Look Is Here', 31 May: 2.

3

'Not a morose type': The Windsor font and *Annie Hall*

J. T. Welsch

Alongside the thick-rimmed spectacles, jazz soundtracks and long takes packed with caustic dialogue, the Windsor typeface used in Woody Allen's title sequences is one of the most recognizable ingredients of his signature style. As type designer Tobias Frere-Jones put it recently, 'If you take Windsor and set it centered, just a couple of words, white on black, you will not be able to think of anything else but a Woody Allen movie' (Spooner 2019, 20). Before any of the star-studded casts or the work of Allen's extraordinary cinematographers grace the screen, viewers are greeted by Windsor's familiar blend of classic and whimsical features, highlighted by simple white-on-black title cards, setting the scene for Allen's own blend of arthouse and commercial aspirations. This chapter will focus on Allen's first use of Windsor for the opening titles of *Annie Hall* (1977), examining its typographical provenance and its place in the history of film title design (Figure 3.1). Attending to the material features and history of the typeface – first produced in 1905 by the industrial type foundry Stephenson Blake – helps us understand the role Windsor plays in the negotiation of art and commerce throughout Allen's oeuvre, in so far as those opening credits frame our expectations for the films that follow. But before diving into Windsor's history and the wild variety of 1970s title design, I want to revisit one of *Annie Hall*'s best-known scenes and the easily overlooked – indeed, nearly imperceptible – reference to typography at its centre.

Figure 3.1 The opening titles of *Annie Hall* (1977).

The McLuhan fallacy

For many viewers, Marshall McLuhan might be better known for his *Annie Hall* cameo than his once-influential theories of media. As Paddy Scannell writes, 'By the end of the 1960s, McLuhan was a spent rocket and in the next decade he fell sharply out of fashion, overtaken by new marxisms and structuralisms which took a disparaging view of him as the ideologue of corporate, capitalist America' (2007, 136). McLuhan's waning authority comes through in accounts of *Annie Hall*'s production, where Allen says he would have preferred someone else for the famous scene. 'I tried many people', he tells Stig Björkman, 'and McLuhan finally agreed to do it. He was not my first choice. My first choice was Fellini, because it would be more natural if people were standing in line talking about movie, that they would be talking about Fellini' (2004, 79). This is clear from the dialogue where the unnamed academic behind Annie and Alvy begins his rant with the assertion that a recent Fellini film was 'not one of his best' and 'lacks a cohesive structure'. It is only after extensive discussion of Fellini as a 'technical' and 'indulgent' filmmaker, and a shift in focus to Annie and Alvy's conversation about therapy and sexual problems, that the man revives his diatribe with a mention of McLuhan. Briefly, McLuhan's views on television are shoehorned in before Alvy addresses the camera, prompting a debate resolved by McLuhan's entrance. The humour still works regardless of McLuhan's reputation, of course. We've all encountered such boors, and McLuhan fulfils the fantasy of having an expert to back us up. But the dialogue complicates the joke, distracting us from the specific error in the man's pontification and from considering implications for the film's aesthetic positions.

Russell Horton, the actor playing the obnoxious man, admits his dialogue 'is essentially all about Fellini, and there's only one last thing about McLuhan because they suddenly had him' (Breznican 2017). That 'one last thing' follows the character's mention of 'the influence of television', explaining to his unfortunate date how 'Marshall McLuhan deals with it in terms of it being a high intensity, you understand, a hot medium'. This is the moment when Allen's Alvy interrupts – 'What I wouldn't give for a large sock of horse manure!' – complaining directly to camera until the man notices. Horton and others have pointed out the nonsensicality of McLuhan's retort, with various opinions on whether the line 'You mean my whole fallacy is wrong!' is knowing satire of academic jargon, and whether it should be credited to Allen or McLuhan.[1] However, no one seems to notice that it also remains unclear whether the man in the queue has actually made a mistake at the point he is interrupted.

The distinction between 'hot' and 'cool' media receives its most extensive treatment in McLuhan's *Understanding Media*. The book, first published in 1964, was enormously influential in the emerging field of media studies, and likely enough to have appeared on the syllabus for 'a class at Columbia called TV, Media, and Culture' taught by a fictional academic in the mid-1970s. In it, McLuhan defines his binary categories by the relative involvement of the audience. Film is a 'hot' medium, he suggests, because it offers a large amount of sensory information, compared to a 'cool one like TV', which leaves more to be 'filled in or completed by the audience' (1964, 24–5). In the movie line man's defence, the audible dialogue leaves it ambiguous whether he has gotten this backwards. (In either case, the error is certainly not egregious enough to suggest he knows 'nothing' of McLuhan's work, as McLuhan quips.) But even if we understand 'it' in the line – 'McLuhan deals with it in terms of it being a high intensity, you understand, a hot medium' – to refer to film, rather than television, the almost inaudible speech that continues under Alvy's complaint suggests a definite point of confusion. The man appears to say ' … as opposed to, uh, as opposed to print, which is essentially linear, or … ', before he trails off, noticing and addressing Alvy.[2]

This is a mistake, though it comes after Alvy has had enough. McLuhan is adamant in *Understanding Media* and elsewhere that print should be considered a 'hot' medium, due to the way it structures thought in a mechanized visual context. His previous book, *The Gutenberg Galaxy: The Making of Typographic Man* (1962), also draws on the work of Walter Ong (his former student) in order to establish print's detachment from speech and handwriting on the basis of its 'increased sophistication in visual presentation' which 'is part of the evolution of typography, showing clearly how the use of printing moved the word away from its original association with sound and treated it as a "thing" in space' (1962, 174). Following these lines of thought, McLuhan emphasizes print's visual orientation in relation to other commercial media:

> Visually, print is very much more 'high definition' than manuscript. Print was, that is to say, a very 'hot' medium coming into a world that for thousands of years had been served by the 'cool' medium of script. Thus our own 'roaring twenties' were the first to feel the hot movie medium and also the hot radio medium. It was the first great consumer age. So with print Europe experienced its first consumer phrase, for not only is print a consumer medium and commodity, but it taught men how to organize all other activities on a systematic lineal basis.
>
> (137)

Thus, this throwaway line by an unnamed character, dismissing print's visual impact through a garbled application of McLuhan's work, raises vital questions we might direct toward the on-screen text at the start of *Annie Hall* and Allen's subsequent films. Recovered from background muttering, the small error gestures to print's 'hot' medium, full of 'high intensity' or 'high definition' visual data. Such visual potency makes title typography an integral part of a film's design, less a matter of conveying information than presenting another visual object or 'a "thing" in space', in Ong's words. Learning from the movie line man's mistake and his latent comparison of TV and film to print in *Annie Hall*, we can begin to see how the mechanized, 'essentially linear' nature of typography as a 'consumer medium and commodity' intersects with negotiations of visual and consumer culture across Allen's oeuvre. More specifically, the Windsor typeface that has become a trademark since its first use in *Annie Hall*'s opening titles can be revisited as a site for these negotiations of uniformity and marketability, in relation to the film's and Allen's more general concern with commercial or artistic status.

'It's just plain chicken'

In interviews from the early 1990s, Woody Allen gives his assessment of movie title design in the years leading up to *Annie Hall*: 'It had really got out of hand in the United States. There was a time during the sixties, when the titles got to be like *The Pink Panther* [1963]. The producers would put aside $250,000 for the title sequence. It would be one of the main things in the movie' (Björkman 2004, 76). This corresponds with Noah Gittell's account, in an article lamenting Netflix's 'skip credits' feature. 'By the mid-1960s', he writes, 'studio movies were paying vast amounts of money for elaborate, animated title sequences that added little of value to the film, such as those featured in the *Pink Panther* movies' (2017). Although Gittell references a scene from *Annie Hall* preceding the one discussed above, acknowledging his affinity with Alvy Singer, 'who refuses to go into a foreign film when Annie arrives to the theater two minutes late', there is, ironically, no mention of how Woody Allen's films fit into his potted history of title design. Nevertheless, the 1970s decline Gittell notes for elaborate animated or narrative sequences, inspired by graphic designers like Saul Bass or directors like Alfred Hitchcock, mirrors the slow evolution of Allen's titles in that same period.

The art nouveau, Aubrey Beardsley-esque opening to *What's New, Pussycat?* (1965), designed by Richard Williams, is typical of the animated *Pink Panther*-inspired title sequences that Allen criticizes, and which Gittell suggests 'added little of value to the film'.[3] Though Allen wrote, acted in, but wouldn't have been responsible for the titles of *Pussycat*, his directorial debut the following year, *What's Up, Tiger Lily?* (1966), is similar in more than its title. At what would have been a relatively high cost for a film made by dubbing and re-editing a Japanese original, the title sequence designed by Phill Norman has a cartoon version of Allen frolicking among colourful pin-up stills reminiscent of James Bond films, accompanied by the first of several original songs by the Lovin' Spoonful, who also appear in the film. Allen's first completely original directorial effort, *Take the Money and Run* (1969), begins with a more straightforward filmed sequence, with credits superimposed over shots of Allen's character being led to his prison cell. From here, the development of his titles can be traced through the vibrant, animated opening of *Bananas* (1971), with Marvin Hamlisch's original song 'Quiero la Noche'; and the word-by-word titles of *Everything You Always Wanted to Know About Sex* (1972), with its credits over footage of rabbits and Cole Porter accompaniment; towards the more staid white-on-black credits of *Sleeper* (1973) and *Love and Death* (1975), with their respective big band and

Prokofiev soundtracks. The shift in the early 1970s is acknowledged by Allen, working towards his use of Windsor for *Annie Hall* (1977):

> I had done some fancy titles on *Bananas* and *Everything You Always Wanted to Know About Sex* ..., and then I thought to myself, 'It's silly to spend money on titles! It's a very American stupid habit. I'm going to get the cheapest titles I can, just a plain announcement.' And I picked the typeface that I liked, and I never changed it after that. Because, what do titles mean? It's just simple information.
>
> (Björkman 2004, 76)

In practice, this money-saving approach meant parting ways with Norman Gorbaty, who designed the titles for *Bananas*, *Everything You Always Wanted*, and *Sleeper*. A company called Computer Opticals produced the title cards for all six films from *Love and Death* (1975) to *Midsummer Night's Sex Comedy* (1982), and Allen has never worked with a named designer since, instead using various New York-based effects firms. But even among those mid-1970s films gradually adopting a simpler design, there is a further evolution in Allen's typeface choices, belying his account of having 'picked the typeface that I liked' and stuck with it. *Bananas* had reverted to *Tiger Lily*'s use of cartoonish Cooper Black, while *Everything You Always Wanted* employed a textbook-like Baskerville in keeping with its mock-educational premise. Although the stark, centred titles for *Sleeper* and *Love and Death* settled on a layout similar to that of later films, their use of Souvenir and Century Schoolbook typefaces show further tweaks en route toward Windsor. Moreover, the notion of finding Windsor and 'never chang[ing] it after that' ignores the fact that *Interiors* (1978), the film immediately after *Annie Hall*, continued to explore other possibilities with its use of News Gothic, and that the title of his next film, *Manhattan* (1979), appears only in a shot of the neon sign on the Manhattan Hotel.

When Björkman suggests to Allen that the Windsor titles 'have become a trademark for your films' and that Ingmar Bergman's later simplified titles might have been an influence, Allen remains practical: 'I didn't know that, I hadn't thought about that. [...] I think it's just fine. It costs no money at all' (Björkman 2004, 76). Without mentioning Allen, however, the French film critic Michael Chion, in his study of *Words on Screen*, identifies a wider mid-century trend:

> The completely black or monochromatic background never goes out of fashion, but it was rare between 1930 and 1960 other than in 'auteur' films. Certain directors created and maintained personal styles for their credit sequences as part of their signature. These were generally frugal looking, on a neutral (often black) background.
>
> (2017, 38)

This chimes with interpretations of Allen's Windsor as part of his 'signature' as an 'auteur', as well as the appeal of something 'neutral' and 'frugal looking', in response to more garish title sequences. The opening of *Annie Hall* can be viewed as the culmination of approaches across Allen's first decade of filmmaking, in the silence and succinctness of its nine single-credit title cards naming main crew and no cast members. Yet, despite his recollection, Windsor's history, its features and wider trends in title design show there was nothing plain or simple about the choice of typeface, or the context for that decision.

''Cause I'm anal'

Filling gaps in Allen's vague account, an online community of typography enthusiasts have conducted more detailed investigations around his use of Windsor. Some of this has drawn out fascinating possibilities. When the Romanian graphic designer Kit Paul published a short post about Allen and Windsor on his blog in June 2006, an American student named Randy J Hunt replied with this anecdote within a couple of hours:

> I'm currently taking a typeface design course with Ed Benguiat, and just last night he described a time when he would have breakfast at the same New Jersey diner every morning. Among the others that would dine there was Woody Allen. On one occasion, referring to Benguiat as a 'printer', Allen asked him what a good typeface was. Benguiat had an affinity for Windsor and suggested it to him that morning.
>
> (Paul 2006)

Benguiat and Allen would certainly have had plenty to talk about. The artist and type designer grew up in Brooklyn, and was an accomplished jazz musician, who performed with Allen's namesake and idol, Woody Herman. More importantly, Benguiat also had an impressive record in film, having designed the logotypes for blockbusters like *Planet of the Apes* (1968) and *Super Fly* (1972). Furthermore, his work with Photo-Lettering Inc (or PLINC) and the International Typeface Corporation (ITC) and their pioneering developments in photo-composition and digital typesetting would have given Benguiat a unique sense of the way different typefaces perform on screen. Benguiat's interpretations of older faces like Caslon or Bookman, his own Souvenir (used in Allen's *Sleeper*) and other 'Benguiat' named designs for ITC now typify a 1970s visual style, establishing the nostalgic vibe for films like Quentin Tarantino's *Jackie Brown* in 1997, using Benguiat's Caslon variant.

Given Windsor's comparable blend of classic and modern touches, the story of Benguiat's recommendation seems entirely plausible. Further internet detective-work around Allen's title design appears to muddy the history of Windsor itself, however. Alongside the Benguiat story, many accounts, from Kit Paul's blog post to newspaper items about Allen's love of Windsor, refer to the specific variant as 'EF Windsor' and either Elongated or Light Condensed. A *Guardian* article from 2011 acknowledges the debates online, asking, 'Which one is it really – Elongated or Light Condensed?' (Glancey 2011). Another emergent consensus is the sole attribution of Windsor as having been 'designed by Eleisha Pechey in 1905 for the Sheffield type foundry Stephenson, Blake', according to that same *Guardian* write-up. These points of simplification not only mask a more complex background but together suggest a cultural attitude towards type design that privileges individual authorship over its industrial context. In this regard, the fragmented history of Windsor echoes tensions between commercial and auteur cinema in *Annie Hall*.

The designation of 'EF Windsor', wherever it began, implies that Allen uses a licensed version of Windsor produced by the German design firm Elsner+Flake, which was only founded in 1986 and whose main business is in publishing a library of more than 2,500 digitized typefaces, old and new. While it is easy enough to see how the mistake might proliferate with someone comparing Allen's titles to whatever images are available through online font libraries, the small slippage is also symptomatic of the type industry's changing fortunes. Allen's adoption of Windsor for *Annie Hall* coincides with a prolonged upheaval as traditional 'hot metal' printing gave way to photographic and digital methods. In that sense, the notion of Allen's Windsor being attributed to either Elsner+Flake or Stephenson Blake as the original owner of the design is neither more nor less accurate than saying his Windsor belonged to the digital effects company, Computer Opticals – who would have produced *Annie Hall*'s title cards from their own images of Windsor, and without any physical type involved. Debating the difference between the Elongated or Light Condensed styles or weights similarly overlooks the fact that these are images of letters, rather than actual printing from Stephenson Blake's named variants, and easily stretched or modified as needed in its photographic form. Moreover, it suggests an authorial consistency not borne out by the films themselves. The sizes of Allen's titles have fluctuated throughout his career, with no subsequent film coming close to the height of 'Annie Hall'. The weight varies too, with those from the mid-1980s, *Broadway Danny Rose* onwards (when Allen primarily used another New York firm, The Optical House), noticeably heavier than earlier films. If the uppercase

'H' of *Annie Hall* looks more or less like the Windsor Light Condensed on Stephenson Blake's specimen sheets, with its wider stance and longer crossbar, the same letter in *Hannah and Her Sisters* (1986) is both narrower and heavier (Figure 3.2), more consistent with the 'H' at the start of *Hollywood Ending* (2002). There is a sense in which each film's titles, if not each title card within each film, must be taken on its own terms as a visual composition.

Crediting Windsor to a single designer, aligned with this projection of authorial consistency, is more tenuous. The claim that the typeface was 'designed by Eleisha Pechey in 1905' is first undercut by the fact that Pechey died in 1902. Some sources, including Wikipedia and Luc Devroye's encyclopaedia of type design information, specify that William Kirkwood was responsible for actually cutting the Windsor punches (used to make the moulds for casting type) from Pechey's designs posthumously. Legal records for a copyright case I will return to in my conclusion show that Windsor was registered on 2 March 1904, which conceivably pre-dates Stephenson Blake's first offering of the type the following year. In any event, the nature of industrial type design and Stephenson Blake's company structure means that although 'Windsor's design has often been attributed to Eleisha Pechey (1931–1902)', as Paul McNeil writes in his *Visual History of Type*, 'it is more likely that the type was drawn by anonymous staff members in the foundry's drawing office' (2017, 177). While questioning Pechey's attribution as Windsor's individual creator, however, we can also see where his role in the company may have influenced its design in legible ways.

Figure 3.2 The opening titles of *Hannah and Her Sisters* (1986).

'What is that your business?'

John Stephenson and James Blake established what was originally a file and tool-making company in the summer of 1818, with a £600 inheritance from Blake's recently deceased uncle. Over the next two centuries, Stephenson Blake & Co. would become the largest and last of the UK's industrial type foundries, introducing influential designs like Impact, Granby and Playbill, while gradually acquiring other foundries and licenses for Baskerville, Clarendon, Georgian, and other classic English typefaces, before ceasing type production in 2005. Elisha Pechey (it's unclear where the misspelling of his first name is introduced, with only one 'e' in all historical documents) joined the company in 1863, serving as chief clerk in Sheffield until 1873, when he was sent to manage its London office. Following Pechey's transfer, 'the London Manager and his staff became the true antenna of the company', Roy Millington writes in his comprehensive history of Stephenson Blake (2002, 83). Tensions between the sales office in London and foundry in Sheffield are personified in the relationship between Pechey and director (and son of founder) Henry Stephenson. As Millington writes: 'Pechey was not one to hold his tongue and his all too frequent demands commercially and typographically fell on deaf ears' (85). An 1887 letter gives some sense of the gap between Pechey's commercial drive and Stephenson's emphasis on maintaining quality and good working conditions: 'There is no doubt in my mind', Pechey writes, 'that the effects of your engineers and fitters must be unrelaxed to keep pace with the growth of your business. ... I am afraid this is the only foundry that has ever found it necessary to adopt stunting and repressive measures of this kind, but I fancy you have never had sufficient faith in the growth of your business' (Millington 2002, 84). Debating a new design in 1894, Pechey is even more passive aggressive, giving a clearer sense of the intersection between creative and commercial concerns:

> Your deference to my view as to the new Old Style is flattering, but puzzling. You have a more or less definite ideal in your mind, which I am afraid is different from mine. You agree as to the fatness of hairline and mainstroke and gauge being as now, and I agree to the De Vinne form of letter being adopted. My ambition had been to get a distinctly new character of Old Style, but I see no reason why I should desire to further my own views on such a speculative subject against your opinion and those you have consulted.
>
> (Millington 2002, 85)

Neither man lived to see Windsor in production. Pechey died still working aged seventy-one in 1902, after falling ill on a trip to North America, where he hoped to expand the company's business. Henry Stephenson died two years later, still working at age seventy-seven. From their correspondence, we see the importance of specialized language and attention to detail with regard to a typeface's physical features. In many ways, Windsor reflects Pechey's ambition (and Stephenson's resistance) towards 'a distinctly new character of Old Style'. These factors may have delayed its production until after their deaths. Like the Old Style series and other turn-of-the-century typefaces, Windsor combines modern touches with an intricate serif style. Both are loosely related to eighteenth-century neoclassical ancestors like Baskerville or older variants of Garamond, whose serifs maintain a closer link with handwritten styles than the industrial, modernist sans serifs increasingly used for display texts in advertising throughout the twentieth century. More specifically, Windsor shares with Old Style what are known as 'adnate' (as opposed to 'abrupt') serifs, where the transition from the main part of a letter to the serif is more gradual. Both typefaces have an 'oblique axis' as well, meaning its rounded shapes appear to be rotated slightly anti-clockwise, so that the thinner parts at the top and bottom are slightly off-centre. But other features also give Windsor what Pechey might have thought of as 'a distinctly new character'. The crossbars on its uppercase, for instance, are generally quite low, relative to the standard 'x-height' – meaning the height of lowercase characters with no ascending strokes, such as 'n' or 'e'. The 'A' in 'Annie Hall' or 'Woody Allen' is a clear example. Many characters have their own flourishes, such as the tails on the upper 'Q' or lower 'g', the large bowls of the upper 'P' and 'R', or the distinctive curl of the upper 'J' and hooked arch of the lowercase 'f'. Cumulatively, these touches define the Windsor look. The sharp angle of its lowercase serifs, when combined with its rounded 'beaks' and stubby feet, further marks the typeface's unique personality. But Windsor's signature quirk, I would suggest, is the exaggerated slope of its lowercase 'shoulders', which make the lowercase 'm', 'n', or 'h' appear as if they're kicking out their right 'legs', and which, along with the teardrop shape and modulated stroke of rounded characters like the upper 'O' or lower 'b' and 'd', make the letters much thicker on the bottom, giving an overall impression of sitting more heavily upon or almost sagging into the baseline.

Again, the effect of these features is anything but plain or simple. Its 'many odd forms in both cases', as described in a 1962 *Encyclopedia of Type Faces*, are also what make Windsor better suited to use in titling than for a longer main text (Turner Berry 1962, 196). In Stephenson Blake's own specimen books, used for advertising available typefaces, Windsor is included with other display faces, intended for titles, advertising and signage. Viewers will note that the scene on Annie's balcony uses a simple sans serif for its subtitles, and the more eagle-eyed might spot that the small copyright notice under 'A Jack Rollins – Charles H. Joffe Production' in the end credits of *Manhattan* also retains a sans serif. Such decisions adhere to the paradox at the start of Robert Bringhurst's authoritative *Elements of Typographical Style*: 'In a world rife with unsolicited messages, typography must often draw attention to itself before it will be read. Yet in order to be read, it must relinquish the attention it has drawn' (2012, 17). A mid-century brochure for Windsor attempts to bridge these competing needs, insisting it 'ATTRACTS ATTENTION' (in uppercase and its outline variant) but also 'reads so well' (in its standard weight). Despite such claims, Windsor's idiosyncrasies have left it rarely used as a composition face for a body of text. In Bringhurst's terms, its design quirks mean it attracts too much attention. In McLuhan's terms, Windsor exemplifies the overload of visual information that makes print such a hot medium.

'Seems like old times'

Another general effect of Windsor is its sense of nostalgia, partly due to the historical layers in its design and partly due to associations accrued in use. While McNeil's *Visual History of Type* finds in Windsor 'a distinctly English, Edwardian feel', Bethany Heck describes it for the *Font Review Journal* as a 'bit of a grab-bag': 'its formal elements feel haphazardly pilfered from various trends from Art Nouveau as well as more conservative and versatile serifs from the era' (2018). Indeed, the brochure mentioned above has Windsor 'shewn [sic] here with stock ornaments of the period' in the form of Mucha-esque women with flowing gowns and flowers. Windsor's 'odd blend of refinement and whimsy', Heck suggests, 'have made it a go-to choice for designers seeking to tap into nostalgic undertones'. Ingrid Haidegger's study of 'the art of movie titling' – where Allen's Windsor is the 'most notable' among 'rare cases' in which a typeface becomes linked to a director (2015, 433) – says this innate quality of Windsor's design 'suggests a certain feeling of nostalgia, which is a central element in almost every [Allen] film'.

Windsor's vague, 'grab-bag' sense of nostalgia is complicated, however, by its renewed popularity at the time *Annie Hall* was made. Four decades later, it becomes impossible to disentangle whatever historical hodgepodge was worked into its design at the turn of the twentieth century from the connotations accrued through use by Allen and others. In Andy Sturdevant's reading, the adoption of Windsor from *Annie Hall* onward was less about looking back to a previous era than following contemporary trends. When Allen 'began using it in the 1970s', he writes, 'it was a much more common typeface, and was visual shorthand for a certain cosmopolitan deadpan quality prevalent in that era' (2016). For many, Sturdevant suggests an immediate reference point would have been the awning of Max's Kansas City, a New York club frequented by famous artists, writers and up-and-coming rock and punk acts throughout the 1970s. Others would have encountered Windsor on the covers of Stewart Brand's era-defining *Whole Earth Catalog*, first published in 1968. A third, even more ubiquitous appearance was the credit sequence for the sitcom *All in the Family*, the most-watched television show in the United States each year between 1971 and 1976. Of course, the idea that *Annie Hall* might have been knowingly following these trends is muddied by the fact that the film itself rejects all three cultural forms so explicitly. We might think of Alvy's wariness of Shelley Duvall's character's *Rolling Stone* crowd or his teasing Annie about a 'rock concert' date. At other points, Alvy is literally sickened by Rob's *All in the Family*-like sitcom and TV in general, and we can imagine the hippyish aura of the *Whole Earth Catalog* typifying much of what he despises about LA, from its health food to the far-out guests of Tony Lacey's party, along with the film's frequent spoofing of drug culture. Rather than suggest that Allen's adoption of Windsor is therefore ironic, these incongruities – along with its use in toy and food packaging of the period (Heck says, 'McDonald's was quite fond of it in the late 70s and early 80s') – point to the typeface's versatility. While the link between Allen's nostalgic content and Windsor's nostalgic design might seem straightforward, the typeface's popularity in the period in which it becomes his 'signature' typeface again shows the complexity of that choice.

Moreover, Allen was hardly the only filmmaker using Windsor for titles at the time nor the only one using it to connote nostalgia. Mark Rydell's 1969 adaptation of William Faulkner's final novel, *The Reivers* (subtitled *A Reminiscence*), put Steve McQueen in a 1905 setting, curiously coincidental with Windsor's initial production, while George Roy Hill's *The Great Waldo Pepper* (1975) employed a heavy Windsor to set the scene for a 1920s flying drama with Robert Redford. Westerns set in the late 1800s, like *Billy Two Hats* (1974) and *Heaven's Gate* (1980), also used Windsor prominently enough to make it a pointed echo for *City Slickers*' titles in 1991. Amidst these wider contexts, Heck's essay on Windsor shows it becoming 'a visual shorthand to signal "this is about the 70's"' without ever mentioning Allen. Other recent uses on the US cover of Eimear McBride's 2016 coming-of-age novel *The Lesser Bohemians* or *New York Magazine*'s 'Doomed Earth Catalog' issue in 2017 attest to this delayed retro effect, similarly tapped into by the cover of Allen's *Mere Anarchy* (2007), his first collection of new writing since 1980's *Side Effects*. Allen's 2020 autobiography, *Apropos of Nothing*, also uses a staid variant of Windsor in white-on-black for its cover.

'It's like a visual poem'

Beyond a nostalgia either inherent in design or accumulated in use, Ed Benguiat's recommendation of Windsor may have stemmed from his experience with text on screen. Windsor's bottom-heavy strokes and shapes are arguably more conducive to vertical presentation on screen, for instance, giving the impression of physical weight. Heck also finds its distinctive shoulders 'make the line of text feel as if it's a living thing, crawling across the page', which might be experienced as a cinematic tension between its kinetic design and static layout, retaining the subtlest hint of those earlier animated sequences. In any case, Windsor's abstract material features mean its visual presence usurps its function as 'simple information', in Allen's words. As Eric Gill writes in his celebrated *Essay on Typography* (1931): 'a good piece of lettering is as beautiful a thing to see as any sculpture or painted picture' (122). Here, 'a good piece of lettering' refers not only to the design of the typeface but also to its setting. Rather than view Windsor as a choice made for *Annie Hall* and 'never changed' since, every title card for every Woody Allen film is the result of countless decisions. I mentioned variations in weight and size above, but these decisions include relative sizes too – where 'Starring' or 'Edited by' for individual credits are always smaller, for example. Perhaps uniquely, the 'and' in *Crimes and Misdemeanors* is also noticeably smaller than the two nouns. Design decisions include the space between individual letters (compare the tight *Midnight in Paris* with *To Rome With Love* among consecutive examples[4]), as well as word-spacing (compare *Hannah and Her Sisters* to the more cramped *A Midsummer Night's Sex Comedy*), and line-spacing (compare the words of *Mighty Aphrodite*, almost touching, to the gaps in *Vicky Cristina Barcelona*). The latter is also contingent upon line-break choices, of course, given that there's no practical reason why *The Curse of the Jade Scorpion* should fit on a single line while *You Will Meet a Tall*

Dark Stranger should isolate the 'a' so unusually amidst three lines. These tiny decisions, however conscious or unconscious, contribute to an overall effect for each film.

Keeping Gill's words in mind, a full appraisal of Allen's commitment to Windsor depends on viewing those title cards as visual compositions – or 'a thing to see' – as much as mere announcements. As for McLuhan and Ong, the words become 'a "thing" in space'. In that regard, the choice of Windsor for *Annie Hall* also needs re-situating within historical and aesthetic continuities between the simple white-on-black titles of the 1970s and the rise of bespoke 'logotypes' in the same period. The work of influential designers bridges what might seem like a disconnect between the 'auteur' style noted by Michael Chion and brand-savvy image-text creations like Benguiat's *Planet of the Apes*. Two of the most prolific title designers, Wayne Fitzgerald and Dan Perri, mix their love of Windsor with logotypes quite freely. Fitzgerald used Windsor for three films directed by Michael Cimino – *Thunderbolt and Lightfoot* (1974), *Heaven's Gate* (1980) and *The Sicilian* (1987) – as well as hits like *Funny Lady* (1975) and the later *City Slickers* (1991). But he is also responsible for the distinctive logotypes of *Escape to Witch Mountain* (1975), *Battlestar Galactica* (1978) and *Footloose* (1984). The contrast is even more striking between Dan Perri's use of Windsor for Robert Zemeckis's debut, *I Wanna Hold Your Hand* (1978), Oliver Stone's *Platoon* (1986) and Adrian Lyne's *Nine 1/2 Weeks* (1986) and his instantly recognizable logotypes for *Taxi Driver* (1976) and both *Star Wars* and *Close Encounters of the Third Kind* in the same year *Annie Hall* was released. Just as importantly, Fitzgerald and Perri both worked on films with cinematographer Gordon Willis – Fitzgerald on the first two *Godfather* films and Perri on *All the President's Men* (1976) – in the years just before Willis and Allen began their long collaboration with *Annie Hall*.

These working relationships mean that even when Allen stopped using title designers, ostensibly to save money, his surprising choice to work with Willis – and their successful partnership on his next eight films – meant a greater emphasis on visual possibilities in general, while retaining a link to designers whose work defined the period. The fluidly with which Willis and others move between a seeming categorical divide between plain text titles and logotypes helps emphasize their visual equivalence, bringing together the 'hot' media of print and film in the intricacies of typographic and cinematographic design. Rather than see Windsor as a simple rejection of industry trends, viewing it within this spectrum links it to tensions between art and commerce in *Annie*

Hall and much of Allen's work. In an interview from 1978, Allen describes *Annie Hall* as a 'weird hybrid of very dramatic influences on a funny film', before going into detail:

> All the devices of *Annie Hall* are devices one generally associates with films of Bergmans or Buñuels. It's not shot like a comedy. It's low-lit. There's long master shots that go on forever. It's not edited like a comedy. The devices – the split-screen devices and subtitling – are things you don't associate with comedy, but the film itself is a comedy. So it becomes an odd kind of experiment.
>
> (Linehan 1978)

He might have mentioned the silent titles among 'things you don't associate with comedy'.

'The cast of *The Godfather*'

At a time when titles were becoming both serious art and serious business – after 1960s titles had gotten so 'out of hand', in Allen's estimation – the openings for the first two *Godfather* films become a useful final comparison. The centred white-on-black titles at the start of *The Godfather* (1972) are even more basic than *Annie Hall*'s, with only 'Paramount Pictures Presents' followed by the famous logotype (Figure 3.3). *The Godfather Part II* (1974) begins with a silent close-up of Al Pacino having his hand kissed, though the opening titles are similarly restricted to a studio credit and the logotype with 'Part II' added. The gravity of what is to come is obvious, balanced with the marketability of such a striking design. The original Gothic typeface that S. Neil Fujita created for the cover of Mario Puzo's 1969 novel establishes a consistent brand for Coppola's series, and for posters and other advertising. Although the *Godfather* joke in *Annie Hall* might be a playful reference to Gordon Willis's resumé and of course the presence of Diane Keaton in both films, the film's titles show Allen responding with his own brand, with a more subtly ornate, but similarly distinctive typeface.

On the other hand, early wavering in his use of Windsor and the fact that it has only been used on Allen's posters since *Whatever Works* (2009) highlight the degree to which a strictly commercial reading of Allen's Windsor might be another backward projection. Notwithstanding the minor variations noted above, it is only through its persistence across five decades that Windsor becomes a brand aligned with his nostalgic style. In other words, the reading of its design as inherently nostalgic becomes tautological when we cannot avoid reading it

Figure 3.3 The opening titles of *The Godfather* (1972).

as a callback to his own earlier work. When a younger filmmaker like Alfonso Cuarón observes in 2015 that Allen 'is such an important and unique link in cinematic history, connecting the traditions of Old Hollywood with those of French cinema and linking them to the most contemporary film-making styles', that link is partly a matter of content and partly a matter of sheer longevity (Solomons 2015, 7). Allen and Windsor offer a material connection to the early decades of the twentieth century in which they were 'born' and the period in the 1970s and 1980s when they both assumed a new prominence.

Yet, any simple identification between them is also troubled by this tangled history and the tangled relationship between art and industry. Just as it would be impossible to give sole credit for the *Godfather* logotype to Francis Ford Coppola, Gordon Willis, Wayne Fitzgerald, S. Neil Fujita or Mario Puzo, the dubious attribution of Windsor solely to Elisha Pechey or the choice for *Annie Hall* solely to Woody Allen masks the manner by which such decisions and designs emerge collaboratively in an industrial context, driven home by the anonymity of Allen's title design firms since the mid-1970s and of poster designers adopting Windsor in recent years. Rather than view his Windsor credits as an unassuming throwback, the use of then-new computer effects technology to fashion cheaper title sequences gestures towards the constructed nature of nostalgia in general. At the same time, re-evaluating our authorial or auteur-bound investments in Windsor as a 'signature' allows us to see how the 'high intensity' of print itself persists in the face of industrial and technological changes.

As Eric Gill finally admits, 'our argument here is not that industrialism has made things worse, but that it has inevitably made them different' (1931, 74). Gill remains convinced, however, of the 'incompatibility' between 'the typography of industrialism' and what he calls 'humane typography' (1931, 69–70). If this seems analogous to an apparent divide between arthouse and mainstream cinema, it is also clear that the thrill of Allen's best work lies in the 'weird hybridity' of seemingly incompatible elements, mixing genres, styles and conventions. Windsor retains a parallel hybridity in its 'grab-bag' of physical features. In a 1916 court case regarding Stephenson Blake's copyright on Windsor, the question of whether type design should be categorized as 'fine art' or 'industrial design' is finally decided on that grounds that, legally, the latter supersedes and includes the former (Pain 1916, 666–9; Williams 1916, 55–6). Conceptually, however, McLuhan shows that print has been 'a consumer medium and commodity' at least since Gutenberg, offering a stream of visual data in a mechanized 'hot medium'. In that sense, separating a typographical choice from cinema's visual composition or treating a particular typeface as somehow anti-commercial would repeat the movie line man's unheard mistake.

Notes

1   Philip Marchand, in his biography *Marshall McLuhan: The Medium and the Messenger*, suggests this was McLuhan's 'favorite put-down for hecklers' (270).
2   The latter part of this line is omitted from online transcriptions and the published screenplay in *Four Films of Woody Allen*.
3   In addition to those reproduced here, screenshots of many of Allen's title sequences can be viewed at Christian Annyas's *Movie Titles Still Collections* online.
4   The letter gaps in *To Rome With Love* are the result of the lowercase Os and the I following uppercase T, R and W, which a typesetter or graphic designer would normally adjust for visual consistency.

Works cited

Allen, Woody, 1982. *Four Films of Woody Allen*. London: Faber.
Allen, Woody, 2020. *Apropos of Nothing*. New York: Grand Central Publishing.
Berry, William Turner. 1962. *The Encyclopedia of Type Faces*. New York: Pitman.

Björkman, Stig. 2004. *Woody Allen on Woody Allen: In Conversation with Stig Björkman*. New York: Grove Press.

Breznican, Anthony. 2017. 'The Movie Theater Blowhard from Annie Hall Finally gets his say', *Entertainment Weekly*, 5 April.

Bringhurst, Robert. 2012. *The Elements of Typographical Style* (4th edition). London: Hartley & Marks Publishers.

Chion, Michael. 2017. *Words on Screen*. English edition. New York: Columbia University Press.

Gill, Eric. 1931. *Essay on Typography*. London: Sheed and Ward.

Gittell, Noah. 2017. 'Why Netflix's "Skip Intro" Feature Is Bad News for Classic Films', *Guardian*, 15 May 2017.

Glancey, Jonathan. 2011. 'Windsor Is Just Woody Allen's Type', *Guardian*, 5 April.

Haidegger, Ingrid. 2015. 'What's in a name? The Art of Movie Titling', *Word & Image* 31 (4): 425–41.

Heck, Bethany. 2018. 'Windsor – Designed by Eleisha Pechey', *Font Review Journal* 25, November.

Linehan, Brian. 1978. 'Woody Allen', in *City Lights*. Toronto: CityTV.

Marchand, Philip. 1998. *Marshall McLuhan: The Medium and the Messenger*. Cambridge, MA: MIT Press.

McLuhan, Marshall. 1962. *The Gutenberg Galaxy: The Making of Typographic Man*. Toronto: University of Toronto Press.

McLuhan, Marshall. 1964. *Understanding Media: The Extensions of Man*. New York: McGraw-Hill.

McNeil, Paul. 2017. *The Visual History of Type*. London: Lawrence King.

Millington, Roy. 2002. *Stephenson Blake: The Last of the Old English Typefounders*. New Castle, Delaware: Oak Knoll Press.

Pain, W. P. 1916. 'Stephenson, Blake and Co. vs Grand, Legros, and Co. Limited (17, 18, and 25 October 1916)', *The Law Times* 115 (1916–1917): 666–9.

Paul, Cristian (Kit). 2006. 'Woody Allen's Windsor', *Kit.blog*, 14 June.

Scannell, Paddy. 2007. *Media and Communication*. London: SAGE.

Solomons, Jason. 2015. *Woody Allen: Film by Film*. London: Carlton Books.

Spooner, Erik B. 2019. 'What's Your Type?' *Advertising Age* 90 (14), 15 July.

Sturdevant, Andy. 2016. 'Windsor: A "Cosmopolitan Deadpan" Quality Carries This Throwback Typeface into the 21st Century', *MinnPost*, 8 July.

Williams, S. E. 1916. 'Stephenson, Blake & Co. v. Grand, Legros & Co. (28 October 1916)', *Solicitors' Journal and Weekly Reporter* 61 (1916–1917): 55–6.

4

Annie Hall as a memory-film

Sue Vice

Annie Hall is all about memory, as is evident from the opening moment of Alvy Singer's (Woody Allen) monologue and confirmed by the matching address to camera at the film's end. Approaching Allen's film as a memory-text (Kuhn 2010) allows the audience to consider with a new emphasis those elements that have attracted the most commentary, ranging from questions about Alvy's reliability as a focalizer to the use of obtrusive cinematic techniques, and to view afresh some of the visual and verbal sequences that have become most celebrated in the decades since its release (see for instance Bradshaw 2017).

Indeed, as such a stance suggests, in extra-diegetic terms *Annie Hall*'s memorious state includes the implicit recall of its own textual history as part of the final form. The film has in turn become a memory-object, with a global influence on romantic comedy and self-representation, in examples that extend to autofictional British television drama such as Simon Amstell's *Grandma's House* (Christine Glennon 2010–12), in which the comedy relies on the exposure of the central character's failings, and Phoebe Waller-Bridge's *Fleabag* (Harry Bradbeer 2016–19), where the protagonist's audience-soliciting glances to camera were described as the series' 'hallmark' (Ovenden 2019). Waller-Bridge has described this 'breaking of the fourth wall' as indebted not only to Michael Caine's eponymous character in *Alfie* (Lewis Gilbert, 1966) but also to 'a few films by Woody Allen […] early stuff' (Waller-Bridge 2019). Since Waller-Bridge adds that the technique was 'useful' for her television series because of its potential to represent 'really flawed characters' (Waller-Bridge 2019), we can only imagine that *Annie Hall* was prominent among the 'early' Allen films that influenced her. In this chapter, I will ask whether the questions of the film's unreliability and heterogeneous form are resolved by considering them as expressions of memory, and if assigning *Annie Hall* to that genre, as much as to one of romantic comedy, generates new meaning.

Looking back

The film is framed by Alvy's pair of monologues in a way that highlights the deliberate casting of the protagonist's mind back over the period of his relationship with Annie (Diane Keaton), in an attempt to determine why it ended, as Alvy says straight to camera at the opening:

> ALVY: (*Sighing*) Annie and I broke up, and I – I still can't get my mind around that. You know, I keep sifting the pieces o' the relationship through my mind – and examining my life and tryin' to figure out where did the screw-up come, you know, and a year ago we were ... tsch, in love.
>
> (Allen 1983, 4)

The detail of Alvy's phrasing, including his lamenting the inability to 'get [his] mind' around the end of his relationship, and therefore attempting a 'sifting [of] the pieces', has a more direct relevance to the film's representation of memory than at first it might seem. *Annie Hall* itself takes exactly the fragmentary and non-linear form that Alvy describes as his mental mode of looking back. Equally, the longer roots of the factors involved are invoked in the unfolding of the story, sometimes as memories-within-memories, as part of a process that Alvy describes here as 'examining' the entirety 'of [his] life'.

All the film's varied techniques, including address to camera, voiceover, split screens, subtitling and animation, can be considered as methods for presenting memory's subjective view of past events. Each is drawn from filmic genres that expand the present film beyond its comic type (McBride 1977), suggesting that this is the way a filmically oriented individual might recall their past. Such techniques augment the more conventional methods used in *Annie Hall* to convey memory, including the subject's appearance as an onlooker in the scenes of his history, and the replaying of what we know to be flashback sequences as if they were unfolding in the present. Viewing the film in such a way, as one both about and structured in order to imitate memory, allows the audience to consider anew such questions as the extent of the subjective or even one-sided image of the romance that emerges, as well as whether the conundrum introduced by Alvy at the outset, to find out 'where the screw-up came', can be fully addressed.

The notion of a relationship reflected upon 'in pieces', as Alvy puts it, unites the 'impressionism' of form with that of the workings of memory, in a manner reminiscent of the practice described by the Modernist writer Ford Madox Ford, whose conception of the act of looking back is one that takes place in 'disordered pictures', rather than as a straightforward 'report' (Ford 1924, 72). As Ford argues, since even everyday recall's impressionistic pattern demands of the artist a high degree of narrative experimentation, 'just imagine how it will be with your love-affairs, that are so much more complicated' (Ford 1924, 73). Indeed, the form of Allen's film is most disrupted when it is 'complicated' emotions that are recalled. By contrast, the fondness of nostalgia, rather than the retrospective strictures of self-scrutiny and blame, renders the 'courtship' scenes of the film's mid-section the most conventional in form and order (Schatz 2006, 129). Such a combination of voiceover from a point in the future offering a romanticized view of the past appears in other works by Allen, notably *Radio Days* (1987). Yet in *Annie Hall* even such orderliness is enfolded within a broader achronistically presented narrative (Genette 1980, 50), conveying that romantic nostalgia is itself framed by what might seem to be ambivalence and regret.

When chronology is most disrupted in *Annie Hall*, so are the realist codes of classical cinema. The presence of both together indicates the ambivalence of memory and the uncomfortable judgements it might entail. The greatest linearity is therefore evident when the 'courtship story' is unfolding, in those sequences that occur between Alvy and Annie's first meeting at the Wall Street tennis club, up to the moment of their first separation. In this centrally located 'movement', in Thomas Schatz's term (2006, 128), the exertions of memory are not directed at ironic or bitter self-scrutiny which characterizes the sections before and after that of the courtship, and are more suited to the mode of filmic stand-up that entails the presence of Alvy's self-conscious addresses to camera. Rather, this central movement is characterized by a pleasurable or wistful memory and consequently takes a form that is close to the 'concealed artistry' of classical Hollywood cinema (Bordwell, Staiger and Thompson 1988, 24).

The first scene in *Annie Hall*'s diegesis proper (Lee 2001, 40), following straight on from the opening monologue, remains with Alvy alone. It delays Annie's eventual appearance, which is prepared for by Alvy's monologue and a subsequent dialogue between him and his friend Rob (Tony Roberts), who warns him that he – like the audience – risks being 'late for meeting Annie' (Allen 1983, 10). The first scene after his monologue shows us, rather, Alvy's recalling his much younger self at school. This look back not only forms part of the far-reaching search for the origins of the 'screw-up' in Alvy's past but establishes the way in which the audience is to be presented with his recall of that history, delivered in his customary comic style. Although such humour has a disarming effect, we might be suspicious at the condescension or manipulation it implies, as suggested by Alvy's second wife Robin (Janet Margolin), who admonishes him in a flashback, 'No jokes, these are friends, okay' (Allen 1983, 27). Humour, it seems, is reserved for one's enemies.

The conceit of a bodily return to the past is enacted in the school-room scene, since Alvy is present as both his younger and older selves. Later, when a flashback to his parents arguing in his childhood home provokes Alvy to exclaim, 'You're both crazy!', Rob reminds him, 'They can't hear you, Max' (Allen 1983, 73). However, in the present case, it seems that the figures of the past can both hear and reply. This casts further doubt on the flashback's reliability, since the past is shown as it responds to and is altered by the present, for instance in the aftermath of the six-year-old Alvy's attempt to kiss another pupil. While the child responds with adult wisdom, Alvy is present in the form of an adult:

> 1st GIRL: For God's sakes, Alvy, even Freud speaks about a latency period.
> ALVY (AS ADULT) (*Gesturing*): Well, I never had a latency period. I can't help it.
>
> (Allen 1983, 8)

Alvy follows this exchange by musing, 'Sometimes I wonder where my classmates are today.' This makes even clearer that the mode of this scenario is that of memory augmented by what might seem to be the opposite mental actions of supposition or imagination. His question is met with a series of responses whose absurdity or banality seems to redeem his failure at school and justify his present life:

> *One at a time, the young students rise up from their desks and speak.*
>
> 1st BOY: I'm President of the Pinkus Plumbing Company.
> 2nd BOY: I sell tallises.
> 3rd BOY: I used to be a heroin addict. Now I'm a methadone addict.
> 2nd GIRL: I'm into leather.
>
> (Allen 1983, 8)

However, this imaginary scenario is viewed by Alvy's mother (Joan Newman), who appears in the scene as its judge, as a ruse to justify misanthropy: 'You always only saw the worst in people […] Even when you got famous, you still distrusted the world' (9). If these are the constituent voices in the 'microdialogue' of Alvy's inner world (Bakhtin 1963, 74), the inclusion of his mother's equally imaginary reproach makes them convey not only a solipsistic but a self-critical view.

Annie

It is no accident that the stylized memory of Alvy's childhood set in the schoolroom precedes our first encounter with Annie, which is set at a moment some time into their relationship when it is already foundering. The elements of Alvy's manipulation of events, both cinematically and emotionally, appear in more implicit form in this scene where he waits for Annie outside the Beekman Theatre art cinema. These are now a part of the characterization and action, rather than a stylized enactment. Annie's arrival initiates a sequence of responses that fall into what are clearly well-worn patterns of friction and misunderstanding. She is late and in a 'bad mood', while her having missed a therapist's appointment earlier that day is described by Alvy as an act 'hostile' to him, a presumption that she calls 'egocentric' (Allen 1983, 14–15).

However, the inflexibility and intolerance on Alvy's part in this scene are by no means concealed, but acted out as part of the comedy. His refusal to enter the cinema to watch the film they were due to see, Bergman's *Face to Face* (1976), since they have missed the first two minutes, means he suggests instead seeing Marcel Ophuls's *The Sorrow and the Pity* (1969), despite Annie's not being, as she puts it, 'in the mood' to watch again a 'four-hour documentary on Nazis' (Allen 1983, 13). A cut to the queue for ticket-holders outside another cinema economically conveys that Alvy's preference has prevailed. His being able to scotch the pretentious assertions of another man in the queue (Russell Horton) about Marshall McLuhan by enlisting the philosopher in person concludes with an admission that such a scenario represents not only wish-fulfilment but artistic licence:

> ALVY (*to the camera*): Boy, if life were only like this!
>
> (Allen 1983, 16)

The to-camera addresses such as this give an impression of honesty, of 'levelling' with the audience (Bailey 2001, 33), as part of Alvy's effort, in Christopher Knight's phrasing, to curry a spectatorial 'interpretive favour' (2004, 214). However, as the scene's concluding utterance, the present example is a belated admission of an artifice that the viewer might take to refer to a wider wish on Alvy's part, not just to get his own way, but to create an art-work with a coherence absent from reality. Ironically, the works that do appear in the film under his authorship, notably the play whose rehearsal we witness near the film's end, simply reinforce the 'lifelike' nature of *Annie Hall* itself, with its bittersweet rather than conventionally romantic ending.

The role of the fantasied moment in which the opinionated man in the cinema queue is silenced by McLuhan seems to be compensatory, since it allows Alvy and his views to be endorsed. Yet it also takes its place in a portrait of his ambivalence about intellectual endeavour, since Alvy's distaste for its overt and self-aggrandizing expression, in relation to the luckless man in the film-queue as well as to his ex-wife Robin, coexists with his urging self-improvement of this kind on the insecure Annie. Even the flashback to an uncomfortable scene with Robin seems motivated by a need to disprove Annie's claim that 'you really like those New York girls' (Allen 1983, 26), or indeed to suggest the bleaker truth that neither Robin, the cosmopolitan sophisticate, nor Annie, the Wisconsin ingénue, is quite suited to him. Knight includes in a reading of Alvy's persona as 'unyielding and coercive' his twice-repeated comment about romantic impasses, 'usually attributed to Groucho Marx [...], "I would never wanna belong to any club that would have someone like me as a member"' (Allen 1983, 4, see also 22), concluding that loving 'the ideal, but hat[ing] the actual' is 'a dismal recognition and a sorry fact' (Knight 2004, 215).

Alvy's opening with the Groucho Marx joke sets the scene for the film's mode, in which humour depends on his being self-deprecating without necessarily recognizing his actual shortcomings. Indeed, such a failure on his part to understand fully is shown to be an element of what went wrong between him and Annie. These revelations are not always part of conscious memory, and indeed they are given quite different meanings in Alvy's framing of them, but his obliviousness emerges nonetheless. This is evident in other instances of sharp juxtapositions between scenes, for instance the abrupt cut between one that concludes with Alvy's praising 'adult education courses', and the next one starting with his self-avowedly 'spying' on Annie and her tutor David:

> ALVY: I think [adult education]'s a wonderful thing. You meet wonderful, interesting professors.
> CUT TO:
> EXTERIOR. STREET.
> *Annie stands at the open door of a cab, Alvy next to her gesturing as people and cars move by.*
> ALVY: Adult education is such junk! The professors are so phony. How can you do it?
>
> (Allen 1983, 63)

If *Annie Hall* is indeed a Pygmalion story, as critics have claimed (Knight 2004, Shone 2015, 83), in which the protégée outstrips her instructor, the bridge between these scenes conveys a trajectory that Alvy sums up to his therapist as, 'her progress is defeating my progress' (Allen 1983, 81). Even more significant is the look back that these incidents encode. The film-scape of Alvy's memory offers comically unflattering revelations which appear with increasing frequency as the relationship declines, culminating in his flying to Los Angeles to propose to Annie at a time when she is living and recording music with Tony Lacey (Paul Simon). It might seem that such moments suggest an honesty or self-awareness that challenges the image of Alvy's otherwise presiding perspective, and the slanted orientation of his memory as we have experienced it. However, it offers rather an extension of the persuasiveness conveyed by the to-camera addresses and the comedy itself, both of which turn the audience into Alvy's confidant. Making us share in his failings aligns us further with his view of the past. Indeed, his apparent lack of self-awareness is itself comic. Alvy protests his innocence aloud in the spying scene, after Annie, having declared, 'I just think we oughta call this relationship quits!', rides off in the taxi:

> ALVY: Well, I just don't know what I did wrong. (*Gesturing*) I mean, I can't believe this. Somewhere she cooled off to me.
>
> (Allen 1983, 63)

On this occasion, one of the voices enlisted as commentary, that of '*an older woman walking down the street carrying groceries*', supports Alvy's disinclination to assume responsibility for Annie's departure. The passer-by's verdict, 'Never something you do. That's how people are. Love fades' (Allen 1983, 63), conveys a truism that might offer solace to Alvy, but is not accurate here. The voice of the 'woman on the street' is the first sign of a return to the non-classical cinematic code with which *Annie Hall* began, and which was in abeyance during Alvy's remembering the start of the relationship and its early episodes. Annie's departure in the taxi prompts the resumption of a more fractured, self-conscious mode consistent with uneasy recall.

(Un)reliability

Alvy's status as the film's focalizer and narrator, in relation to what he says is the case both within and outside the narrative, often conflicts with his role as a character and what we see him do. Although we are not directed to invoke a radical scepticism about what are presented to us as 'scenes from a relationship' (McBride 1977), the comic exposure of Alvy's partiality means that our judgement is solicited about whether his memory is either deluded or obliquely self-aware. The orientation of his perspective towards eliciting the viewer's allegiance is typified by moments in which the dialogue or imagery itself seems to conform to his viewpoint. Such an effect is only redoubled when it is implied that such moments are not reliable reports on reality but Alvy's exaggerated perceptions. To note such unreliability is in one sense simply to reiterate the fact that this is a memory-film located in the recall of one of the protagonists. In another sense, we might consider the viewpoint itself to be tainted, in its exhibiting such a conventionally masculine standpoint that it is, as Knight argues, 'less perspectival than normative' (2004, 214). Considering Alvy's perspective in terms of the distortions of memory does not sidestep its aspects of normativity of this kind, but does take for granted its unreliability. Indeed, to suspect inaccuracy is to identify the presence of memory.

The intertwinement of memory with unreliability is evident for instance in the sequence in which Alvy is invited for 'Easter dinner' at the Halls' home, and a series of shots at the table between Grammy Hall and Alvy seems to reveal her estimate of him. Yet any objective revelation about someone else's viewpoint in a film so consistently tied to one individual's subjectivity and recall is impossible. The camera cuts from Alvy, dressed in what he clearly believes to be the 'correct attire' of a sports jacket and checked shirt (Abrams 2017) for this gentile occasion, to Grammy, looking straight at him with an expression of 'utter dislike' (Allen 1983, 55), then back to Alvy, who is now dressed Hasidic-style in black coat and hat with a full rabbinical beard. The viewer might be aware that this is Alvy's imagining how Grammy sees him, or how he is made to feel, in the wake of Annie's breezily saying of her grandmother, 'You're what Grammy Hall would call a real Jew ... She hates Jews' (Allen 1983, 38–9). Yet it is hard not to believe in the judgement that Grammy Hall (Helen Ludlam) is what Alvy calls 'a classic Jew-hater' (Allen 1983, 56) as conveyed by this image. The shot-reverse-shot formation implies the depiction of a reaction, yet in this instance it exists rather for the sake of comic timing, to delay and then suddenly reveal an image that seems to vindicate what Rob calls Alvy's 'paranoid' fears. The scene's shorthand of a 'sight gag' (Lee 2001, 43) to convey discomfort makes greater sense if we consider it as the product of Alvy's looking back, since unreliability and exaggeration together make clear the presence of memory.

It is not just the viewers' vision that is drawn into Alvy's ambit in a way that demonstrates and profits from its unreliability but also their perception of dialogue recalled. His viewpoint is at times initially endorsed and then comically undermined, for instance in his recall of Annie's recounting her dream about Frank Sinatra, at a moment soon before their first separation. Although it might seem that Alvy's version of events, or at least the way they are recounted, is ultimately triumphant, this comes at the cost of a larger loss. This scene is significant in signalling Annie's turning away from Alvy to the self-determination encouraged by her therapist, a process acted out by the shifts in the dream's interpretation as she gradually reveals its details. Annie appears to jog Alvy's memory and motivate the sequence's appearance, as she says at the end of the previous scene:

> ANNIE: You're the one who never wanted to make a real commitment. You don't think I'm smart enough! We had that argument just last month, or don't you remember that day?
>
> (Allen 1983, 60)

The sequence follows Alvy's recall of 'that argument', rather than Annie's, so that its import is not as clear as she implies. If Alvy's assumptions about her intellectual eligibility are at stake, this is in the context of an interpretive battle centring on Annie's dream in which Frank Sinatra is 'holding his pillow across my face and I can't breathe' (Allen 1983, 63). The process of deciphering the dream shifts from Alvy to Annie. While Alvy reads the dream's drama as suggesting that Annie, a singer just like Sinatra, is 'trying to suffocate [her]self', her interpretation relates instead to Alvy's surname, Singer, implying that, on the contrary, as he indignantly recognizes, 'So whatta you saying that I – I'm suffocating you?' (Allen 1983, 62). As we watch, the couple's presence on-screen enacts the rhetorical shifts: a mid-shot of Annie arriving home from the screen's left and discussing her therapy session cuts to a two-shot, as Alvy appears from the right and eagerly hails his own 'perfect analytic … kind of insight' (Allen 1983, 62) about her self-suffocation. Annie moves off-screen to the right to offer her opposite interpretation, meaning that they have changed places rhetorically and physically. They meet again in the middle in a two-shot only to disagree about something else, in the form of an individual word.

In this scene, the viewer's own memory and perception is called upon, in relation to the dream but also the subsequent clash. This takes place not only between Alvy and Annie's different interpretation of her dream and of their interaction but their recall of the same event. It is one that occurs in our hearing and centres upon what we might take to be the verifiable status of a single word:

> ANNIE: I don't think I mind analysis at all. The only question is, will it change my wife?
> ALVY: Will it change your wife?
> ANNIE: Will it change my life?
> ALVY: Yeah, but you said, 'Will it change my wife'! [...]
> ANNIE: (*Yelling out, angry*): Life. I said, 'life'. *Alvy turns toward the camera.*
> ALVY: (*To the audience*) She said, 'Will it change my wife.' You heard that because you were there so I'm not crazy.
>
> (Allen 1983, 62)

The soundtrack to the sequence, and, as we see above, the screenplay itself, appears to reveal that Alvy was not 'crazy' but correct in his insistence on Annie's slip. Nonetheless, this moment is a small but crucial instance that is metonymic of the film's relying on, yet seeding doubt about, Alvy's view of a shared past. It seems that he returns to this moment as a manifest attempt to show that he was right, but such a return's latent meaning, in the terminology of the two-tier signification of the dream-work, in this instance applying to memory, relates to mourning the loss of Annie. She did want to change her 'wife', assuming that Alvy can be considered to occupy that role, in the process of changing her life. Although Alvy's recall is vindicated in the local terms of the isolated signifier, the larger currents of responsibility and regret go unaddressed.

Time

In *Annie Hall*, the disordered chronology, as motivated by the memory of what Ford Madox Ford calls a 'love-affair', takes two forms. The first is that of stylized flashbacks to Alvy's childhood and his previous relationships, some of which take place as if they were accounts given to Annie, while others are introduced solely to the audience. The second is the deliberate recall of the relationship, often in the form of episodes that are narrated and linked associatively rather than in the order of their occurrence. Even in the film's courtship section, the precise chronology and links between scenes are not always made clear. This establishment of a new kind of connection between temporal moments other than linear cause and effect arises from Alvy's quest to locate the moment of breakdown, since it is not amenable to logical analysis. Rather, it allows him to consider events in this memorial 'album' (Shone 2015, 83), depicting a relationship in terms of their affective priority.

Following such a pattern, the moment of the very first meeting between Alvy and Annie at the tennis court is not shown until a quarter of the way through the film, by which time it has, as its editor Ralph Rosenblum puts it, the 'refreshing effect' of a 'new beginning' (Rosenblum 1986, 282). Since this scene is preceded by others revealing the fault-lines in their relationship, we are already familiar with Alvy and Annie by the time we see the moment they met. Their being known to us, even though they are strangers to each other, gives even their first meeting and early enthusiasm a sense of nostalgia on the audience's part that parallels Alvy's own. Disrupted or even reverse chronology can be a means of ironizing or judging a relationship, by showing it 'from divorce to wedding', as A. O. Scott puts it of François Ozon's 2004 film *5x2*. In the present case, however, the fact that such temporal disorder is motivated by the intradiegetic narrator's memory fills it with feeling, rather than its constituting a formal device imposed from the outside. Psychology is thus united with artwork.

After Annie invites him into her apartment for the first time, Alvy's viewpoint is presented as if it were complemented by hers. Their first lengthy conversation on the apartment terrace takes place as if we had access to her subjectivity as well as his. In reply to Alvy's asking if she took the photographs displayed on the walls, we witness the following:

> ANNIE (Nodding, her hand on her hip) Yeah, yeah, I sorta dabble around, you know. (Annie's thoughts pop up on the screen as she talks: *I dabble? Listen to me – what a jerk*).
> ALVY: They're ... they're ... they're wonderful, you know. They have – they have, uh ... a ... a quality (*As do Alvy's: You're a great-looking girl*)
> (Allen 1983, 39)

In the terms of a comedy, the subtitles constitute a formal and romantic disruption beneath the surface of the official dialogue. In relation to the representation of memory, the fact that they are less a version of reality than a reconstruction of it is made a part of the plot. While Knight regrets what he sees as a gendered imbalance in Annie and Alvy's thoughts (2004, 216) – she worries about her intellectual standing, he wonders '*what she looks like naked*' (Allen 1983, 39) – if this exchange is the product of memory, its being infused with both pleasure and regret informs what we know to be Alvy's look back. It is therefore his supposition that is responsible for the nature of the 'thoughts' depicted. For a seasoned spectator, this is made clear by repeated viewings and the film's drawing on the memory of its own performance. Thus Annie's phrasing towards the end of their relationship appears prochronistically, that is, too early, in the scene of their first meeting, as she responds to Alvy's comment about the uncertain 'aesthetic criteria' for photography:

> ANNIE: Aesthetic criteria? You mean, whether it's, uh, good photo or not?
> (*I'm not smart enough for him. Hang in there*)
>
> (Allen 1983, 40)

As the subtitles show, Alvy's look back takes the form of suggesting that Annie's thoughts, even at the moment they first met, already gave voice to what he only later came to recognize as her constant anxiety: 'You don't think I'm smart enough to be serious about.' Since the viewpoint is Alvy's, we know that the representation of Annie's thoughts arises from his supposition. Indeed, to backdate the appearance of such a sentiment to this meeting is to absolve himself by giving it life independent of his influence. Alvy's apparently garbled reply, which he too fears will reveal him as '*not knowing what I'm saying – she senses I'm shallow*', is in fact a metacritical comment on the film in which they both appear, signalling his role in charge of the narrative: 'The – the medium enters in as a condition of the art form itself' (Allen 1983, 40). This insight could aptly be applied not only to the film itself, but to its representation of memory. The utterance's wording that so displeases Alvy here equally suggests that he is not after all so different from the pretentious man in the film-queue whose comments later enrage him.

Although the film's disordered chronology might mean that the relationship's end appears pre-determined or even inevitable, the effect in this case is, rather, one of poignancy. The viewer is affected by eagerness for the relationship to start, combined with nostalgia in advance in the knowledge of its end. Indeed, a selective memorious gaze, as embodied by Alvy's look back at this moment from the past, could be said to highlight what turned out to be its pitfalls. His is the only viewpoint to which we have direct access, and his unreliability is a topic on which even he comments, admitting early on that his analyst says he 'exaggerate[s his] childhood memories' and that his 'hyperactive imagination' means that he has 'some trouble between fantasy and reality' (Allen 1983, 6). Although this seems to be a self-reflexive comment originating in the film's first cut, in which prolonged surreal narratives emerged from the protagonist's contemplation of his life, in the present case, it functions as a warning to the audience in relation to the information they gain about Annie.

Intertextual memory

Annie Hall as a whole contains vestiges of its first version, before it was edited to represent an individual's memory, but it is the disruptive opening section where these are most evident. Although Thomas Schatz aptly notes that the first third of the film imitates the format of 'the stand-up-comedy-routine' in which 'the comic narrator's life' is the organizing principle (Schatz 2006, 128), it is also a palimpsestic memory-trace of an earlier version of the text in which the relationship was not central. This first cut, at two hours and twenty minutes, related the 'surrealistic and abstract adventures of a neurotic Jewish comedian who is reliving his highly flawed life' and 'in the process satirizing much of our culture', in the form of a 'visual monologue' (Rosenblum 1986, 275). Allen's description of the action all 'supposed to take place in my mind' supports his summation that 'It was originally a picture about me, exclusively, not about a relationship' (quoted in Rosenblum 1986, 283). In *Annie Hall*'s final ninety-three-minute running time, the portrayal of a romance, which has now taken centre-stage, both focuses the plot and widens its scope beyond the 'reliving' of a single life.

In Rosenblum's account of the original version, the romance with Annie is simply the prompt for 'innumerable flights into the past', in a reverse of the priority in the released film, where the past is enlisted in relation to her (Rosenblum 1986, 279). Instead of a consistent internal 'monologue', the perspective is one of personal memory. The film's title conveys this shift from an individual's life to that of his recall of a relationship, in a way that its other discarded titles, including *Anhedonia* – the inability to feel pleasure – and *Annie and Alvy*, would not have accomplished. Yet, by the film's end, the title might seem to convey a portrait of an individual, in its reference to the self-fulfilment of the eponymous subject. In that sense, *Annie Hall* is a filmic version of a dramatic monologue, in which the narrator's biases are revealed in the very process of recalling the object of address.

Some traces of the longer 'surreal' scenes from the original version of the film remain as the basis for more naturalistic details in the final release. While we might, for instance, regret the decision to omit a sequence in which Alvy's parents 'speak with the Halls' civility' about a martini cocktail served 'on white bread with mayonnaise' (Rosenblum 1986, 280), this surreal satirizing of gentile dining preferences appears in a different form in *Annie Hall*. The counterpart to Alvy's praising the 'dynamite ham' (Allen 1983, 55) at the Halls' Easter dinner table is Annie's ordering 'a pastrami on white bread with, uh, mayonnaise and tomatoes and lettuce' (Allen 1983, 43) in a New York deli. In response, '*Alvy involuntarily makes a face*', drawing our attention to Annie's failure to ask for her pastrami 'properly', on rye with mustard (Abrams 2017). As Nathan Abrams points out, this 'WASPish meal' in a kosher deli is itself recalled in *When Harry Met Sally* (1989), where Sally (Meg Ryan) likewise disconcerts her rye-bread-eating Jewish companion Harry (Billy Crystal) in New York's Katz's Deli by ordering a turkey sandwich on white bread with mayonnaise (Abrams 2004, 91). In the case of *Annie Hall*, rather than its being an element of the comically exaggerated differences between the Halls and the Singers, as in the original version, this visual routine has been turned into an element of the film's subjective memory-scape and Alvy's recall of the relationship's dynamic.

Likewise, in the original a discarded sequence was devoted to Alvy's dream about his 'cowardice' in the face of interrogation by the Gestapo (quoted in Rosemblum 1986, 278), in a flight of introspective fancy motivated by his preoccupation with Ophuls's *The Sorrow and the Pity*. In *Annie Hall*, it is Annie who says, 'sometimes I ask myself how I'd stand up under torture' (Allen 1983, 17) when they have come home after watching Ophuls's film. Alvy's response is enmeshed within the narrative of their divergent sexual expectations:

> ALVY (Offscreen): You? You kiddin'? (*He moves into the frame, lying across the bed to touch Annie, who makes a face*). If the Gestapo would take away your Bloomingdale's charge card, you'd tell 'em everything [...]
> ANNIE: I – you know, I don't wanna.
>
> (Allen 1983, 17)

Although Annie had not wanted to see Ophuls's film again, she remains true to its spirit while Alvy attempts to change the mood. Her not wanting to respond to Alvy's advances precedes his joke about the 'Bloomingdale's charge card', but their different registers here typify her fear that 'You don't think I'm smart enough to be serious about' (Allen 1983, 49). His memory of the incident reveals this disjunction despite itself. The scene is resolved not on its own terms but by a flashback within this past-tense occurrence, prompted by Annie's saying, 'I mean, you've been married before, you know how things can get. You were very hot for Allison at first' (Allen 1983, 18). Alvy's look back at his first marriage seems to credit the justice of Annie's words, even though it concludes with his repeating the Groucho Marx comparison of the opening monologue, rather than his reflecting that this time someone seems to see him as the wrong kind of club.

In both cases, that of the pastrami sandwich and the Gestapo interrogation, the editing of cultural and surreal gags has not only shortened and transferred them to the dialogue but has made Annie their object. Even the respective grimaces, by means of which dissent takes the form of 'making a face', have a different orientation in each case. While it assumes the form of a 'sideways glance' (Bakhtin 1984, 108) at the audience from Alvy in the deli, it is a firmly intradiegetic sign from Annie in the bedroom scene. Her 'mak[ing] a face' takes up a role in the story of her physical reaction to Alvy's emotional withholding, and the enabling nature of her therapist. These small instances typify the transformation of a solipsistic film into one about a romance viewed from one side, in their first soliciting (the deli) and then undermining (the bedroom) our allegiance with Alvy's recall. The process of editing the film's first cut was undertaken to 'find the plot', as Rosenblum puts it (1986, 290), which turned out to be that of a relationship – viewed from the perspective of memory.

Conclusion

Viewing *Annie Hall* as a memory-scape, rather than in such other guises as an extended therapy session (Lee 2001, 59) or urban romance, allows us to recognize more sharply but also to accept that the viewpoint is thoroughly subjective. All unreliability, whether involuntary or strategic, can be ascribed to the workings of recall. The ending of *Annie Hall* maintains the focus on memory by offering several different ways of looking back as part of the plot. These include Alvy's play and a final montage, but also his visit to Los Angeles after Annie has moved there. The greatest gap between Alvy's perspective and that of the audience occurs in relation to his changing attitude towards Annie's singing. At first he encourages her in relation to his own performance career – 'I know exactly what that's like', as he puts it of an early audition (Allen 1983, 41) – then becomes increasingly resentful as her circumstances change while his do not. In this sense, memory becomes a symbol of failure to progress, as summed up by Annie's resistance to such allegiance to the past when they divide up their belongings on her moving out for the second time:

ALVY (looking down at a book): This *Denial of Death*. You remember this? […] This is the first book that I got you […] Remember that day?
ANNIE: Right. Geez, I feel like there's a great weight off my back.

(Allen 1983, 94)

Alvy's insistence on a particular kind of remembrance, as his repetition of the term suggests, is subverted by Annie's wish to leave the past behind.

Indeed, Alvy's disinclination to renounce their history, since, as he put it, 'I miss Annie. I made a terrible mistake' (Allen 1983, 95), motivates a geographical journey, as if back to the past yet also to Annie's new home in Los Angeles. Alvy's persona here is neither that of the stand-up comedian summoning up surreal visits to the locations of his history, as in the schoolroom scene, nor that of the wise-cracking misanthrope whom we encountered in New York, but a fully fledged 'urban schlemiel' (Feuer 2013, 96), whose very motive for travel to Los Angeles, let alone his behaviour there, is suspect and even slapstick. It seems that a rueful and honest kind of recollection is at play here in Alvy's look back at his unaware earlier self, as conveyed by our witnessing the encounter in which his proposal of marriage is turned down, and Annie's conclusion by invoking the benefit of not always keeping the past in mind: 'Just forget it, Alvy, okay? Let's just forget the conversation' (Allen 1983, 100).

Alvy's play uses verbatim some of the dialogue we have just heard between him and Annie, before a volte-face ending in which the actress declares her love for the Alvy-within-the-play and agrees to return to New York with him. As soon as the lines are uttered, Alvy *'looks straight into the camera'* as if in response to spectatorial disbelief:

> ALVY (*To the audience, gesturing*) Tsch, whatta you want? It was my first play. You know, you know how you're always tryin' t' get things to come out perfect in art because, uh, it's real difficult in life.
>
> (Allen 1983, 102)

In autofictional terms, we might imagine *Annie Hall* to be the second play by the implied dramatist, in its representation of life's inconclusive imperfection. Such a metacinematic moment is followed by the real resolution, in which, some time later after a chance encounter, Alvy and Annie meet for lunch at the Lincoln Center and 'kick around old times' (Allen 1983, 104). Alvy's phrase 'old times' is repeated in the soundtrack to the montage that follows, as we hear Annie singing 'Seems Like Old Times', a motif of this film with its invocation of varied kinds of memory. In this case, there is a reprise of Annie and Alvy's relationship in the form of a series of scenes playing silently *'in quick succession'* while *'Annie continues to sing'* (104). Memory and cinema come fully together in the unspooling of *'a series of flashbacks'*. The montage consists of what Rosenblum calls the 'pieces of film' that constitute what are, in this case, at the same time shared memories (1986, 288).

The sequence of flashbacks starts with Annie and Alvy going to her apartment in her car up the FDR Drive on the day they met, followed by a series of other moments presented in an even more impressionistic, temporally disordered form. This constitutes a version of the film in microcosm, even though, as Sander Lee points out, what we see here are not just old but good times, each individual vignette edited to exclude any discordant note (2001, 43). Yet because this montage relies upon the viewer's memory of each event, the omissions and selectivity on this occasion are clear to see. They do not spoil the viewer's own fond reviewing of the film in this way, and assent to Alvy's estimate of Annie in his concluding monologue, 'I realized what a terrific person she was and – and how much fun it was just knowing her' (Allen 1983, 105). Lee claims that the 'we need the eggs' joke with which the film ends, where Alvy justifies the reasons to 'keep goin'' despite the 'irrational and crazy' nature of relationships, marks a renunciation of any logical approach to the topic of romantic love (2001, 41). However, it also marks a temporal development, even in this film about the past and 'old times', beyond the moment of the opening monologue and its preoccupation with the 'terrible mistake' or 'screw-up'. The very act of remembrance has enabled Alvy to move on into the future.

Works cited

Abrams, Nathan. 2004. '"I'll have whatever she's having": Jewish Food on Film', in *Reel Food*, ed. Anne L. Bowers, 87–100. New York and London: Routledge.

Abrams, Nathan. 2017. 'We all love *Annie Hall* 40 years on', The *Jewish Chronicle*, 27 April 2017. https://www.thejc.com/culture/film/annie-hall-woody-allen-1.436957

Allen, Woody and Marshall Brickman. 1983. *Annie Hall*, in *Four Films of Woody Allen*. London: Faber.

Amstell, S. and D. Swimer. 2010–12. *Grandma's House*, dir. Christine Glennon, BBC2.

Bailey, Peter. 2001. *The Reluctant Film Art of Woody Allen*. Lexington: University of Kentucky Press.

Bakhtin, Mikhail. 1963. *Problems of Dostoevsky's Poetics*. Translated by Caryl Emerson. Minneapolis: University of Minnesota Press, 1984.

Bordwell, David, Janet Staiger and Kristin Thompson, 1988. *Classical Hollywood Cinema*. London: Routledge.

Bradshaw, Peter. 2017. 'Annie Hall at 40: Ranking the Film's Funniest Moments', The Guardian, 20 April. https://www.theguardian.com/film/2017/apr/20/annie-hall-at-40-funniest-moments

Feuer, Menachem. 2013. 'Woody Allen's Schlemiel: From Humble Beginnings to an Abrupt End', in Woody on Rye: Jewishness in the Films and Plays of Woody Allen, ed. Vincent Brook and Marat Grinberg, 79–99. Waltham, MA: Brandeis University Press.

Ford Madox Ford. 1964. 'Joseph Conrad' (first published in 1924), in The Critical Writing of Ford Madox Ford, ed. Frank MacShane, 72–88. Lincoln: University of Nebraska Press.

Knight, Christopher. 2004. 'Woody Allen's Annie Hall: Galatea's Triumph over Pygmalion', Literature/Film Quarterly 32 (3): 213–21.

Kuhn, Annette. 2010. 'Memory Texts and Memory Work: Performances of Memory in and with Visual Media', Memory Studies 3 (4): 298–313. https://doi.org/10.1177/1750698010370034

Lee, Sander H. 2001. 'Existential Themes in Crimes and Misdemeanors', in Woody Allen: A Casebook, ed. Kimball King, 225–44. New York and London: Routledge.

McBride, Joseph. 1977. 'Film Review: Annie Hall', Variety, 29 March 1977. http://variety.com/1977/more/reviews/annie-hall-1200424062/

Ovenden, Olivia. 2019. 'Fleabag Episode 3 Proves Phoebe Waller-Bridge Is Still Two Steps Ahead of Us', 17 May. https://www.esquire.com/uk/culture/tv/a26881008/fleabag-priest-fourth-wall-twist/

Rosenblum, Ralph and Robert Karen. 1986 [1979]. When the Shooting Stops, the Editing Begins: A Film Editor's Story. Cambridge, MA: Da Capo Press.

Schatz, Thomas. 2006. 'Annie Hall: The Issue of Modernism', in The Films of Woody Allen, ed. Charles L. P. Silet, 123–32. Lanham, MD: Scarecrow Press.

Scott, A. O. 2005. 'An Unhappy Marriage, from Divorce to Wedding', New York Times, 10 June. https://www.nytimes.com/2005/06/10/movies/an-unhappy-marriage-from-divorce-to-wedding.html

Shone, Tom. 2015. Woody Allen: A Retrospective. London: Thames and Hudson.

Waller-Bridge, Phoebe. 2016–19. Fleabag (Harry Bradbeer), BBC3.

Waller-Bridge, Phoebe. 2019. Interview with Kevin Jacobsen, David Montgomery and Susan Wloszczyna, Gold Derby, 23 August. https://www.goldderby.com/article/2019/phoebe-waller-bridge-fleabag-emmy-nominee-video-interview-transcript/

5

I love speaking to you: Narcissism in *Annie Hall*

Reidar Due

Forms of authority

This chapter explores the representation, and performance, of a special kind of authority in Woody Allen's film *Annie Hall*. This is an authority that can be termed narcissistic. It is embedded in the semiotic fabric of the film. It is also embodied in its protagonist, Alvy, played by Woody Allen. The following interpretation is not the application of a theory of narcissism to the film *Annie Hall*. My approach in this chapter is hermeneutic. The chapter describes the structure of narration and character relationships in the film and then seeks to interpret this structure through reflection and philosophical contextualization. Hence, the chapter may be read, also, as an intervention in the ongoing film studies debate between critics and theorists (Wood 2006, 3; Zizek 1992, 1–10). The hermeneutic method as practised here is one that begins in criticism and ends in philosophy.

Central to this interpretation of the film is a confrontation between Woody Allen and a range of philosophers, particularly Stanley Cavell, who formulated influential reflections on moral subjectivity and its limits. According to Cavell, the human subject learns to mitigate its pretensions, moderate its views and listen to authorities other than its own within everyday linguistic exchange (Cavell 1999). In the web of ordinary conversation, the subject may thus experience a moral education that has as its immanent ethical goal a kind of perfection. The state of perfection is never fully attained, but it provides orientation to the subject. Cavell illustrates this by reference to classical Hollywood films (Cavell 1981). In the banality of their banter, Hollywood spouses adapt and adjust, because they discover that by doing so they may become slightly better people than they would have been, had they clung to their initial certainties – their class consciousness and social prejudice. Given this theme, we can construct a virtual dialogue between Woody Allen and Stanley Cavell.

The negative ideal that Cavell's moral perfectionist seeks to overcome, or avoid, is the figure of a moral narcissist. This would be someone who jealously guards the realm of his own opinions against foreign intrusion. In this chapter I aim to show that Alvy, the protagonist of *Annie Hall*, is a flamboyant representative of just such a moral narcissism. Yet, this character is not silent. He is not confined within his own solitary thoughts, as he speaks continuously. The chapter then encircles the following paradox: moral narcissism may not only *not* be tempered by ordinary language exchange, as Cavell claims it will; rather, it is in fact on the very stage of ordinary language that a narcissistic subject – such as the character Alvy – celebrates its best victories. I believe this paradox to have implications for any philosophy that sees ordinary language as posing a limit to subjective authority.

Turning now to *Annie Hall*, we may say that its style and charm are grounded in two well-defined methods: intellectual gags (originating in Woody Allen's own career as stand-up comic and writer of jokes) and a sophisticated metacinematic and autobiographical use of the medium reminiscent of early Godard in films such as *Une femme est une Femme* (A Woman is a Woman, 1961), an autobiographical love story with slapstick elements. The two styles, gag and meta-cinema, are combined in *Annie Hall* in various intricate ways. The film achieves this effect by producing cartoonish versions of transposed autobiographical life segments, alternating furthermore between two modes, each with a different tone. The first mode is comical and cynical and consists in refining the construction of a type, or a brand, the Allen character – Alvy in the film. He is a complaining, self-obsessed intellectual who is keenly interested in his cultural and social identity as a New York Jew from a socially modest background. The other mode is romantic and has mise en scène elements from the cinema of the 1920s. We see this in a scene where the two future lovers awkwardly begin a conversation at a tennis club. This scene develops space dynamically in a way that is characteristic of Woody Allen's filming of interior scenes generally. The scene is a medium-distance reverse-shot montage across a diagonal line, where the two characters talk to each other from the two corners of a public space, the foyer of a tennis club. The spatial arrangement appears as a very literal symbol of the indirectness of their incipient flirtation.

The aesthetic charm of the film resides in a tension between these two modes, of comic cynicism and romantic innocence. Neither of the two tendencies of tone in the film is allowed to dominate the film entirely and the film hovers between the two. For instance, two comic flashback sequences, depicting failures in Alvy's former love life, are ambivalent. They exhibit a caricature style and portray the Alvy character as set on a course of programmed repetition. Alvy's refusal to engage fully with others finds different modes of expression in these stories. Yet, these repetitive, and hence cynical, stories of Alvy as a failure also form part of his courtship with his new girlfriend, Annie (Diane Keaton). They are vignettes narrated in the present tense of the diegesis. They form part of the web of stories that the two lovers tell each other in order to get to know each other. Hence, we are presented also with two of Annie's former lovers. One is a very young man from Keaton's own youth. The other is an artistic character, a handsome and charismatic actor. He is shown, both culturally and physically, to be the direct opposite of Alvy, who in fact judges him as such and then effortlessly goes on to claim, during a romantic walk with Annie along the beach, that she is lucky that he, Alvy, 'came along'. This assertion of authority in relation to Annie's past cements the film's narrative alignment with the protagonist's point of view.

These flashback stories about Alvy and Annie's former lovers can seem puzzling. Why do these lovers entering a new, and possibly fragile, relationship find that they need to fill their common space with other people? Why they need to do so explicitly, in speaking, finds an answer in the very texture of their courtship. In the most romantic scenes of the film, such as the scene at the tennis club referred to above, we see how the two characters fall in love because they speak and act in synchrony. They follow each other along the same syncopated path of half-interrupted speech. One could also say that they meet at the site of a common interest, as they are both quite interested in themselves. During their first romantic evening, we see Annie, standing on a balcony and throwing Alvy a challenging glance over her wine glass, as she repeats something that he said: 'fifteen years'. This refers to his declaration previously that he had been in therapy for fifteen years.

The ethical questions that the film could inspire in the viewer are nested in its charm. As the film gradually seduces us into the web of its own internal references, it becomes clear that the film's narrative point of view is closely aligned with the psychological point of view of its protagonist, Alvy. Indeed, in an earlier version, as Allen explains in his autobiography, the film 'was supposed to be [Alvy's] stream of consciousness, but that was yet another of life's great dreams that did not work out' (Allen 2020, 189). The film thus defends and supports its protagonist even when it appears to be making fun of him. In return, Alvy at times seems to serve as a vehicle, or mouthpiece, for the director himself.

Even if we distinguish, as is conventional, between the Allen persona in the film and the biographical subject Woody Allen (Jacobs 1982; Hösle 2007), there are moments when the two seem to echo each other. As we will see shortly, these are moments in which the film, and the character, take sides within a local – social and cultural – battle for recognition within the world of New York intellectuals. The film, both within its semiotic construction entailing a subject of enunciation (not to be confused with the director) and in the speaking voice of its protagonist, asserts in these moments a stance of defiance in the face of a New York mandarin cultural establishment. The film is thus both a reflection *of* and *upon* the life of the New York artist that the director and the protagonist both are part of, tapping into the director's own project of self-assertion at a moment in his life where he was at the point of becoming a global star. Here, I am interested in the intra-filmic or textual dimension of this structure, as it informs the Alvy character and his place within the diegetic world of the film.

Annie Hall can be read as the objectification of a subjectivity that has difficulty entering an objective world. An objective world would be one, for instance, where the subject thinks that the roles, which other subjects attribute to it, are reasonable, predictable and acceptable. This would be a world of shared norms and values. The story world in *Annie Hall* is in fact a microcosm of shared values and concerns. It depicts a very particular segment of more or less bohemian, more or less familial, intellectuals in New York. This shared social and cultural setting does nothing to appease the protagonist, however. Since he casts himself in the role of an outsider, Alvy experiences social life as an arena of combat, conquest, self-assertion and threats. He speaks incessantly to others – in order to demarcate his turf, to remind himself of his opinions, to hedge his feelings against the probable emergence of other, possibly divergent, opinions. He is thus a fighter and a solitary being who is also, for this very reason, energetically pursuing a career as a settled man and as the boyfriend of a girlfriend. The ease with which we see Alvy establishing domesticity with his girlfriend – even though the fact of living permanently together with a woman in one flat is something that he recoils from – suggests that it is the liturgy of the everyday, more than the actual identity of his partners, which matters to Alvy. One senses that he falls in love easily and women seem to find his air of being intelligently lost attractive.

Love is thus important to Alvy, but the questions that love poses to him are framed within his general search for identity. He identifies himself as someone who loves many different women. It is not surprising therefore that within the diegesis, the two lovers seem unable fully to reach each other. Moreover, one has the impression that they are both trapped in certain images that they have of themselves – although, as we shall see, Annie's perception of herself evolves in the course of the story. That is not the case with Alvy. His unchanging self-perception is performed throughout the film in efforts to assert authority, erotic as well as intellectual. I shall for the remainder of the chapter discuss the relationship between the narcissism of the Allen character's search for identity and his construction of authority.

Narcissism as narration

Even as Alvy is constantly ridiculed, the film is rarely narratively ironic about his point of view. Even if the spectator can see Alvy's perspective from the outside, and judge it to be partial or incomplete, the character's overall narrative trajectory is also that of the film. Thus, in a highly controlled way, *Annie Hall* aligns the viewer with the point of view of its protagonist.

Alvy's various monologues are in fact strongly supported by the subject of enunciation established within the fabric of the film. Thus, in the cinema queue episode, early in the film, the film quite suddenly produces a conceptual gag, breaking the ontological frame of the fiction and allowing the Allen character to 'win' over his 'opponent' through a metacinematic device. We hear a college professor talking with authority about Marshall McLuhan. Alvy challenges him and ultimately breaks out of the frame of the fiction by fetching the real Marshall McLuhan, who has conveniently been waiting in the wings. The cameo McLuhan now appears in the scene as a superior authority on the subject of himself, a voice of truth who can put the talkative intellectual in his place. We see in this attitude that the film shares with its protagonist a sort of personal politics, a project of fighting the perceived authority of an exclusive and self-referential cultural establishment. This lends a certain depth of authenticity to Alvy's speech: it is supported both by the subject of enunciation and implicitly by the director, who is also a New York intellectual. Hence, the alliance of protagonist, subject of enunciation and director protects the character from too close scrutiny – by the film or by the viewer. This is a hint that the viewer will also be positioned so that she may find it difficult to question the authority of the film's protagonist.

Throughout, we get a sense that the fighter Alvy insulates himself within his own words. He speaks in order to assert himself. Yet, his words, at the same time, confirm his separation from others. This lends to his authority a brittle and at times futile quality. This vulnerability adds to the film's charm, of course, and thereby obscures somewhat the robust structural coherence of the character's construction of authority within the diegesis.

The two characters, Annie and Alvy, meet and separate at the site of a shared attitude towards life, as they appear concerned with themselves, yet not quite at peace with themselves. One could say that they fall in love because of their shared narcissism. We could also more prosaically say that it is Annie's gradual self-discovery that slowly leads her away from Alvy. As they begin a relationship, Alvy persuades Annie to start psychoanalysis. The result will be that Annie discovers her own desires and aversions. This discovery further leads to her embarking on a music career, which Alvy encourages. Therapy and music then lead Annie to California and to her gradual separation from Alvy. This plot is presented in a mixed tone. The plot of a lover, bringing his lover to therapy, which then makes her discover that she does not love him, seems on its own a kind of New York joke, as if the whole story were an extended gag. But if so, this would be one of Allen's existential absurdist jokes, since for the two characters, there is nothing funny or lighthearted about their falling in love and failing to remain lovers. In its tone, the film is, we might say, respectful of this ambivalence, as it moves between comic detachment and romantic empathy.

In following their relationship, our point of view is aligned with the Alvy character and with his stories and obsessions. We see Annie through his eyes, sympathetically. This is so even when they drift apart. We can observe a turning point of tone in the film, however, when we see the screen split in two and they each talk to their therapist. We discover that Alvy is more interested in making love than Annie is. They are both, as we hear, meticulously counting how often they sleep together. During her analytic session she says that they make love all the time, three times a week. To his therapist, Alvy says that they never make love, only three times a week. The distancing effect of this simple joke is supported, diegetically, by a difference in life projects, which is also reflected in the two characters' divergent perceptions of their relationship and its significance in their life. Alvy gives the impression of seeking through the act of making love to give volume to the relationship and thereby make it into an extension of himself. She, on the other hand, is searching for what she wants to do, what she will be able to do. The relationship supports her in that endeavour, but for that very reason, the relationship is for her not an end in itself. The relationship is there for her, alongside something else that she tries to do or tries to find. At this point in the narrative, even as we see them moving away from each other, we still see and hear enough of her life to sympathetically appreciate the difference between him and her, and between their life situations – and to see this difference not *only* from his point of view. In their conversations, we thus see that she is neither completely absorbed into his world view nor is she positioned within the film in a comic, or otherwise inferior position. This equality of point of view gradually deteriorates in the later parts of the film.

A little further in their relationship, an affable music producer called Tony Lacey (Paul Simon) invites Annie and Alvy to a party. They sit in a night club where Annie has just performed a song. She is elated by the producer's attention and eager to accept his invitation. Alvy's reaction is different. He appears in the grip of panic as if his erotic authority is now definitively threatened. Alvy contrives, and in fact manages, to avert what to him seems an absolute disaster, a party with a glamorous rival expressing an interest in his girlfriend. The disaster would consist in a scenario where Annie would be talking to a man who is better positioned to give her what she wants, that is, a career in music. Alvy's initial victory in averting the party in fact appears illusory since he not only loses face in front of Annie but also must embrace the unglamorous role of a possessive lover. His victory is also short-lived. Soon after this incident, Alvy and Annie break up, and she travels to California to be with Tony Lacey and record music with him.

Ethics of speech

Alvy travels with Annie to Los Angeles before their relationship is officially over. They have tried at this point to break up but have resumed the relationship. The California episode turns out to signify a reversal of that decision: on the plane back, they peacefully agree to split up.

The California episode appears as an extended version of the McLuhan episode earlier in the film. Here we follow in satire mode a comedic Alvy character who enacts his aversion towards what the film portrays as the free and sunny lifestyle of California – the theme of Alvy's allergy towards California is in fact brought up at the very beginning of the film, before he meets Annie. The world of Californian artistic leisure and pleasure is set up in contrast with a very stony and often grey New York, which Alvy sees as his natural habitat. In New York, Alvy finds his own pleasures, his childhood memories and the trajectories of his love life. New York offers a map of his desires and longings. We see this for instance in the motif of Coney Island, that both in the film and in popular culture generally appears as an emblem of New York nostalgia. California, on the other hand, offers Alvy no memories, no immediate points of recognition. His own work ethic is opposed to the hedonism of the drifting characters they meet at a party in Tony Lacey's expansive villa. One typical gag shows Alvy overhearing a phone conversation during which a distraught young man talks to his spiritual mentor, complaining that he has forgotten his mantra. This farcical presentation of the beliefs of characters far removed from the protagonist again aligns the subject of enunciation with the protagonist.

In the California episode, we in fact witness a kind of personal political and cultural battle that the film engages with the very existence of California: in his systematic rejection of everything that surrounds him, Alvy manifests an instinctual aversion against its entire cultural mores and aesthetic values. This battle is expressed in a battery of jokes, some of them at the expense of Alvy himself. These jokes, which drive the momentum of the film in this episode, and entirely dominate its mood, are central to the subject of enunciation holding the strings of the diegesis together. With these jokes, the film uses the counter-world of California to semiotically mythologize New York as a mental territory. In this episode, narrative attention thus becomes identified with the emotional point of view, and narrative goals, of the protagonist. We are offered no reasons for Annie's interest in the music producer, or in California, apart from the diegetic knowledge that we already have. We know that she is a searching and artistically ambitious character who, we may assume, finds inspiration in this new environment, but the film goes out of its way to show her choice as frivolous. The film thus sacrifices the 'other' diegetic point of view to a cultural politics of self-assertion, thereby also drifting away from the dialogical structure of the middle of the film, which grew out of their courtship and Annie's and Alvy's initial equality as lovers.

As this equality is gradually put under strain through Alvy's effort to assert authority, it is logical, one can say, that Annie, at the point when she no longer submits to his authority, will also, from the point of view of the film itself, and its subject of enunciation, appear as an alien. The ethical implication of this sudden ostracization of the other from the semiotic fabric of the film, is that of a rejection, on the part of film and protagonist alike, of any world outside of New York. Since that city is portrayed as the metaphorical extension of the protagonist's identity, this also amounts to a *rejection of the other's voice in general*.

We may see this as a kind of narcissism that consists in a refusal, on the part of the subject, to perceive anything that is new or external to it. The new can for this subject only be seen as a threat to what it already is, or to what it already has – and which it is therefore defined by. If the new and different is a threat to the subject's identity, narcissism would be expressed as a territorial assertion of identity: the performance of a symbolic production that aims to make it seem as if any new reality does not in fact exist or does not *legitimately* exist. The Alvy character is therefore not just self-obsessed in a moral or colloquial sense. In his stance of refusal to perceive difference, he also exemplifies a position of radical subjectivism. Such a stance has been discussed within philosophy.

In philosophy, subjectivism was first discussed as a topic by Hegel in his criticism of Kant for failing to appreciate the moral subject's dependence on a shared ethical world (Beiser 2002, 356). In twentieth-century philosophy, following Martin Heidegger's pragmatic philosophy and Wittgenstein's philosophy of ordinary language, many philosophers have sought a pragmatic response to the subjectivism of the earlier philosophical tradition.

It was in this vein that Cavell developed his criticism of subjectivism. It is grounded in an original interpretation of the philosophy of René Descartes, who is often thought to initiate the Western philosophical tradition of self-consciousness considered as a separate arena of enquiry (Cavell 1999, 131–2; Williams 2005, 34). Cavell sees the Cartesian search for internal authority to open the door to a moral abuse of authority that would be on display in Shakespeare's dramas such as *King Lear*. According to Cavell, classic Hollywood films, by contrast, display a space of moral reciprocity between two equally autonomous, but emotionally interdependent characters. This mutual moral emotion unfolds, in the Hollywood films that Cavell interprets, within the realm of marriage. Marital reciprocity is seen there as an alternative to the kind of unchallenged internal authority that Descartes justifies and Shakespeare dramatizes (Cavell 1981, 2003).

Speech is the medium and instrument of moral education in Cavell's philosophy. The arena on which a subject is brought to acknowledge its feelings and measure them against the claims of another subject within a love relation is therefore ordinary language. It is by speaking – and not for instance by making love, going for walks, cooking, playing with dogs or through any other not necessarily linguistic activity – that the Hollywood lovers come to be constituted as moral subjects on a journey of incrementally growing reciprocity (Cavell 1981).

Paradoxically, Alvy is neither short of words nor unable to listen, to understand and encourage the beloved other. It is in fact because of Alvy's kind and understanding encouragement that Annie gains faith in her music career. However, within the relationship between Alvy and Annie, speech appears centred on, and dominated by, Alvy's intellectual authority – and by his less successful effort to exert erotic authority. An emblematic bedroom scene opposes Annie's smoking a joint to Alvy's putting a red bulb in the bedside lamp: the drug and the red light are equally elements in their shared erotic space, yet Alvy verbally denigrates Annie's part of that space. In return, we see the Annie character as a ghost moving away from her own body lying on the bed with him.

Now, on a different stage, the stage of therapeutic conversation, speech can be conducted outside the reach of, or untouched by, the spell of Alvy's authority. It is on this other stage that Annie makes discoveries about herself that were not open to her previously. These discoveries concern her emotions and also her aspirations and plans. It is thus only outside of her relation to Alvy, and his authority, that Annie can actually think about herself. In the film we therefore see in speech not just an arena of possible self-limitation and reciprocity, as Cavell advocates, but an arena of authority, which for *one* of the conversation partners constitutes a block against herself.

Let us now turn to another thinker who has sought an alternative to subjective authority in ordinary language. The social philosopher Jürgen Habermas developed in his treatise *Theory of Communicative Action* (1981) a conception of language considered as an arena where social agents are made to acknowledge their moral bonds with one another. In speaking, we enter an intersubjective social space in which both speakers tacitly entertain expectations as to the meaningful linguistic behaviour of the other. In acknowledging our participation in this web of reciprocal expectations, we are by the same token, compelled to accept that our own subjective pretentions must always be expressed within entrenched social conditions of mutual interpretation. These are conditions which are not controlled by me as a subject and hence do not fall under my subjective authority.

Now, reading Habermas' text critically, and from a feminist point of view, we can see the *family*, and the social authority expressed within it, as taking place in an ambivalent and liminal space. The family appears to the participants as intimate but is also implicitly a political arena (Baehr 2018, 183). Within this seemingly intimate space, the display of gendered authority embodies more general structures of authority. In fact, gendered authority thrives, just as any other form of social authority, just as long as it is not being questioned.

Equality, on the other hand, is for Habermas a matter of accepting others as participants in a kind of dialogue, which may require of the subject that it examines itself *critically*. For a dialogue to manifest equality, and to be an arena that enhances equality, it further has to be based on an exchange of reasoned opinion, which Habermas calls 'argument'. Of course, a couple that would spend all its time on intellectual arguments, would end up arguing about everything. We see this happening in *Annie Hall* when Annie and Alvy's relationship increasingly becomes dominated by his opinions. It might therefore be interesting to reflect on Annie's and Alvy's relationship from this Habermasian perspective of equality in communication.

According to Habermas then, critical dialogue challenges the subject's preconceived opinions. Hence, it requires of the subject that it exposes its values and criteria of judgment, its ideals and basic opinions, to criticism by the dialogue partner. We can speculate how this ideal of exposure through dialogue applies to the gendered asymmetry of authority in *Annie Hall*. For Annie to challenge Alvy's authority she would need to be able to ask him to evaluate his own basic points of view. However, it seems unlikely that the searching and shy character Annie who admires Alvy as a sort of educator, would be able to challenge him on the stage of language. Such a challenge would require of him, on the other hand, that he would take up a detached viewpoint in relation to his own opinions. He would then have to ask himself, for instance, why he is so obsessively interested in the theme of death. However, it seems hardly possible for the Alvy-subject in the film to reflect critically upon the framework of thought provided by his own basic beliefs, or for that matter, to think outside of this frame. Thus, when Annie leaves him in order to live in California, Alvy makes a last attempt to bring her back, and convince her to return to New York with him. In his speech of persuasion, Alvy refers mainly to himself and to his own opinions. When she refuses his invitation, he immediately switches tack and aggressively utters a series of invectives against her new chosen habitat. Just as Alvy earlier was barred from perceiving in California anything other than a threat to his own identity, he now cannot perceive in Annie's life plan any legitimate reason for her choice.

It would seem, therefore, that in the face of a serious subjectivist such as the Alvy character in *Annie Hall*, the speech cures offered by Cavell and by Habermas do not take the full measure of the threat to communication posed by subjective authority. Especially, this is the case when the subject develops a kind of authority that is already prepared for being performed in speech. In order to challenge such a performative authority on the level of speech, the other subject needs to establish a kind of *counter* speech, as one would do in a political situation, when for instance, a trade union imposes a new way talking about, or to, management. How could something like this be possible in the love relationship that we witness in *Annie Hall*? If Annie loves Alvy *she also loves his authority* and would therefore not be out to destroy it. If she would talk to him as a social worker talking to a client, or as a trade unionist talking to management, she would step outside of the circle of speech that defines their relationship. It is therefore quite logical that, within the diegesis, Annie challenges Alvy only by leaving him and that she can find the courage to leave him only by establishing a counter stage of speech, in therapy.

Thinking further about speech and the performance of authority, we come to see that narcissistic authority in *Annie Hall* is performed and established through a kind of speech, which is fundamentally charming and seductive. Against the moral interpretation of speech in Habermas and Cavell one may dwell on this element of speech seduction. Narcissistic authority performed on the stage of ordinary language means also the following for the subject who has the inferior part in the speech relation, the subject who finds itself seduced: before *I* speak the other has already spoken – and spoken well. It is a merit of *Annie Hall* that in spite of aligning itself so thoroughly with the authority of its protagonist, the film nevertheless grants enough independence to the character of Annie for us to prolong the story within our own reflection and think through what the film does not directly show, which is what it would mean for Annie, as a subject, to confront the seductive authority that the Alvy character performs for her. This would mean that she would be able to disentangle herself from the seduction of his continuous speech.

We may now shift the angle of investigation and turn our attention to the subject of seductive speech. What kind of need does this performance of authority fulfil for the subject of speech? In order to address this question, we may look at Freud's theory of narcissism as discussed by the philosopher Paul Ricoeur. In his work *Freud and Philosophy*, narcissism appears in a complex way to be characterized as subjective authority.

Narcissism as authority

In his study of Freud, Ricoeur analyses in detail the evolution of psychoanalytic theory (Ricoeur 1965, 81–169). He undertakes to trace the breaking points in Freud's texts, moments where the underlying philosophical stakes of psychoanalysis come to the surface. There was a period when Freud moved from an *energy* to an *agency* model of the psyche. It turns out that Freud's theory of narcissism is at the core of that development. The focus of the mature agency model with its distribution of psychic power between the three agencies of the Ego, the Id and the Super-ego relies on the earlier theory of narcissism as an immediately preceding theoretical moment.

In its move through the Oedipal complex, an unconscious subject discovers how to set limits to itself. The structure of narcissism consists for Freud in the production of an internal libidinal object. By investing energy in an Ego Ideal, or Imago, which is set up as a ideal for the subject to live up to, the subject comes to position itself, within itself, in relation to a limit, which it at the same time experiences as external – since the Ideal Ego represents limits imposed by moral authorities. In Freud's early theory of sexuality, which is at the heart of his energy paradigm, sexual evolution was seen to move from autoerotic to reproductive sexuality. With the establishment of the canonical topic model of Ego, Id, Super-ego, Freud sees the endpoint of development as being one where the subject breaks free of its material sexual origins, and identifies itself as a social subject. Freud's theory of narcissism forms a precarious and ambivalent moment in this trajectory – and this is reflected in the life and development of the subject itself, since for the subject, narcissism marks a liminal moment, at the border between sexual energy and social morality. Along this trajectory, narcissism comes to provide for the subject a source of nearly limitless *internal* authority.

This authority is experienced simultaneously as a tyrannical law and as the potential for the subject to occupy a social position of great significance. Importantly for the theme of love relations, this is a subject which does not need to measure itself in relation to a desired object, since, in the field of love, the libidinal object of a narcissistic subject is implicitly its own Ego Ideal. The loved one will then appear unconsciously to the amorous subject as being at the service of its own Ego Ideal. Hence, narcissistic authority would consist in the absence of awareness of the other as actually external to the amorous subject. Such an amorous subject would express its love in efforts at symbolic incorporation of the loved object. Only if the other is incorporated can he or she be of service to the Ideal Ego.

Within this narcissistic position, it is certainly possible for the subject to put itself in the other's social shoes, to acknowledge her or his reasons and arguments, as a good language user might do – according to Cavell or Habermas. Yet this sort of everyday speech is only on the surface a relation between a subject and another subject, or between a subject and a desired object, since the narcissistic subject has invested its libidinal energy primarily in its own, internal, Ego Ideal.

Returning to *Annie Hall* we may now ask how such a narcissistic form of authority and incorporation play themselves out in the Alvy character's performance and within the semiotic fabric of the film. We shall see that incorporation expresses itself as demarcation: that which cannot be incorporated is rejected. We saw this logic at work already in the California episode.

Authority and assertion

In *Annie Hall*, the authority of the speaking subject within the Alvy-Annie relationship is grounded in a structure of narcissistic incorporation and demarcation. In order to deepen that discussion, we may dwell for a while on a carefully crafted sequence in the film, devoted to Alvy's encounter with Annie's family. Annie is portrayed as the restless child of very calm, Midwest, middle-class parents. The film makes much of the cultural difference between this family and the Alvy character. This difference is described during a family meal of Easter celebration. We see this meal and this contrast played out entirely from Alvy's perspective. During this scene, the Alvy character at one point enters a *reverie*, which the film picks up and supports, allowing us to see the scene not just from his perspective, or visually aligned with his point of orientation, but to see visualized also his cogitations and mental reactions to the family. This is achieved through the creation of a conceptual space, and by a break with the ontology of the fiction, that by now we are very familiar with. Stand-up comedy style, the Alvy character addresses the viewer in order to explain: he seeks to explain the difference between his identity and the alien territory that he is invited to enter and on which he himself will inevitably be construed as an alien. This conceptual filmmaking device here serves to further integrate the dual authority in the film, the subject of enunciation and the subject-protagonist. In this sequence, the protagonist actually comes for a certain time to occupy the place of the subject of enunciation and thus be granted supreme authority over how to interpret elements within the fiction.[1]

In the space of an interruption of the diegetic flow, the momentary intra-diegetic narrator enlists the spectator as his witness and shows him just how alien this other family is. Alvy is invited to a first dinner with his future parents in law. This is a conventional, somewhat ceremonial family dinner. Present are the husband, his wife, two children (Annie and a brother Duane, played by Christopher Walken) and, last but not least, a grandmother. The dinner is conducted in theatrical mode as a social set piece. Nothing remarkable is being said, but in this unremarkable ordinariness, certain boundaries are subtly on display. The mother starts a round of praise of her own mother's cooking, which is of course also a ritual way of praising her. Others join in, and even Allen interprets his own role to be that of someone who should add to the chorus. Unfortunately, he misses his cue, and so reveals that he is at the other side of some invisible fence. As the conversation meanders on, Alvy soon realizes that he cannot easily join the flow of family anecdotes. That is when he starts reflecting on the difference between them and him. In a conceptual shot, we see him through the eyes of the grandmother, in the way that he imagines that she sees him, namely as an orthodox Jew with a long beard. Then the screen splits and the elegant home of quiet decorum competes with a scene from Alvy's childhood. We see his family as he remembers it. His family is loud and boisterous and strikingly different in rhythm of speech and emotional register from the new territory that Alvy now has to enter. Finding support within this memory image, Alvy, as narrator, also establishes this image, for us. The image does not belong *in* the diegesis but comes directly from a subject of enunciation who has the authority to interpret the story for us. In the diegesis, the image offers a buffer of identity-knowledge that can protect the subject against novelty, in a similar way to what we saw in the California episode.

This attitude is confirmed in the following scene, which forms a small parenthesis within the flow of narration. During a brief conversation, Alvy shares a moment in a separate room with Annie's brother, Duane. The brother confesses to having some personal problems and tells Alvy of them. Duane prefaces his confession by saying that he thinks that as an artist Alvy will be able to understand. He then says that, when he is driving by night, he is haunted by fantasies of suddenly turning the wheel and crashing his vehicle into the cars driving in the opposite direction. One is reminded of the famous hiking scene in Sartre's *Being and Nothingness*, where the happy wanderer is suddenly gripped by a strange urge to throw himself into the abyss below. Sartre reflects that since nothing stops the wanderer from doing so, this *nothing* is precisely his freedom (Sartre 1943, 66). The brother thus reflects upon freedom, his imaginary experience of a freedom that would be opposed to his secluded life in a family that seems quite certain of its beliefs and rules of behaviour. One could think at this point that Alvy, who is himself a character far removed from those social and cultural certainties, would have much in common with the troubled brother. Yet, for reasons of his own, Alvy does not seek communication with the other man. He does not rise to the challenge. He uses a joke to protect himself and leaves the room. In this scene, we see that the brother addresses Alvy from a position of weakness. The brother appeals to his understanding 'as an artist', but this fact of being asked for help seems threatening to the Alvy character.

Superiority and inferiority appear throughout *Annie Hall* equally threatening to the Alvy character, since neither allows him a channel of symbolic assertion. He can only assert himself if the other neither actively demands something from him nor requires him to occupy a position of inferiority. Such a symbolic channel of self-assertion, which he seeks to establish with the character of Annie, is not based on equality, exactly. Rather, to open this channel requires for Alvy a situation, in which the other subject does not ask of him anything that would be *different* from his own assertion of authority. In other words, we can say that narcissism consists for the Alvy character in a generosity that can only express itself when it coincides entirely with his own assertion of authority.

Note

1   This motif of a subject that longs for the kind of authority that only an author can have in relation to the characters that he has himself created is developed further by Woody Allen, as a fantasy, and treated in a comic mode, in his later film *Deconstructing Harry* (1997).

Works cited

Allen, Woody. 2020. *A Propos of Nothing. Autobiography*. New York: Arcade Publishing.
Baehr, Amy R. 2018. 'Feminism', in *The Habermas Handbook*, ed. Hauke Brunkhorst, Regina Kreide and Cristina Lafont. 183–187. New York: Columbia University Press.

Beiser, Frederick. 2002. *German Idealism: The Struggle Against Subjectivism*, 1781–1801. Cambridge, MA: Harvard University Press.
Björkman, Stig. 1993. *Woody Allen on Woody Allen*. New York: Grove Press.
Cavell, Stanley. 1981. *Pursuits of Happiness: The Hollywood Comedy of Remarriage*. Cambridge, MA: Harvard University Press.
Cavell, Stanley. 1999 (first published in 1978). *The Claim of Reason: Wittgenstein, Skepticism, Morality and Tragedy*. New York: Oxford University Press.
Cavell, Stanley. 2003. *Disowning Knowledge in Seven Plays of Shakespeare*. Cambridge: Cambridge University Press.
Habermas, Jürgen. 1981. *Theorie des Kommunikativen Handelns*. Frankfurt: Suhrkamp Verlag. English edition. 1984. *The Theory of Communicative Action*. Boston: Beacon Press.
Hösle, Vittorio. 2007. *Woody Allen, An Essay on the Nature of the Comical*. Notre Dame Indiana: University of Notre Dame Press.
Jacobs, Diane. 1982. *The Magic of Woody Allen*. London: Robson Books.
Ricoeur, Paul. 1965. *De l'interprétation, essai sur Freud*. Paris: Editions du Seuil. English edition. 1970. *Freud and Philosophy: An Essay on Interpretation*. New Haven: Yale University Press.
Sartre, Jean-Paul. 1943. *L'être et le néant*. Paris: Gallimard.
Williams, Bernard. 2005 (first published in 1978). *Descartes: The Project of Pure Enquiry*. Abingdon, Oxfordshire: Routledge.
Wood, Robin. 2006. *Personal Views: Explorations in Film*. Detroit: Wayne State University Press.
Zizek, Slavoj, ed. 1992. *Everything You Always Wanted to Know about Lacan (but were afraid to ask Hitchcock)*. London: Verso.

Filmography

Annie Hall. Film. Directed by Woody Allen. Hollywood: United Artists, 1977.
Deconstructing Harry. Film. Directed by Woody Allen. USA: Sweetland Films, 1997.
Une femme est une Femme. Film. France: Euro International Films. Directed by Jean-Luc Godard. 1961.

6

Narrative transformations of joke-work in *Annie Hall*

Ruth D. Johnston

Critics have claimed that the title of Woody Allen's *Annie Hall* is misleading because the film is more about Alvy than Annie. They also remark upon the similarities between Allen and the character he plays, Alvy Singer (DeLeyto 1994–95, 47; Mast 1987, 131; Fabe 2004, 181). Frank Krutnik assumes that the extra-diegetic status of the comedian as 'a misfit-hero' disrupts the classical notion of a protagonist, which is ultimately resolved 'in terms of narratively articulated problems and the generic field' (1984, 54–5). Celestino Deleyto comes to a similar conclusion regarding the function of narrative logic in Allen's later films; in contrast, the early films draw upon his stand-up background and use narrative merely to provide 'filmic wrappings' that serve as an excuse to tell jokes (1994–95, 41–2). Such commentaries tend to focus on explaining the jokes' significance or thematic relevance rather than how jokes work.

This calls to mind Lacan's use of a Jewish joke to explain how trompe l'oeil dupes the subject by telling the truth. The Jewish joke demonstrates how the trick is done. One character accuses another of lying 'by saying you're going to Cracow so that I should believe you're going to Lemberg, when in reality you are going to Cracow' (Freud 1960, 115). Trompe l'oeil performs this duping visually: whereas Zeuxis paints a basket of grapes which the birds mistake for real fruit, Parrhasios demonstrates how to dupe a human; he paints a veil, thereby inducing Zeuxis to ask what is behind it. Lacan observes that in his exclusive concern for what is behind the veil, Zeuxis overlooks the veil itself (1981, 112). Perhaps this is why Woody Allen's humour is frequently characterized as drawing on the tradition of the schlemiel, a comic character within a narrative who serves as the anti-hero or butt of the joke. Yet the use of direct address indicates 'a recognition of the fictionality of the performance, questioning classical accounts of the cinema as a place of socially sanctioned voyeurism' (Drake 2003, 196). Such comic performance, characterized by its exhibitionism and ostentatious behaviour, acknowledges the viewer's position as onlooker.

This chapter examines *Annie Hall* as a meditation on joke-work as analysed by Freud and elaborated as a form of minority discourse by Homi Bhabha. The film mobilizes joke-work as a cinematic self-critical discourse – formally related to parody – to analyse its own key procedures and mechanisms, many of which resist the constraints of narrative structure. In the process, it demonstrates how the medium of film is eminently suitable for displaying a postmodern, discontinuous proliferation of selves through the deployment of technology and incorporation of other media.

Film itself is fragmented, constituted by a series of still photographs. At the same time, the repeated direct addresses to the camera and the disruption of the narrative call to mind the tradition of the cinema of attractions, which in turn implies that the spectator's relation to the medium can best be described as 'distraction' (as theorized by Tom Gunning and Siegfried Kracauer) rather than 'identification', the classical spectator's mode of engagement with narrative absorption. Gunning conceives of distraction – 'a taste for thrills and spectacle … that defines the [exhibitionist] aesthetic of attractions' – as a response to the fragmentation of modern experience and to the radical transformations of spatial and temporal relations wrought by industrialism (1997, 128–9). He thus contests the notion that the audience's reaction to early cinema was a primitive one. For Kracauer, distraction is a cinematic social/aesthetic vocation: film 'must aim radically towards a kind of distraction which exposes disintegration instead of masking it' (1987, 96). In the context of *Annie Hall*, distraction is a postmodern intertextual rendezvous with modernity. Here, I invoke Linda Hutcheon's conception of postmodern parody, which rejects the 'prevailing interpretation … that postmodernism offers a value-free, decorative, de-historicized quotation of past forms' (2002, 78). She argues that the past is not reduced to the textual but that our connection with the past is mediated by an acknowledgement of our temporal separation by intervening representations that call into question the notion of an original. Accordingly, postmodern distraction does not just cite an earlier cinematic style but transforms it by insisting on its status as re-presentation, copy or reconstruction.

The concern with joke-work is emphatically announced in the opening monologue of the film, which contains two jokes. The cultural stereotypes in the first make a thematic comment by quoting an exchange between two women at a resort in the Catskills. One complains, 'Boy, the food at this place is really terrible', and the other adds, 'Yeah, I know, and such small portions.' The speaker comments, 'Well, that's essentially how I feel about life. Full of loneliness and misery and suffering and unhappiness, and it's all over much too quickly.' The second joke, in contrast, exposes the joke process via its ambivalent attribution to Freud and/or Groucho, which indicates a postmodern approach as it acknowledges the tradition of comedy and the cinema of attractions:

> The other important joke for me is one that's usually attributed to Groucho Marx, but I think it appears originally in Freud's *Wit and Its Relation to the Unconscious*, and it goes like this. I'm paraphrasing. I would never want to belong to any club that would have someone like me for a member. That's the key joke of my adult life, in terms of my relationships with women.

The explicit admission that he is paraphrasing further emphasizes the uncertainty of origin and layering of citations. History is conceived as non-linear, archaeological.

Up to this point the speaker's identity remains suspended until he mentions having broken up with Annie and his inability to figure out why. However, confusion returns with a 1975 clip of an actual Woody Allen appearance on The Dick Cavett Show, which is presented as an appearance of Alvy on the talk show. On the one hand, it seems that Alvy is speaking because the flashback to his public school immediately precedes this TV clip: 'I lost track of most of my old schoolmates, but I wound up a comedian.' On the other hand, it is an actual TV clip of Allen on the show telling a joke about being rejected by the Army because he was classified as 'four-P': 'In the event of war, I'm a hostage.' Note that the scene juxtaposes two comic performances, not an opposition between fiction and reality.

The relation of Woody Allen and Alvy receives yet another turn of the screw in the scene of an encounter on a ticket line outside of the Beekman Movie Theater. Alvy is approached by a man who recognizes him from a TV appearance on The Johnny Carson Show. Claiming to be Robert Redford, Alvy tries to conceal his identity but finally agrees to give the guy an autograph, describing him stereotypically as someone from the cast of *The Godfather* (1972), which features Diane Keaton, who, playing Annie in this film, pulls up in a taxi at just this moment. So the juxtaposition of two performances applies to her as well.

Quite aside from slippery identities that resist diegetic constraints, narrative logic is itself a problem, as Stephen Heath explains: 'the structure of representation is a structure of fetishism' (1974, 106). The disavowal of sexual difference in the clinical description, when transposed to film theory, serves to confirm the subject's 'imaginary coherence' on the one hand (1974, 106) and to deny his production in a position of separation from the text on the other hand. This disavowal is achieved first by identification, which directs attention to the story level (Heath 1974, 121), and second by narrative transparency and continuity, which imply a causal chain that reduces the movement of desire to 'the form of an enigma' (Weber 1979, 161).

Leo Bersani and Ulysse Dutoit revise this conventional clinical/cinematic account by defining fetishism as an iterative textual and psychic process that can generate an enormous diversity of representations (1985, 41). Citing Freud's definition of fetishism in *Three Essays on the Theory of Sexuality*, they emphasize its mobility and contingency:

> [T]he longing for the fetish passes beyond the point of being merely a necessary condition attached to the sexual object and actually takes the place of the normal aim, and ... the fetish becomes detached from a particular individual and becomes the sole sexual object.
>
> (Freud 1953, 154)

This suggests a model of desire that can detach from one object and move to others related to the previous term by metonymic displacement (Freud 1963, 217). It calls to mind Freud's definition of anaclisis in *Three Essays* as a movement that displaces an instinct or vital function and perverts it into sexuality as drive. The process is strikingly similar to fetishism; it involves detachment and substitution, and results in the loss of the 'original' object and endless repetition. Jeffrey Mehlman argues that joke-work is a masked repetition of anaclisis – a form of intertextuality which reveals the operation of the same displacement process, but 'masked' insofar as its function changes with each text, producing figural transformations (1975, 443).

Focusing on the process rather than a fixed structure promotes a reading such as Paul de Man's analysis of irony, which he equates with doubling and the annihilation of fixed identity. De Man rejects the idea of the comic as 'an intersubjective relationship', a struggle between the self and others (1983, 212); instead, he locates 'discontinuity' and 'plurality of levels' as internal to the subject (1983, 213). Moreover, 'the ironic mind is an endless process that leads to no synthesis. In temporal terms ... it engenders a [repetitive] temporal sequence of acts' with 'no movement toward a recovered unity' (1983, 219–20). De Man's theory therefore contests readings that conceive of doubling in terms of an extra-fictional comic performer's control of the diegetic character's actions within the text (e.g. those of Krutnik and Deleyto). As Lisa Trahair maintains, the doubling of character and performer 'eludes both presence and identity' and emerges only at the moment when we laugh (2007, 97–8).

Acknowledging Allen's engagement with the play of multiple selves rather than an intersubjective relation supports a fresh reading of the relationship between parody and joke-work. Whereas Margaret Rose describes parody as a triangular intertextual structure similar to joke-work, a dialogue between two texts that is complicated by the parodist-reader relation (Rose 1979, 149), Elizabeth Ermarth distinguishes postmodern parody by its proliferation – an 'anathematic development that multiplies many times the doubling gesture of parody' (1999, 226). Patricia Waugh considers parody a process that deploys displacement and condensation: the parodist combines the conventions of individual works of a mode or genre to create a template which 'is ... displaced through exaggeration and the substitution of new context, so that the relationship of form to content, as in the joke, is itself laid bare' (1984, 78).

Joking and the issue of doubling have particular relevance for Jewish postmodern identity. Thus Philippe Lacoue-Labarthe and Jean-Luc Nancy's 'The Jewish People Don't Dream' attempts, after Auschwitz, to imagine what would constitute a distinctly Jewish process of identification in lieu of 'identificatory mechanisms' that 'are ... complicitous with fascism' (1990, 307). They locate in Freud's *Der Witz* a distinctly Jewish identificatory process: 'The mocker participate[s] in the defect being mocked ... by means of an identification stretching across a doubled, or collective identity' (Lacoue-Labarthe and Nancy, 1989, 195). At the same time, the authors recognize that such doubling of identity might problematize the notion of identity per se: 'Perhaps one must discern here ... a path ... which *above all* would draw analysis ... beyond any identifiable "Jewishness." One way or another, this path would lead *beyond the identity principle*' (1989, 195; italics in original).

However, an identificatory mechanism deemed problematic in the European context translates into a distinctive mode of minority discourse in Homi Bhabha's analysis, which mobilizes performativity and doubling (1998, xx). Judith Butler's distinction between performance and performativity, especially her insistence on the unconscious aspect of the latter, supports a notion of doubling close to Bhabha's and Freud's:

> The psyche calls to be rethought as a compulsive repetition .... If every performance repeats itself to institute the effect of identity, then every repetition requires an interval between the acts ... in which risk and excess threaten to disrupt the identity being constituted. The unconscious is this excess that enables and contests every performance, and which never fully appears within the performance itself.
>
> (1991, 28)

Joke-work's central mechanisms – condensation, displacement, indirect representation – are the same in dream-work and other operations of the psyche.

As for the second term, the most significant doubling occurs not in the protagonist but in the enunciation or narration, and therefore implicates the spectator. Whereas Freud remarks that the most apt instances 'have grown up on the soil of Jewish popular life' (1960, 111), Homi Bhabha analyses the tendentious, self-critical joke as 'a mode of minority utterance' (1998, xx), thereby extending Freud's cautious designation of 'the subject's own nation' (1960, 111). Significantly, this focus on joke-work as a postmodern communal mechanism shifts the definition of difference from visible or visual marks to 'verbal or rhetorical locutions through which the community hears itself "spoken"' (Bhabha 1998, xvi).

Bhabha isolates four aspects of the tendentious self-critical joke that are relevant to *Annie Hall*: narration, iteration, performance and ethics. He focuses first on the narration of the Jewish joke, which produces 'a doubly articulated subject' – the 'subject of the jest (sujet d'énonce)' or butt of the joke, viewed extrinsically, and 'the subject of the joke-work (sujet d'énonciation)', which is not so much a specific person but a process of narration (1998, xvii). This doubled subject produces a self-critical posture, which Freud describes as 'criticism directed against the subject himself, or to put it more cautiously, against someone in whom the subject has a share – a collective person, that is (the subject's own nation, for instance)' (1960, 111). Freud contrasts such self-critical jokes with comic stories told about Jews by foreigners:

> The Jewish jokes which originate from Jews admit [that Jews are comic figures] too; but they know their real faults as well as the connection between them and their good qualities, and the share which the subject has in the person found fault with creates the subjective determinant ... of the joke-work.
>
> (1960, 111)

Comic stories about Jews told by others indicate a confrontation between cultural insiders and outsiders, between two distinct positions which can be invoked to support the notion of distinct identities (as in de Man's notion of inter-subjectivity [1983, 212]). In contrast, the 'subjective determinant ... of the joke-work' avoids such essentialism because it offers a mode of cultural affiliation that results from ambivalence. Such ambivalence is articulated in the doubling of 'sharing in' and 'to have a share in', as Bhabha explains: 'To share in ... is to participate communally ...; to have a share in assumes ... a contradictory process of division, partialization, separation.' Joke-work is 'caught in the interstices between these double subjects of "sharing"' (1998, xviii). Bhabha also remarks that communal identification involves an *iterative process* – 'compulsive repetition' in Butler's terms (1991, 28), seriality in de Man's (1983, 220) – which 'has initially to turn upon a destabilizing encounter with alterity prior to the affiliative bond' (Bhabha 1998, xviii, xix). Moreover, this iterative process or performativity does not accommodate a transcendent perspective existing apart or prior to the cultural performance.

Annie Hall offers a rich array of techniques that translate the doubled subject's encounter with alterity of Bhabha's theory into specifically cinematic terms, such as the scene in which Alvy produces Marshall McLuhan to challenge the obnoxious pedantic professor on the movie line. McLuhan's nonsensical pronouncement – 'You mean my whole fallacy is wrong' – is followed by Alvy's direct address to the camera acknowledging that this is sheer wish-fulfilment: 'Boy, if life were only like this!' Simultaneously, direct address ruptures the self-sufficiency and self-containment of the diegesis through the introduction of disparate external discourses, including the references to Fellini in this scene. An alternative to direct addresses to the camera is the use of subtitles in the scene at Annie's apartment shortly after Annie and Alvy first meet at the tennis court. Here, the doubled subject of the joke-work is produced by the characters' thoughts printed on the screen undercutting the pretentiousness of their spoken dialogue. As Alvy babbles about aesthetic criteria for judging photography, he thinks, 'I wonder what she looks like naked'. In a later scene the insertion of an animated sequence from *Snow White* caricatures the central conflicts of the story. Annie, presented as a cartoon Wicked Queen, and a cartoon Alvy have their usual fight. She complains that they never have fun anymore, and he says she must be getting her period, to which she responds that cartoon characters don't have periods. In all these instances, the displacement process or perversion of fetishism involves movement to another narrative register, not simply to another object.

The film's innovative use of flashback produces another instance of doubling, one that emphasizes a subject's temporal incoherence by juxtaposing past and present rather than presenting them sequentially, a strategy that also crosses diverse narrative levels. In a flashback to Alvy's public school, young Alvy kisses a schoolmate, is scolded by the teacher and summoned to the front of the room while his adult self, sitting at the back of the room, defends the kiss: 'Why, I was just expressing a healthy sexual curiosity.' The teacher counters, 'Six-year old boys don't have girls on their minds', to which he responds, 'I did'. At this point the girl intervenes with a very grown-up comment: 'For god's sake, Alvy, even Freud speaks of a latency period.' Alvy (adult) replies: 'Well I never had a latency period.' In addition to juxtaposing adult Alvy and the children, the scene presents temporal discontinuity as a conflict between sound and image as his classmates use adult language and present tense to report their diverse occupations, clashing with their youthful appearance: 'I run a profitable dress company.' 'I'm president of the Pinkus Plumbing Company.' 'I sell tallises.' 'I used to be a heroin addict. Now I'm a methadone addict.' 'I'm into leather.'

In other flashbacks, past and present coincide as Alvy and Annie enter the flashback to observe and comment without interacting with the characters from the past, for example Annie's boyfriend Jerry, the over-dramatic actor who claims he would like to die by being torn apart by wild animals, provoking Alvy to remark, 'Heavy! Eaten by some squirrels.' Similarly, a visit to Coney Island leads into a flashback to Alvy's childhood home in which Alvy's parents have a ridiculous argument about the Black cleaning woman's 'right' to steal from them. The scene then shifts to a welcome home party for Alvy's cousin, introducing other family members, including Aunt Tessie, who claims to have been 'a great beauty' and 'quite a lively dancer' in her youth. Rob comments, 'That's pretty hard to believe.' These flashbacks expose the cultural differences between Alvy and Annie as they foreground the discontinuity of time and identity.

Annie Hall is also famous for its split-screen sequences, which use spatial juxtaposition to highlight discordant perspectives. When Alvy joins the Halls for a quiet, elegant Easter dinner, the screen splits in half to reveal Alvy's family crowded around the kitchen table, talking loudly and at once. If this juxtaposition exposes the Singers' working-class status, it also represents Grammy Hall's antisemitism, not from her perspective but as Alvy imagines it via his sudden transformation into a Hasidic Jew wearing traditional garb, a full beard and side locks. Yet the scene ends with the two families addressing each other across the split screen, suggesting the permeability of the boundary that divides them as it calls attention to the split-screen device as such.

One of the most interesting uses of the split-screen shows Alvy and Annie at their psychiatrists' offices. The discordance achieved by the juxtaposition of images is augmented by the dialogue. The visuals emphasize the contrasts in style between the two: the left side of the screen shows a very modern office with stark white furniture and lots of chrome. Annie sits in an easy chair, as does her doctor. On the right side Alvy lies on a couch, his doctor seated in an armchair behind him. This office has leather furniture and wood panelling on the walls. As for the dialogue, though Alvy and Annie give similar replies (both doctors ask about the frequency of sex), their perspectives on the issue diverge radically. Alvy responds, 'Hardly ever. Maybe three times a week.' Annie says, 'Constantly. I'd say three times a week.' This doubling of perspectives is in turn triangulated by the spectator, who is in a position to laugh at the subtle play between identities and differences yet escapes being limited to the sex, gender or sexuality of either. These scenes demonstrate the aptness of Bhabha's analysis for understanding how joke-work functions in Woody Allen's cinema as a distinct mode of narration.

If the representation of joke-work as an iterative process suggests its performativity, Bhabha also discusses joke-work in terms of performance, specifically the importance of timing, an aspect that works in tandem with the joke's ethical dimension, which takes into account the hearer. The first has to do with the contingent temporality of enunciation: the fact that each time the punchline is delivered in a different context (1998, xix). The ethical dimension involves the uncertainty of truth, the question of

> what determines the truth .... Is it the truth if we describe things as they are without troubling to consider how our hearer will understand what we say? ... [D]oes not genuine truth consist in taking the hearer into account[?] ... What [such jokes attack] is not a person or an institution but the certainty of our knowledge itself.
>
> (Freud 1960, 115)

As Bhabha explains, the success of the joke depends on the third person: 'To take the hearer into account is to share in the making of a "collective person" – nation, community, group – from the ambivalent movement that circulates in between first and third persons' (1998, xx). Linda Hutcheon makes a similar observation about parodic discourse, which depends on the spectator's engagement with the text (1985, 93).

Given the importance of the third 'person' and laughter, more needs to be said at this juncture about the ways in which diverse media – film, TV, stand-up, theatre – transform Freud's hearer into a collective audience in a public space with distinct modes of reception (Hanich 2014, 51). Differences include the size and make-up of the audience, whether the performance is live (stand-up, theatre) or technologically mediated (film, TV), the importance of present time in the performance (stand-up, theatre, broadcast TV), whether the laughter serves to unite or exclude members of an audience (Drake 2003, 196) and finally the effects of intermediality – *Annie Hall*'s incorporation of other media. For example, the film's extra-diegetic reception may be doubled by a diegetic audience, yet provoke different responses.

If the narration of the joke is multiple, film viewing is a collective experience that mirrors such multiplicity. As a physical response, laughter is as disruptive as the comedian's direct address to the camera: both interrupt our absorption in the diegesis. According to Miriam Hansen the positive mass psychological effects of collective laughter in the context of early cinema function as a balance between humans and technology: 'the dangerous tensions which technification and its consequences have engendered' may be countered by 'this same technification' which possibly can provide a therapeutic inoculation via collective laughter (Hanich 2014, 57).

The use of multiple media performs the same social function in so far as the film criticizes certain uses of technology in comic practices. For instance, when Alvy visits the control room of Rob's studio in Los Angeles he is scandalized by the use of canned laughter, which has helped make Rob a TV star in a hit situation comedy. Rob instructs the technician when to insert different size laughs over the sounds of the taped show, ranging from a 'tremendous' laugh to 'a medium-sized chuckle'. Alvy calls this mechanical reproduction of fake laughs 'immoral'.

Alvy objects to not only mechanical devices that fake laughter but chemical substances that induce it, as in the love scene in which Annie insists on smoking grass and Alvy objects that 'it ruins it for me if you have grass because, you know, I'm like a comedian, so if I get a laugh from a person who's laughing, it doesn't count. You know, 'cause they're always laughing'. Alvy's low-tech idea of using a red lightbulb to add 'a little Old New Orleans essence' to the sexual experience provokes Annie's distance, presented through the use of superimposition as Annie literally steps out of her body and the bed; she decides to do some drawing 'while you two are doing that [having sex]'. Nevertheless, both mechanically produced laughter and faked sex are realized via cinematic devices that lay bare the materiality of the film image.

This scene leads directly into another about faked laughter in which a theatrical agent introduces Alvy to a comedian who claims that he is classy and not funny looking and therefore needs 'sensational' material. He asks Alvy to duplicate the material of his existing routine and replicate a predictable reception, as predictable as canned laughter. Alvy's reaction echoes Annie's withdrawal in the previous scene but highlights the materiality of film sound. With a fixed smile he talks to himself in a voice overlapping the comic's speech: 'look at him mincing around, like he thinks he's real cute …. If only I had the nerve to do my own jokes'. Accordingly, the scene cuts to Alvy's stand-up performance at the University of Wisconsin, which does not rely on technical mediation to relate to the audience of college students or Annie, who tells him that she is 'starting to get more of his references too'.

Yet some of Alvy's jokes also fail when he repeats content and loses touch with process. After breaking up with Annie, Alvy dates another woman with whom he tries to duplicate the lobster scene in which he and Annie strongly connect. The woman is not responsive; she doesn't know why he's making such big deal about picking up the lobster. When Alvy replies that he hasn't been himself since he stopped smoking, the woman is puzzled: 'Whatta you mean? … you stopped smoking sixteen years ago, is that what you said? oh, I don't understand. Are you joking or what?' Clearly, she doesn't 'get it/him'.

'Getting' is noteworthy as a term associated with the reception of a joke and suggests an instantaneous effect: the coincidence of understanding and induced laughter. As Mary Ann Doane explains, the timing is all important because if one does not 'get' the joke at the moment of transmission, one will never 'get' it, even if one belatedly comprehends it. For in 'getting' the joke, one 'finds oneself' laughing; 'finds oneself' suggests that one is 'beside oneself', other than oneself (Doane 1991b, 40–1).

Thus 'getting' involves a split or doubled subject. The doubling of the listener mirrors the doubling of the subject of the joke-work. In each case, doubling suggests an encounter that prevents one's coincidence with oneself and that therefore enables the construction of a non-essentialized community. Essence implies unity and coherent identity, which doubling or being beside oneself destabilizes.

Another issue that needs further elaboration at this point is gender. Many critics have demonstrated the intersection of racial and sexual categories in

European constructions of the Jew. For instance, Sander Gilman demonstrates a long-standing linkage between Jewish males and women because of the ritual practice of circumcision. The clitoris was regarded as a truncated penis, and Jewish males were considered feminized (1993, 38–9). Consequently, comments Ann Pellegrini, 'the Jewishness of male Jews became as much a category of gender as of race'; therefore, 'in the homology Jew-as-woman, the Jewish female body goes missing' (1997, 17, 18).

In the American context, the representation of the feminized Jewish male transforms into material for humour, and his desire for a gentile woman results in the double displacement of the Jewish female, who is also categorized in terms of gender and ethnicity/race. In another kind of tendentious joke analysed by Freud, the 'dirty joke' or smut, the (Jewish) woman functions as the butt of the joke and is structurally excluded. As Doane comments,

> In order for the dirty joke to emerge in its specificity ... the object of desire – the woman – must be absent and a third person (another man) must be present as witness to the joke – 'so that gradually, in place of the woman, the onlooker, now the listener, becomes the person to whom the smut is addressed'.
>
> (1991, 30)

The 'dirty joke' is certainly operative in the representation of the Jewish woman as a 'Jewish American Princess', or JAP. According to David Biale, the acronym is 'suggestive of anti-Japanese racism' in the post–Second World War era. In contrast to the 'comic and perhaps loveable' male sexual schlemiel, the JAP stereotype is characterized as 'obsessively materialistic ... and utterly uninterested in sex' (1997, 207). Riv-Ellen Prell, who locates the prevalence of JAP humour in the post-assimilationist 1970s, explains that 'Woman's sexuality is, in humor, subsumed by consumerism because she embodies the economic system that depends on manipulation rather than manufacture, consumption rather than production' of the time, specifically Jews' participation in a middle-class economy 'that depends on manipulation rather than manufacture and consumption rather than production' (1996, 84). Consequently, 'Jewish women become the site for projections of all that seems most hateful about Jewish sexuality' (Biale 1997, 207). In *Annie Hall*, the JAP makes a cameo appearance as Alvy's second ex-wife, characterized by her social ambition and lack of interest in sex.

His more appealing first wife, also presented through cultural stereotyping, challenges such labelling. When they meet at a political rally for Adlai Stevenson, Allison resists Alvy's attempt to pin down her type: 'You're like

New York Jewish Left-Wing Liberal Intellectual Central Park West Brandeis University ... the Socialist summer camps and the father with the Ben Shahn drawings, right?' Allison replies, 'That was wonderful. I love being reduced to a cultural stereotype.' Alvy concedes that he is a bigot, 'but for the left'. Nor does she conform to type after they are married, for she urges him to come to bed, but he is too obsessed with the Warren Commission report to do so. In fact, she argues, 'You're using this conspiracy theory as an excuse to avoid sex with me'. At this point, the camera pans left to Alvy, who addresses the camera directly, admitting, 'She's right! Why did I turn off Allison Portchnik? She was beautiful. She was willing. She was real intelligent. Is it the old Groucho Marx joke? That I just don't want to belong to any club that would have someone like me for a member?' The reference to the Groucho Marx joke offers a self-critical acknowledgement of the structural exclusion of the Jewish woman. It simultaneously enables Alvy to avoid engaging with Allison's insight by ascending to the level of enunciation while visually relegating her to 'a hyperbolically diegetic context' – a flashback to the past pushed off-screen by the pan (Silverman 1988, 45). In this scene she is stripped of discursive authority, spatially and temporally contained.

Despite the abrupt cut to the scene of Annie and Alvy bonding through shared laughter as they attempt to catch a group of live lobsters crawling around the kitchen floor, Allison's spoken words resonate with an earlier scene in which Annie recounts her dream after her first visit to a psychiatrist: 'in my dream Frank Sinatra is holding his pillow across my face, and I can't breathe .... he's strangling me.' Alvy's interpretation relies on a reductive one-to-one relation between dream and waking life: 'he's a singer and you're a singer .... so you're trying to suffocate yourself. It makes perfect sense.' But Annie counters by exposing the displacement process: '[the psychiatrist] said your name was Alvy Singer ... in the dream I break Sinatra's glasses.' Alvy proceeds to address the camera to comment on Annie's slip of the tongue (substituting wife for life) in order to avoid owning up to being the Singer who is stifling her. In this scene distraction is deployed to exert control, although unlike Allison, Annie remains on screen albeit moved to the left edge while Alvy commands centre stage and has the last word.

On numerous other occasions Alvy makes fun of Annie's lack of discursive dexterity (her use of expressions such as 'neat' and her failure to tell a joke about her grandmother's narcoleptic brother George). But she compensates for her verbal deficiencies visually with her witty style of dressing. She turns into a live quotation of silent film comedy, specifically Charlie Chaplin's Tramp, whose contradictory costume is re-created by designer Ralph Lauren – half dapper, half tramp: the androgynous baggy khaki pants, over-sized white shirt and tie, fitted suit jacket, bowler hat. Although in some cases androgyny may reduce sexual difference or ambivalence to antithesis or mere opposition and reversal (Weber 1979, 82–3), Annie's citation of Chaplin's costume involves a displacement of function from class to gender. Her costume diverts attention from herself as sexual fetish object to the arbitrariness of her gender presentation, for her image is not an essence but a sign that demands a reading (Figure 6.1) Transforming the sexual into the textual, this access to the site of textual production furnishes a distance between the image and the woman, which Doane defines as masquerade (1991, 39). Hence Annie's dismissively cool reception of Alvy's birthday gift of a red see-through body suit (Figure 6.2).

In resisting fetishism Annie's masquerade resists stereotyping, which, according to Bhabha, is a problem of fixation and insistence on unity and coherence of identity, an attempt to deny difference and mobility and to restore original presence:

> the stereotype is not a simplification because it is a false representation of a given reality … [but] because it is an arrested, fixated form of representation that, in denying the play of difference … constitutes a problem for the representation of the subject in significations of psychic and social relations.
>
> (1983, 32)

Figure 6.1 Annie dressed as Charlie Chaplin's Tramp.

Figure 6.2 Alvy's birthday gift to Annie: a red see-through body suit.

In formal terms fetishism seeks to embrace 'two contradictory beliefs' (Bhabha 1983, 32) by vacillating 'between metaphor as substitution (masking absence and difference) and metonymy (which contiguously registers the perceived lack)' (1983, 27).

According to Doane, undoing fetishism involves the temporal separation of its two components by activating trompe l'oeil: the moment when the eye/I believes the image is real, then the re-cognition which retroactively reveals its status as representation and insists on a reading. The discrepancy between the first and second moments of seeing exposes the splitting of the subject (1991, 195).

Appropriately, the film concludes with an instance of trompe l'oeil in the first of its three embedded endings, each representing a different medium and a distinct approach to undoing fetishism. The scene from Alvy's play incorporates verbatim his conversation with Annie at the health food restaurant in L.A. in a previous scene. At one point the film camera pulls back showing Alvy sitting with two men at a table and behind them a mirror along the wall reflecting the two actors with a script between them, acknowledging the foregoing exchange as representation. The dialogue changes with a cut back to the actual actor and actress; she agrees to go back to New York. At this point Alvy's direct address to the camera reinforces the breaking of the theatrical frame as he apologizes for the phony and implausible resolution of his first play. Next, a montage of flashbacks to earlier scenes with Annie, accompanied by her voice-over singing 'Seems

Like Old Times', provides a cinema-specific critique of the play's conventional closure and teleology. Separating image and sound, the montage undermines any sense of resolution as it abandons narrative logic for an arbitrary serial ordering, followed by the final non sequitur joke, which echoes the first joke in the opening monologue: A guy tells a psychiatrist that his brother is crazy because he thinks he's a chicken. But he can't turn him in, as the doctor suggests, because he needs the eggs.

The use of joke-work to construct postmodern communal identity in Woody Allen's cinema is double-pronged: on the one hand it relates *Annie Hall* to early comedy and the cinema of attractions; on the other, it exemplifies the distinctly postmodern Jewish identificatory process in *Der Witz* described by Philippe Lacoue-Labarthe and Jean-Luc Nancy, which stretches 'across a doubled or collective identity' that problematizes identity per se. For Homi Bhabha such problematic identity offers an assurance that the self-critical joke constructs a non-essentialized collective community. Insisting on the importance of the third person or hearer in a specific, time-bound iteration of the joke, Bhabha foregrounds the performativity and ethical dimension of joke-work by acknowledging the contingency of truth. The film contrasts the inclusiveness of the self-critical tendentious joke with the deployment of the dirty/ethnic joke, which functions to exclude the Jewish woman. Her absence facilitates the forging of a relation between the teller and listener and produces a gender/ethnic imbalance into the joke-work that requires attending to the performative effects of the not-shown, the un- or under-narrated, the un-narratable, as exemplified by Allison's permanent confinement to the invisible off-screen.

In addition to joke-work, this essay extends the understanding of fetishism to include formal narrative constraints as well the stereotypical reductions of identity. Drawing on the theories of Heath, Weber, Bersani and Dutoit, joke-work is presented as an anti-narrative mode that undoes fetishism conceived as a narrative structure by mobilizing the displacement process central to its operation. Gunning's re-thinking of the spectacle-narrative dialectic in early film uncovers alternative definitions of cinematic space, time, and reception. Spatial discontinuity, present time, exhibitionism and direct address to the spectator all function to liberate spectacle from subordination to narrative and to resist the conventions of classical cinema, thereby enabling the play of multiple differences (Bukatman 2006, 75–7). Bhabha's theorization of the stereotype as a form of fetishism also expands previous models of fetishism beyond classical cinema by including racial/ethnic and class differences and exploring alternatives to the assumption of the priority of male-driven narrative over objectified feminine spectacle (which Heath's definition of fetishist structure reinforces). One such alternative is Annie's masquerade, in so far as it resists fetishistic objectification and escapes exile in some off-screen limbo.

These revisions in turn result in the redefinition of narrative pleasure: the viewer is moved by a process that exceeds him/her, ending up in a different position from the expected one, and the fascination with privileged scenes and images is transformed into the pleasure of diversion/distraction per se.

Works cited

Bersani, Leo and Ulysse Dutoit. 1985. *The Forms of Violence: Narrative in Assyrian Art and Modern Culture*. New York: Schocken Books.

Bhabha, Homi. 1983. 'The Other Question ... Homi Bhabha Reconsiders the Stereotype and Colonial Discourse', *Screen* 24 (6): 18–36.

Bhabha, Homi. 1998. 'Foreword: Joking Aside: The Idea of a Self-Critical Community', in *Modernity, Culture and 'The Jew'*, ed. Bryan Cheyette and Laura Marcus, xv–xx. Palo Alto: Stanford University Press.

Biale, David. 1997. 'Sexual Stereotypes in American Jewish Culture', in *Eros and the Jews: From Biblical Israel to Contemporary America*, 204–27. Berkeley: University of California Press.

Bukatman, Scott. 2006. 'Spectacle, Attraction and Visual Pleasure', in *Cinema of Attractions Reloaded*, ed. Wanda Strauven, 71–82. Amsterdam: Amsterdam University Press.

Butler, Judith. 1991. 'Imitation and Gender Subordination', in *Inside/Outside: Lesbian Theories, Gay Theories*, ed. Diana Fuss, 13–31. New York: Routledge.

Deleyto, Celestino. 1994–95. 'The Narrator and the Narrative: The Evolution of Woody Allen's Film Comedies', *Film Criticism* 19 (2): 40–54.

de Man, Paul. 1983. 'The Rhetoric of Temporality', in *Blindness and Insight: Essays in the Rhetoric of Contemporary Criticism*, 187–228. Minneapolis: University of Minnesota Press.

Doane, Mary Ann. 1991. *Femmes Fatales: Feminism, Film Theory, Psychoanalysis*. New York: Routledge.

Drake, Philip. 2003. 'Low Blows? Theorizing Performance in Post-Classical Comedian Comedy', in *Hollywood Comedians: The Film Reader*, ed. Frank Krutnik, 187–98. London & New York: Routledge.

Ermarth, Elizabeth. 1999. 'Finger Exercises: Parody as a Practice for Postmodernity', *European Journal of English Studies* 3 (2): 226–40.

Fabe, Marilyn. 2004. 'Film and Postmodernism: Woody Allen's Annie Hall', in *Closely Watched Films: An Introduction to the Art of Narrative Film Technique*, 173–90. Berkeley: University of California Press.

Freud, Sigmund. 1953. 'Three Essays on the Theory of Sexuality (1905)', in *The Standard Edition of the Complete Psychological Works*, vol. 7, translated and edited by James Strachey et al. London: Hogarth.

Freud, Sigmund. 1960. *Jokes and Their Relation to the Unconscious*. Translated by James Strachey. New York: Norton.

Freud, Sigmund. 1963. 'Fetishism', in *Sexuality and the Psychology of Love*, ed. Philip Rieff, 214–19. New York: Collier.

Gilman, Sander L. 1993. *Freud, Race, and Gender*. New York: Routledge.

Gunning, Tom. 1997. 'An Aesthetic of Astonishment: Early Film and the (In)Credulous Spectator', in *Viewing Positions: Ways of Seeing Film*, ed. Linda Williams, 114–30. New Brunswick, NJ: Rutgers University Press.

Hanich, Julian. 2014. 'Laughter and Collective Awareness: The Cinema Auditorium as a Public Space', *European Journal of Media Studies* 3 (2): 45–58.

Heath, Stephen. 1974. 'Lessons from Brecht', *Screen* 15 (2): 103–28.

Hutcheon, Linda. 1985. *A Theory of Parody: The Teachings of Twentieth-Century Art Forms*. New York: Methuen.

Hutcheon, Linda. 2002. *The Politics of Postmodernism* (2nd edition). London and New York: Routledge.

Kracauer, Seigfried and Thomas Y. Levin. 1987. 'Cult of Distraction: on Berlin's Picture Palaces', *New German Critique* 40 (Special Issue of Weimar Film Theory): 91–6.

Krutnik, Frank. 1984. 'The Clown-Prints of Comedy', *Screen* 25 (4–5): 50–9.

Lacan, Jacques. 1981. *The Four Fundamental Concepts of Psycho-Analysis*. Translated by Alan Sheridan. New York and London: W. W. Norton.

Lacoue-Labarthe, Philippe and Jean-Luc Nancy. 1990. 'The Nazi Myth', trans. Brian Holmes, *Critical Inquiry* 16 (2): 291–312.

Lacoue-Labarthe, Philippe and Jean-Luc Nancy. 1989. 'The Unconscious Is Destructured Like an Affect (Part I of "The Jewish People Does Not Dream")', trans. Brian Holmes, *Stanford Literature Review* 6: 191–209.

Mast, Gerald. 1987. 'The Neurotic Jew as American Clown', in *Jewish Rye: Essays on Jewish Humor*, ed. Sarah Cohen, 125–40. Bloomington: Indiana University Press.

Mehlman, Jeffrey. 1975. 'How to Read Freud on Jokes: The Critic as Schadchen', *New Literary History* 6 (2): 439–61.

Pellegrini, Ann. 1997. 'Jewishness as Gender', in *Performance Anxieties: Staging Psychoanalysis, Staging Race*, 17–38. New York and London: Routledge.

Prell, Riv-Ellen. 1996. 'Why Jewish Princesses Don't Sweat: Desire and Consumption in Postwar American Jewish Culture', in *Too Jewish? Challenging Traditional Identities*, ed. Norman Kleeblatt, 74–92. New Brunswick, NJ: Rutgers University Press.

Rose, Margaret A. 1979. *Parody/Metafiction: An Analysis of Parody as a Critical Mirror to the Writing and Reception of Fiction*. London: Croom Helm.
Silverman, Kaja. 1988. *The Acoustic Mirror: The Female Voice in Psychoanalysis and Cinema*. Bloomington and Indianapolis: Indiana University Press.
Trahair, Lisa. 2007. *The Comedy of Philosophy: Sense and Nonsense in Early Cinematic Slapstick*. New York: State University of New York Press.
Waugh, Patricia. 1984. *Metafiction: The Theory and Practice of Self-Conscious Fiction*. New York and London: Methuen.
Weber, Samuel. 1979. *Unwrapping Balzac: A Reading of Le Peau de Chagrin*. Toronto, Buffalo, London: University of Toronto Press.

7

The mechanical bride: On not-knowing in and after *Annie Hall*

Sarah Kennedy

The mechanical truth, in short, was sometimes first spoken in jest.
– Lewis Mumford

History doesn't repeat itself, but it does rhyme.
– Mark Twain

This chapter argues that *Annie Hall* extends the operational aesthetics of early-twentieth-century American comedy into the psychological realm of the 'nervous romance'.[1] Drawing on the mechanical logic of the gag film, Allen's technical innovations constitute a cinematic super-stunt like the cranks, pulleys and self-complicating mechanisms of those fantastical machines made famous by the American cartoonist Rube Goldberg. The film's narrative contrivances and relational dynamics create a paradigmatic fun-house for the exploration of desire and sexual difference. Yet the filmmaker's fixation on the mechanics of 'how' not 'who' perpetuates a pattern of regressive interpersonal structures that both prizes and stigmatizes feminine ignorance and not-knowing.

Pygmalion on the Upper East Side

The – the other important joke for me is one that's, uh, usually attributed to Groucho Marx, but I think it appears originally in Freud's wit and its relation to the unconscious. And it goes like this – I'm paraphrasing: Uh … 'I would never wanna belong to any club that would have someone like me for a member.' That's the key joke of my adult life in terms of my relationships with women.

(Allen 1983, 4)

Alvy Singer's famous opening monologue introduces the viewer to his central problem when it comes to relationships: an irresolvable asymmetry of desire and value that boils down to the conceit: 'if I'm good enough for her then there must be something wrong with her.' No living, breathing woman can be right for Alvy if she shows any interest in him. Those that do must be lacking in some key respect. Alvy sets out each time to discover the insufficiency in his lovers and to improve them into desirability (the more obvious their faults are – and the more charmingly proffered up for his inspection – the better).

Christopher Knight reads Alvy in relation to the Ovidian figure of Pygmalion, with Annie as his reluctant Galatea (Knight 2004). In the classical myth, Pygmalion sculpted a statue of his ideal bride 'Of such proportion, shape and grace as nature never gave / Nor can to any woman give' (Ovid 2002, 302) who was brought to life by the goddess Venus. Like high-schooler Tracy in Allen's *Manhattan* (1979), Galatea may appear to her mentor as a sensual vision of physical perfection, but she is an innocent, new-sprung into an unfamiliar space and must be taught the ways of things by her worldly older lover. This suggestive story has wide cultural currency in English language literature, television and film. In the early part of the twentieth century it was reframed as a comedy of class and manners in George Bernard Shaw's 1913 play *Pygmalion* and its adaptations, including the 1964 film *My Fair Lady*, in which Professor Henry Higgins attempts to drill cockney flower-seller Eliza Doolittle in manners and elocution. The 1983 film *Educating Rita* formalizes the pedagogical element of the romance further when university lecturer Frank Bryant (Michael Caine) educates hairdresser Susan White (Julie Walters) in the codes, attitudes and behaviours of a bourgeois intellectual milieu far removed from her working-class context.

Annie's inadequacies are established early on in the film. When she gives him a lift after their tennis meet-cute, Alvy notes her poor driving and lack of worldliness, asking 'you're not from New York, right?' (Allen 1983, 33). Annie is from Chippewa Falls, Wisconsin: a mid-westerner in New York, a gauche *shiksa* out of place in the predominantly Jewish cultural and intellectual landscape of the Upper East Side. She is acutely aware of what she understands to be her intellectual inferiority: 'You don't think I'm smart enough to be serious about', she says, or 'why are you always pushing me to take those college courses like I was dumb or something?' (49). When Annie takes up Alvy's suggestion and enrols in college, he accuses her of having an affair with her professor ('That jerk that teaches that incredible crap course "Contemporary Crisis in Western Man"!' (59)). As the argument escalates, Alvy neutralizes Annie's indignation by mocking her mid-western expressions: '"Neat!" There's that – What are you – twelve years old? That's one of your Chippewa Falls expressions! 'He thinks I'm neat'" (60). When Annie makes a subtle claim to equality with her professor through the use of his first name, Alvy renders her ridiculous by repositioning her as Bathsheba to the biblical King David. She is reframed as a figure of sensuous femininity positioned to elicit the lust of older and more powerful men (the shadow of sexual violation hangs over the comparison, as Bathsheba could hardly have refused her "seduction" by the King).

As Christopher Knight argues, 'Alvy punishes Annie for the sin of taking him seriously' (216). Knight in turn quotes the critic Foster Hirsch, who writes: 'Their relationship is based on the premise that Annie is an idiot; and once she begins to question that, once she begins, however tentatively, to strike out on her own … the affair is doomed' (Hirsch 1981, 86). According to Judy Berman, *Annie Hall* is prescient and entirely self-conscious in its portrayal of the damaging effects of Pygmalion-syndrome (2017). She writes:

> Decades before Rebecca Solnit's work inspired the 'mansplaining' meme and Sheila Heti made a refrain out of 'he's just another man who wants to teach me something,' in her novel *How Should a Person Be?*, Allen understood how destructive men's urges to educate and shape women could be.
>
> (n.p.)

That may be so, but destructive to whom? Hitchcock explored similar psychological territory in *Vertigo* (1958) when he had Scottie Ferguson importune Judy Barton to reconstruct herself as the unknowable dead woman Madeleine Elster, dying her hair and adopting Madeleine's style of dress. Allen riffs on *Vertigo* when he returns to Annie and Alvy's world in *Manhattan Murder Mystery* (1993), a film that is itself created from the reconstituted remnants of the original, rambling Ur-script of *Annie Hall*. Where Hitchcock's Judy ends up dead, Allen's Annie winds up 'living in SoHo with some guy' (Allen 1983, 104). We do not see what it might have meant for Annie to be the subject of Alvy's improvement project – we only see that she is taking her new partner to see *The Sorrow and the Pity*, a point that Alvy counts 'as a personal triumph' (104). Indeed, Annie is never granted the opportunity for retrospection of any sort. It is Alvy who is left alone, Alvy who remains, watching and reminiscing, as Annie disappears. We are offered the pathos of Alvy's final voiceover as the screen fades, and it is Alvy whom we will follow into the next heartbreaking chapter (as we do, typologically, in the form of Ike in *Manhattan* and many times thereafter).

Contra Berman's statement, we might recall that we are doomed to repeat the histories that we don't understand. Allen's films engage deeply with cinematic histories of genre and style, yet when it comes to his preoccupation with shaping women, his films suffer from repetition compulsion. Allen approaches the myth of Pygmalion and Galatea most explicitly in *Mighty Aphrodite* (1995), but the pattern forms a bass note in much of his earlier, more celebrated work. The drama critic Terry Teachout describes *Annie Hall* as 'the first on-screen manifestation of Allen's Pygmalion complex, which in *Manhattan* would explicitly reveal itself as an obsession with malleable young women' (Teachout 2004). In *Manhattan*, Ike Davis (Allen) is moved by the beauty of his high-schooler girlfriend to say:

> you're – you're God's answer to Job … you know. You would've ended all – all argument between them. I mean, H-H-He would've pointed to you and said, you know, 'I do a lot of terrible things, but I can also make one of these,' you know. And then – then Job would've said, 'Eh okay – well, you win.'
>
> (1983, 227)

The scene recalls Alvy's use of biblical imagery in his argument with Annie, but it is revealing in two further respects. First, it echoes the hubris of Pygmalion in presuming to fashion a woman for himself out of lifeless matter. For Ike, God and Man alike may woman make, since this is exactly the project that Ike embarks upon in Tracy's cultural education. She echoes this sense of his semi-divine Adamic status in her definition of love: 'Your concerns are my concerns' (245). Second, it offers us a vision of idealized womanhood – beautiful, youthful and malleable – as endlessly reproducible. Ike's formulation – 'I can also make one of these' – points simultaneously to Tracy's uniqueness and to her nature as a type to be repeated and commodified (as indeed she is, as the ingénue who reappears in so many of Allen's films, given body variously by actors like Scarlett Johansson, Emma Stone, and Selena Gomez).

In *Mighty Aphrodite* Lennie Weinrib (Allen) goes so far as to rewrite Linda's biography, designating the porn actress and prostitute 'practically incidentally a virgin' as well as quite literally reclothing her for a date. Allen draws on a chequered pattern of knowings and not-knowings to create the dramatic tension. The plot of *Mighty Aphrodite* is motored first by Lennie's need to account for the brilliance of his adopted son by tracking down his birth mother, and later – once he has found Linda and realized that she possesses no extraordinary genius – by his need to reconfigure her as clever, articulate and demure.

A much earlier prototype exists in *Sleeper* (1973), the fourth film written and directed by Allen and the first of the trio of films he co-wrote with Marshall

Brickman in the 1970s (together with *Annie Hall* and *Manhattan*). *Sleeper* also marks the first of Allen's films as director to star Diane Keaton. In this dystopian post-apocalyptic comedy caper Miles Monroe (Allen) wakes up 200 years into the future in a sleek but sinister minimalist world populated by home-assistance robots, blissed-out poets and a few terrified scientists working to create a movement to resist the totalitarian government. When he first meets Luna Schlosser (Keaton) she is a complacent party girl. 'Do you think I'm stupid?' she asks him (she prefigures Annie Hall in this). Later, at his instigation, Luna joins the resistance and immerses herself in Marxist theory, prompting Miles to decry:

> I created a Bohemian monster. Next thing you know, she'll want to have sex with the robots. ... Give her a couple of books to read and right away she's Miss Pseudo-Intellectual, Neo-Fascist, Hegelian, Freudian, Marxist.

The irony is that Miles first encounters Luna when he disguises himself as a robot to escape from government reprogramming. The humour of these scenes stems from his failure to be anything other than fully human. Luna, however, is always in danger of being revealed as a synthetic object. She relies on an 'Orgasmatron' for brief and incurious sexual fulfilment. Her persistent blankness and programmability accounts for Miles's fear that an improved Luna will be more inclined to sleep with robots than with her chaotic human counterpart.

This early prototype of the Pygmalion pattern in Allen's films reveals an underlying logic and structure that is not organic but mechanical. Allen's interest in magic is well known; he practised close-up magic as a child (Allen 2020, 4–5) and card tricks often feature in his films. Yet the enduring patterns of relational failure in his work veer away from the magical paradigm of Pygmalion and into a techno-realm of beeps, clicks and automata. Allen surrenders the irreproducible, organic magic of the Pygmalion mythos to the reproductive efficiencies of the assembly line.

From their first appearance in *Sleeper*, robots are associated with generic female inadequacy and frigidity. On encountering a 'domestic service menial', Mile says: 'These robots are uncanny ... they're alert and they respond, you know, I've gone out with girls who had less movement than that.' He goes on: 'Are there female robots? 'Cos the possibilities are limitless.' On first meeting Keaton, Allen is reported to have described her as 'a blank' and 'a coat-check girl' (Dowd 1993). Perhaps this accounts for his choice in casting her as the first (and later the most enduring) of his Galateas. The figure of the robotic menial offers a model for Allen's ongoing project of female improvement. He is not a magician but a technician, a monstrous inventor, Oz meets Dr Caligari. His plots are crank-shafts churning out female bodies: educated, neurotic and interchangeably unique. Further, as the next section will show, his blueprints are built into the aesthetic structures of his films. Allen's gendered dehumanizations are inextricable from the formal comi-tragic artistry of his most celebrated cinematic work.

Married to the machine

Sam Girgus sees Allen's film oeuvre as working out a 'stuttering poetics of insecurity' (2002, 35) that dramatizes social, cultural and personal problems of desire. Like Girgus, Peter Bailey locates Allen's insecurities in the realm of the aesthetic, noting 'a sort of teasing artistic self-referentiality' (2001, 3) and observing that Allen's films are full of impeachments of art and artists. He describes Allen's conflicted 'intransigently skeptical, highly conflictual attitude' to his own creative productions counterbalanced by his films' 'visual calculation, their formal balance and symmetry' as 'the central tension of Allen's cinematic art' (4–5), observing:

> each Woody Allen film from *Play It Again, Sam* onward constitutes the director's highly self-conscious reconfiguring of the relationship between the chaos of experience and the stabilising, controlling capacities of aesthetic rendering.
>
> (2001, 5)

For Bailey, *Annie Hall* navigates this relationship through its recourse to what he terms the film's 'anti-mimetic emblems' (37), those formal contrivances (subtitles, split-screen elements, impossible vox pops and animated segments) that serve to foreground the artifice of the film medium and break the viewer's immersion in the film's reality. While I agree with Bailey's analysis, it avoids any consideration of the roles of desire and sexual difference as determining motives in the shaping of Allen's formal contrivances.

Annie Hall makes the point explicit in showing us Alvy's play, which operates as a straightforward artistic revision and salvation of his failed romantic relationship. Unable to win Annie back, Alvy writes a play-script in which Sunny returns to Arty and the lovers reconcile. 'Tsch, whatta you want?' Alvy asks the viewer. 'It was my first play. You know, you know how you're always tryin' t' get things to come out perfect in art because, uh, it's real difficult in life' (1983, 102). Desire, identity, sexual difference and artistic anxiety are entangled in Allen's work, which should be understood less as a binary interplay between art and life and more as an assemblage of multiple entwined discourses. In *A Thousand Plateaus* (1980) Deleuze and Guattari articulate their concept of the assemblage in relation to ideas of the machine (a system of multiple interacting parts and axes):

> On a first, horizontal, axis, an assemblage comprises two segments, one of content, the other of expression. On the one hand it is a *machinic assemblage* of bodies, of actions and passions, an intermingling of bodies reacting to one another; on the other hand it is a *collective assemblage of enunciation*, of acts and statements, of incorporeal transformations attributed to bodies. Then on a vertical axis, the assemblage has both *territorial sides*, or reterritorialized sides, which stabilise it, and *cutting edges of deterritorialisation*, which carry it away.
>
> (102–3)

This description helpfully incorporates the oppositional placement of (ordered) form and (chaotic) content that Bailey notes in Allen's films. But it also offers a more encompassing figure for the entanglement, intermingling and reactivity that are such energizing features of Allen's comi-tragic cosmology. Additionally – and especially important for my purposes – Deleuze and Guattari found this concept of the assemblage on the figure of the machine, with its open system of multiple interacting components and moving parts.

Annie Hall imports the 'operational aesthetic' (Harris 1973, 57) of the gag film extending right back to its phylotypical original, the Lumière brothers' *L'Arroseur arrosé* (1895) into a psychological space replete with neuroses and libidinal energies. Tom Gunning describes the basic schema of the gag film as a dyad of schemer and victim linked by a device or apparatus: 'a detour is taken through an inanimate object, or [...] arrangement of objects. As a mediatory visual element which takes some time to operate, the device possesses its own fascination, one which brings us back [...] to the operational aesthetic' (1995, 90–1). The overt machinery of *Sleeper* is absent, but *Annie Hall* is still a mechanical assemblage of desire in which the film itself is the linking device. Its complex and complicating comedic mechanisms offer viewer and creator alike a formalist pleasure even as its self-defeating exertions inevitably result in relational failure.

Allen struggled to choose a title for the film. One of the less successful options, 'A Rollercoaster Named Desire', points to the automated processes that underlie the film as well as to the inextricability of the mechanistic and the libidinous within its cinematic world. Alvy spends his early life beneath the Coney Island Thunderbolt Rollercoaster. Machine turbulence forms a multi-sensory backdrop to the narration of his childhood sexual urges, and he is shown to 'get his aggression out' through the bumper cars (1983, 6). Both of these fairground rides are engineered to create mis-directional motion: their function is to offer human participants a pleasurable yet controlled experience of tumult and disorder, whether on the vertical axes of the rollercoaster or on the horizontal plane of the bumper cars. As Joseph Lanza writes:

> [The rollercoaster] represents all of America's jittery ambitions, love of sensationalism and eroticised violence packed into a single pleasure device [...] rollercoasters offer the vim and violence of the movies, the rising action and denouement of drama, the calculated terror of speed racing, and a kind of demented arrhythmical symphony that places our smug perceptions of person, place, and thing in *controlled danger*. The rollercoaster is, in short, an icon to which the bastions of high-art, academia, pop culture, and pornography can simultaneously relate.
>
> (1992, 53)

For Allen, such visual and spatial patterning offers a dynamic model for the impossibilities of desire. The pattern repeats in *The Purple Rose of Cairo* use of the abandoned fun park (where Jeff Daniels's matinée idol come-to-life hides out) and in *Deconstructing Harry* (where the roadside amusement park is the site of emergence of Harry Bloch's fictional creations into his reality). Explaining their typology of the machine, Deleuze and Guattari write that each type 'has its own singularities and operations, its own qualities and traits, which determine the relation of desire to the technical element' (473). Taking inspiration from the mad-cap energies of the Coney Island rides, *Annie Hall* can be read as a cinematic Rube-Goldberg machine: a self-confounding complexity engine, part-labyrinth, part-pin ball machine.

Rube Goldberg was an American cartoonist and engineer best known for his comic-strip 'The Inventions of Professor Lucifer G. Butts'. Professor Butts invented zany, complicated fictional machines to perform simple tasks in over-elaborate ways. The machines are works of brilliant absurdism, such as the 'Self-Operating Napkin' machine, but they are often also darkly satirical, as in the 'Automatic Suicide Device for Unlucky Stock Speculators'. Goldberg wrote that the machines were 'symbols of man's capacity for exerting maximum effort to accomplish minimal results' (Wolfe and Goldberg 2000, 53). They incorporate chain reactions that are counterintuitive and needlessly complex, but that have an inexorable – if surreal – logic to them. Goldberg had toured with a troupe of vaudeville comedians. Like Allen, he worked as a stand-up comedian in New York and had an interest in slapstick. He was friendly with Charlie Chaplin and designed the 'Billows Feeding Machine' that features in Chaplin's 1936 film *Modern Times*. Goldberg machines are farcical and futile, full of self-sabotaging complications. Their linear (il)logic maps neatly to the contours of the gag film's connection device. Their tongue-in-cheek mechanics are the perfect foil for the banality and self-inflicted misfortune of the bungling *schlemiel*, while offering up industrial production as an active, yet indifferent, supervening force, a deus ex machina made comically literal. What better or more appropriate blueprint could Allen have used as a model for his irresolvable relationship-in-process film art than the concept of the Rube Goldberg machine?

Early in his career Allen was heavily influenced by the tradition of American comedy exemplified by Chaplin, the Marx Brothers, Buster Keaton and Harold Lloyd. Films like *Bananas* (1971) and *Sleeper* are full of allusions to the Marx Brothers – *Duck Soup* (1933) in particular – and *Sleeper* recalls elements of *Modern Times* (Alvarez 2009). In *Bananas*, Fielding Mellish (Allen) is a tester of Goldbergian devices, including a coffin that serenades its occupant, and a machine designed to enable office workers to exercise at their desks. Allen's robot kitchen in *Sleeper* with its sleek but opaque gadgetry is juxtaposed with the equally ludicrous appearance of the Drinking Bird as foyer art in Luna's futuristic apartment. The Drinking Bird or Insatiable Birdie, which uses the heat-driven oscillation of liquids to tip the bird's head repeatedly over a glass of liquid, was a frequent component of Goldberg's cartoon machines. *Sleeper* is, Allen says, 'a great big cartoon' (Carroll 2006, 4). Like Chaplin's feeding machine in *Modern Times*, the instant pudding episode of *Sleeper* satirizes the absurdities of automation, especially in circumstances where the process being automated relates to primal desires for nourishment or satisfaction. As is evident in the scene where Miles dangles at great height from a tangle of magnetic tape as Luna frantically tries to stop the haywire tape machine, the films share a double consciousness, at once animated by machine kinetics and beset by anxieties as to the implications of the machine age for human functioning.

In *The Mechanical Bride* (1951) Marshall McLuhan writes about 'the interfusion of sex and technology' as 'one of the most peculiar features of our world' (94). He describes this 'strange marriage' as a desire 'born of a hungry curiosity to explore and enlarge the domain of sex by mechanical technique, on one hand, and, on the other, to possess machines in a sexually gratifying way' (94). Connecting the rhythms of the production line with the aesthetics of the chorus line, McLuhan notes that 'there is intoxication in numbers and also release from personal responsibility' (96):

> one answer to the ad's query: 'What makes a gal a good number?' is simply 'looking like a number of other gals'; to the query 'What's the trick that makes her click?' the answer is 'being a replaceable part'.
>
> (96)

This vision of a streamlined series of well-formed women emerging from an infinite conveyor-belt recalls Allen's blithe description (in a draft of his 1977 story 'The Kugelmass Episode') of his 45-year-old antihero fascinated by college 'coeds', abstract and undifferentiated. Allen wrote in the margin, '*c'est moi*' (Morgan 2018). Or the scene in *Mighty Aphrodite* when Mira Sorvino's obliging call girl instructs Lennie (Allen) to 'Pull the string' to undress her. Although he patronizingly complains that he's 'not so mechanical', when her top flies open Lennie marvels 'That's amazing. Science is'. Given his ongoing immersion in the fever dream of the mechanical bride, it should come as no surprise that Allen's anxieties and fixation on women and machines should collide in determining the relation of desire to the technical elements of his film-making.

The not-knowing girl

Sianne Ngai points out in her theory of the gimmick (in which category she includes Goldberg's inventions) that 'comedy's special tie to the present lies in the way in which it shares the gimmick's operational aesthetic, its interest in showcasing how things function or the way things go' (59). Gimmick aesthetics are serial; they cannot account for the complex multidimensional processes of transmutation and change. Allen takes this aesthetic to anatomical extreme in *Everything You Always Wanted To Know About Sex* (*But Were Afraid To Ask)* (1972), where male ejaculation is shown to be the product of a frenetic computerized control centre and a steam-fuelled engine room full of driving crank-shafts. As Ngai argues, the machine as gimmick creates the suspicion of fraudulence, complicating the affective response of both creator and audience. This is why the critiques of art offered by Allen's movies so often end up invoking an onanistic masculine-coded shame, as for example in *Stardust Memories*, when Sandy Bates observes 'You can't control life. It doesn't wind up perfectly. Only – only art you can control. Art and masturbation. Two areas in which I am an absolute expert' (Allen 1983, 335). Control is a central feature of Allen's onscreen alter egos' relationships with women, but it is a control exerted through the medium ('the medium enters in as a condition of the art form itself' (Allen 1983, 40)). Art and masturbation both involve a dynamic of control over – and release of – the self: a dynamic that rebounds on the governing consciousness in the process of its making. Neither activity is primarily collaborative, at least in Allen's filmic world.

Allen's equation of art and masturbation follows in the comedic tradition of Chaplin, Keaton and the Marx Brothers. But it also speaks to a much more intrinsic dynamic in Allen's inner life. 'Bliss comes from the success of denial', Allen has said. 'Movie-making is an immense distraction, which is a godsend. If you weren't killing that time and you weren't distracted, you'd be sitting home confronting issues that you can't get second-act-curtain lines for' (Lahr 1996). This recalls Ike's moment of revelation towards the end of *Manhattan* when he is brainstorming a new writing project, 'a short story … about, um, tsch, people in Manhattan who, uh, who are constantly creating these real, uh, unnecessary neurotic problems for themselves 'cause it keeps them from dealing with, uh, more unsolvable, terrifying problems about, uh, the universe' (Allen 1983, 267).

Annie Hall pays homage to its cartoon underpinnings in its animated sequence based on Stuart Hample's comic strip *Inside Woody Allen*. But by the time of its production, Allen had moved beyond the comedy of exteriorized mechanics, and the submerged machine processes in *Annie Hall* are indicative of this shift. They are the patterns you might expect of a writer who features Marshall McLuhan in his film, built into the processes of the medium itself. As Allen has acknowledged:

> Keaton and Chaplin reflected an era where the anxieties and underlying vocabulary of people's longings were physical. It was a physical era. It was trains and machines … I came along after Freud, when the playing field had shifted to the psyche. It was interior. What was interesting to people suddenly was the psyche. They wanted to know what was going on in the mind.
>
> (Lahr 1996)

Meghan O'Gieblyn (2021) observes that writing is itself an act of transmutation, as thoughts move from the psychic interior to an exterior world capable of recording and reproducing them: 'Words, once they leave the mind, become part of the material, mechanical world: they keep saying the same things.' Allen's shift away from the shoe-shuffle slapstick of his physical comedy and towards a rhetorical celluloid narrativity is reflective of his awareness of the point. But *Annie Hall* is so effective as a film in part because it retains a consciousness quite beyond that of its maker, of the uncontainability of the desires (and minds) it seeks to order and record – it knows that machines, too, run riot.

The mind that Allen concerns himself with in *Annie Hall* is his own, in proxy form as Alvy Singer. Alvy begins by outlining his method, which is the diagnostic approach of the engineer: go back over the process, take the pieces apart, reorganize the sequence and see where it all went wrong:

> Annie and I broke up and I – I still can't get my mind around that. You know, I – I keep sifting the pieces o' the relationship through my mind and – and examining my life and tryin' to figure out where did the screw-up come.
>
> (Allen 1983, 4)

The film attempts to create a relationship-schematic, rehearsing, reordering and revising Alvy's romantic failure in the hope that the error can be detected and resolved. Allen's self-confounding storylines follow a Goldbergian logic that enacts and occludes the desperate desire for control that is the film's most basic driver. This mania for control reflects Allen's position as an inventor-filmmaker. For all the deft construction of story and plot that his work exhibits, he is still enamoured with the apparatus of cinema and invested in 'the display of new technologies as entertainment' (Gunning 1995, 88). The labyrinthine structure of the film puts its artifice on show, pulling off the consummate metaphysical double-bluff: it foregrounds its own subjectivity, yet in appearing so guileless it slyly assimilates the viewer into the shared experience of Alvy's musings. The structure of the film's narrative apparatus means that Annie has no personhood or independent standing within the open field of the film's reality. She only ever exists as a series of memory snippets, reordered by Alvy, deliberated over, and made coherent through the uniting effect of his narration.

There is something very sinister in the way that the operational aesthetics of Allen's films elide the distinctions between plot/person and woman/machine, and none more so than *Annie Hall*. The non-chronological ordering of the story, Alvy's narrative dominance, the wide shots that maintain a strict distance from Keaton and never allow her to be viewed alone straight to camera and the frequent irruption of media gimmickry all amount to a meta-cinematic apparatus of control. Rob King sees the 'mechanical spectacle' of Keystone slapstick as crucial in the formation of twentieth-century mass culture due to 'the primacy of technique and technology over issues of social meaning' (2007, 272). Drawing on Adorno's critique of technical virtuosity as the highest value of modern mass culture (1991, 79), King writes that 'the popularisation of a "machine aesthetic" during the early twentieth century often came at the cost of the social and political themes that had infused the work of earlier Progressive artists' (272). Allen's magnificent filmic machine recreates the operational aesthetics of Keystone's contraptions, playing it again in a psychological key. The combination of mechanical contrivance with relational neuroses speaks to a post-Freudian culture in a technological language both familiar and fascinating. That is why there's so much emphasis placed on mechanism, technology, automation and technique. Think of the tape splicing episode in *Manhattan Murder Mystery*, where a recording of Helen Mosse is recut so that a technological phantom can be made to say anything the main characters want. In a simulation of the process of editing a film, a female antagonist is reformatted into an accomplice (before she is further neutralized by being seduced by Ted, in a throwaway line). Like the camera, the tape recorder's effects are double-edged. Tape recorders have the potential to offer up an undistorted reflection of (mostly masculine) narcissism, as in the figure of the director Lester in *Crimes and Misdemeanors*. Even here, however, Allen's character, Cliff, uses editing techniques to make himself look better and his rival worse.

It is revealing that Allen credits Keaton with his gradual realization that women are people:

> When I started writing professionally, I could never, ever write from the woman's point of view. It was when I met Keaton that I started. She has such a strong personality and so many original convictions. I became interested in her and interested in her sisters and her mother as people.
>
> (Lahr 1996)

Annie Hall and her 'la-de-da' ditziness took root in the cultural imaginary so profoundly in spite of Allen, as other contributors in this book amply demonstrate. Keaton's hybrid persona surpasses the material that was written for/about it just as Keaton surprised Allen by having a strong personality and original convictions. Yet in *Annie Hall* the audience is encouraged to take on Alvy's understanding of Annie's blankness and dysfunction (as Miles says to Luna in *Sleeper*: 'For a minute there I thought you didn't know how to work the machine'). Instead of reading her hesitancy and coltishness as characteristic of an immense and energetic mind in constant multiple dialogues with the world around it, we become trained to the rhythm of Alvy's consciousness to perceive Annie's mannerisms as signs of moon-calf malfunction. His attitude to Annie is glib and domineering ('I – I – I'm gonna buy you these books, I think, because I – I think you should read them. You know, instead of that cat book' (45)). We are never told why the 'cat book' would have been such a problem for Annie to read, except that cats are used in the film as synecdoches for lonely, repressed – and possibly independent – womanhood. When Annie confesses to an empty social calendar, Alvy jokes that she might be plague-ridden; she responds that men can be jerks: 'But I'm thinking of getting some cats' (41).

The moment is tongue-in-cheek, but we glimpse an alternate version of the story in which Annie makes her own journey of self-discovery outside of the psychological contortions and sexual mechanics of Alvy's 'nervous romance'. The scene represents a lost opportunity. Just as the rollercoaster of desire is a 'parody of that proverbial train ride to success', and a structure in which 'the tired, linear dichotomy of top versus bottom can be twisted into a Rube Goldberg labyrinth' (Lanza 1992, 53), so too the film could have used its carnivalesque structures to disrupt and subvert the relational power dynamics between Annie and Alvy. That it chooses not to speaks to the crucial importance of power and control to the film's project.

'I have control of everything, and I mean everything' (Lahr 1996). This is the way that Allen describes his approach to film-making. As Dale Bauer says, 'the act of storytelling [is] an act of power. It is a way of reconceiving interpretation as a forceful method of social control' (31). Interviewing Allen, John Lahr notes:

> Even when he was growing up, Allen was more formidable than he liked to show; the dissimulation of powerlessness appealed to him in the same way that the fantasy of being invisible gives a thrilling sense of power. 'I didn't want to play Bogart,' he says. 'I didn't want to play John Wayne. I wanted to be the schnook. The guy with the glasses who doesn't get the girl, who can't get the girl but who's amusing.'
>
> (1996)

Allen's creative inability to allow his women their humanity suggests a deep fear of replacement. It recalls Allen's 'Mechanical Objects' routine from *Standup Comic: 1964–1968*, in which Allen finds himself at the mercy of a well-spoken female elevator: 'I have never in my life had good relationships with mechanical objects of any sort. Anything that I can't reason with or kiss or fondle, I get into trouble with.' To suggest that Allen is aware of these elements within his work is in no way to identify any points at which the irony becomes disruptive to the work's coercive project. Allen is part of a long line of creative but contemptuous male artists who transmute their self-loathing into hubris: a kind of bright perversion that offers to expiate the sins and dysfunction of the prevailing culture – its hunger, its superficiality and its exploitative indifference.

The long-standing working title of the film (and Allen's preferred option) was *Anhedonia*, the inability to feel pleasure. Whose inability is being pointed to? We might assume it is the poor schmuck who believes that life is 'divided up into the horrible and the miserable' (45) and who must keep searching for romantic fulfilment despite the heartbreak ('we need the eggs' (105)). But the term *anhedonia* is equally appropriate for Allen's prototypical inhibited woman, from the up-tight Luna in *Sleeper* ('in the future, everyone is frigid') to the hapless woman at the cocktail party in *Manhattan*, a portrait of sexual misery framed by curtain bangs ('I finally had an orgasm and my doctor told me it was the wrong kind' (205)).

McLuhan connects the 'ideal of the frigid woman' to the barrage of cultural messages that view 'the human body as a sort of love-machine capable merely of specific thrills [...] which reduces sex experience to a problem in mechanics and hygiene' (99). The psycho-sexual mechanics of Allen's storytelling requires that women like Annie and Luna be sexually unavailable, despite his artistic assertion of them as libidinous. An unpublished fictional alter ego observes that 'unlike the Jewish girl – the *shiksa* is not guilt-ridden – not a complainer – she is abandoned, fun-loving, and above all promiscuous. The *shiksa* will perform any sex act' (Morgan 2018). Their sexual unlocking is framed as an almost mechanical challenge for Allen's anti-heroes. Alvy complains that Annie relies on marijuana to relax her before sex because her presence as well as pleasure 'doesn't count' if he is no longer solely responsible for eliciting it (52). He jokingly suggests she should be rendered inert before sex – 'I'll give you a shot of sodium pentothal. You can sleep through it' (50) – but then is dissatisfied when Annie seems distant, becoming literally disembodied.

Something slips through Alvy's fingers here. Annie assures Alvy that he has her body. 'Yeah', he says, 'but that's not – that's no good. I want the whole thing' (52). The 'whole thing' is elusive, and Annie's inner mechanisms remain a mystery. By confining Annie to a role in which she must remain intellectually subordinate, Alvy denies her the possibility of bliss. Allen's assertion that bliss comes from the success of denial reinstates the conditions of the Fall: to know and be known requires a loss of innocence. You can't be in denial if you don't possess the knowledge which is its precondition. Annie is never granted the opportunity to become fully knowing, because doing so would render her equal with Alvy. Even her apparent evolution at the end of the film is compromised because her gesture of intellectual independence reveals a debt to Alvy's influence (he calls it 'a personal triumph'). In *Annie Hall*, sexual frigidity and intellectual entrainment both serve to contain and neutralize the potential of the female subject for self-determination. It stages a drama of female innocence that vests male power in superior knowledge even as it expresses dissatisfaction – perhaps even disbelief – at the naivety of young women. Yet they must remain credulous, because failing to do so would threaten the narrative dominance that Alvy exerts through the film's machinery, as Allen does throughout his oeuvre.

What makes *Annie Hall* such a deeply flawed masterpiece is that it does its job too well. The apparatus of disguise is so deft and effective, its simulation so convincing, that we are in danger of mistaking its fascination with process for true feeling. Annie's lack of independent access to knowledge is idealized and fetishized: she is the foremost Not-Knowing Girl of our time. The Not-Knowing Girl laughs and ingratiates when her intelligence is insulted by a higher wit. The Not-Knowing Girl wants to learn, and therefore must please. The Not-Knowing Girl leans forward when she should be scanning for exits. The Not-Knowing Girl smiles and nods. The Not-Knowing Girl learns to say: 'I believe my friend.'[2] *Annie Hall* is at its heart a cold film. It is a film in which life aspires to art, so long as art aspires to the condition of the assembly line. For all Diane Keaton's flustered charm and Annie's nervous grace, it is a film that fetishizes the shame of not-knowing, and that punishes women first for their ignorance and then for their presumption in acquiring knowledge. It is a film that for forty years has been telling us that when it comes to relationships, ignorance is the closest we can get to bliss.

Notes

1 The tagline 'a nervous romance' appears on the promotional posters for the film's original theatrical release.
2 Keaton's response, when asked in an interview whether she believed the allegations of child molestation made against Allen by his daughter Dylan Farrow (Brockes 2014).

Works cited

Adorno, Theodor. 2001. 'The Schema of Mass Culture', in *The Culture Industry*, ed. J. M. Bernstein, 61–97. London: Routledge.

Allen, Woody. 1983. *Four Films of Woody Allen: Annie Hall, Interiors, Manhattan, Stardust Memories*. London: Faber and Faber.

Allen, Woody. 2020. *Apropos of Nothing*. New York: Arcade.

Alvarez, Joseph. 2009. 'Woody Allen: A Red-Headed Marx Brothers Stepchild?' in *A Century of the Marx Brothers*, ed. Joseph Mills, 151–63. Newcastle: Cambridge Scholars Publishing.

Bailey, Peter J. 2001. *The Reluctant Film Art of Woody Allen*. Lexington: University Press of Kentucky.

Berman, Judy. 2017. 'Does *Annie Hall* Actually Suck?' https://www.vice.com/en/article/mgyvgb/does-annie-hall-actually-suck

Brockes, Emma. 2014. 'Diane Keaton: "I love Woody. And I believe my friend"', *Guardian*, 3 May. https://www.theguardian.com/film/2014/may/03/diane-keaton-i-love-woody-allen-i-believe-my-friend

Carroll, Kathleen. 2006. 'Woody Allen Says Comedy Is No Laughing Matter', 1974. Reprinted in *Woody Allen: Interviews*, ed. Robert E. Kapsis and Kathie Coblentz, 3–6. Jackson: University of Mississippi Press.

Deleuze, Gilles and Félix Guattari. 2013. *A Thousand Plateaus: Capitalism and Schizophrenia*. Translated by Brian Massumi. London: Bloomsbury.

Dowd, Maureen. 1993. 'Diane and Woody, Still a Fun Couple', *The New York Times*, 15 August. https://www.nytimes.com/1993/08/15/movies/diane-and-woody-still-a-fun-couple.html?pagewanted=all

Feldstein, Richard. 1989. 'Displaced Feminine Representation in Woody Allen's Cinema', in *Discontented Discourses: Feminism / Textual Intervention / Psychoanalysis*, ed. Marleen S. Barr and Richard Feldstein, 69–86. Urbana and Chicago: University of Illinois Press.

Girgus, Sam B. 2002. *The Films of Woody Allen*. Cambridge: Cambridge University Press.

Gunning, Tom. 1995. 'Crazy Machines in the Garden of Forking Paths: Mischief Gags and the Origins of American Film Comedy', in *Classical Hollywood Comedy*, ed. Kristine Brunovska Karnick and Henry Jenkins, 87–105. New York: Routledge.

Harris, Neil. 1973. *Humbug, The Art of P. T. Barnum*. Chicago: University of Chicago Press.

Hirsch, Foster, 1981. *Love, Sex, Death and the Meaning of Life*. Boston, MA: Da Capo Press.

King, Rob. 2007. '"Uproarious Inventions": The Keystone Film Company, Modernity, and the Art of the Motor', *Film History* 19 (3): 271–91.

Knight, Christopher J. 2004. 'Woody Allen's Annie Hall: Galatea's Triumph over Pygmalion', *Literature Film Quarterly* 32 (3): 213–21.

Lahr, John. 1996. 'The Imperfectionist', *The New Yorker*, 9 December. https://www.newyorker.com/magazine/1996/12/09/the-imperfectionist

Lanza, Joseph. 1992. 'Female Rollercoasters: (And Other Virtual Vortices)', *Performing Arts Journal* 14 (2): 51–63.

McLuhan, Marshall. 2011. *The Mechanical Bride*. London: Duckworth.

Morgan, Richard. 2018. 'I Read Decades of Woody Allen's Private Notes. He's Obsessed with Teenage Girls', *The Washington Post*, 4 January. https://www.washingtonpost.com/outlook/i-read-decades-of-woody-allens-private-notes-hes-obsessed-with-teenage-girls/2018/01/04/f2701482-f03b-11e7-b3bf-ab90a706e175_story.html

Ngai, Sianne. 2020. *Theory of the Gimmick: Aesthetic Judgment and Capitalist Form*. Cambridge, MA: Harvard University Press.

O'Gieblyn, Meghan. 2021. 'Know Thyself', *The Paris Review*, 13 May. https://www.theparisreview.org/blog/2021/05/13/know-thyself/?mc_cid=16eb9c8cdb&mc_eid=794bb8b413

Ovid. 2002. *Ovid's Metamorphoses*. Translated by Arthur Golding and edited by Madeleine Forey. London: Penguin.

Patton, Paul. 2000. *Deleuze and the Political*. London: Routledge.

Teachout, Terry. 2004. 'Absent without Malice', *Arts Journal*, 29 February https://www.artsjournal.com/aboutlastnight/2004/02/tt-absent-without-malice.html

Wolfe, Maynard Frank and Rube Goldberg. 2000. *Rube Goldberg: Inventions!*. New York: Simon and Schuster.

8

'I'm not haunted by *Annie Hall*. I'm happy to be Annie Hall': The tangled relationship between Annie and Diane

Julie Lobalzo Wright

In 2014, the Hollywood Foreign Press bestowed the Cecil B. DeMille lifetime achievement award upon Woody Allen, who was not present at the Golden Globes ceremony to accept his award. Instead, Diane Keaton, in addition to Emma Stone, star of his film *Magic in the Moonlight* (2014), accepted the award on his behalf, praising the remarkable actresses that have appeared in his films and ending with a verse from the Girl Scouts song 'Make New Friends', dedicating it to her one-time partner and long-time friend. Allen has never been a dedicated award show attendee, but the decision to miss this particular ceremony coincided with an escalation of criticism towards the writer-director in regard to his past relationships with Mia Farrow's (his partner for twelve years) children,[1] one of whom he married in 1997 (Soon-Yi Previn). Many questioned whether Allen should receive the award with Hadley Freeman asking in *The Guardian*, 'Is it OK to celebrate Woody Allen?' (2014). Keaton's speech was deemed inappropriate by Freeman due to her emphasis on the positive presentation of women in Allen's films and by ending with a 'creepy childish song about friendship' (2014). In the face of public outcry over Allen's private life, Keaton has always presented herself as a friend in awe of his filmmaking and comedic talent.[2]

Keaton's relationship with Allen is both professional and personal. The two met when she auditioned for the Broadway production of Allen's play *Play It Again Sam* in 1969, which was adapted into a Herbert Ross-directed film in 1972. Keaton and Allen dated for many years and, eventually, Keaton appeared in seven of Allen's films between 1973 and 1993. The early films with Allen helped solidify the actress' reputation in Hollywood, in addition to her role as Kay in *The Godfather* (Francis Ford Coppola, 1972) and *The Godfather Part II*

(Francis Ford Coppola, 1974), but no film was more instrumental in defining her star image than *Annie Hall* (Woody Allen, 1977). For many, Keaton *is* Annie Hall and this perception endures even forty years after the release of the film: a 2017 *Radio Times* article (Dougary 2017), promoting the romantic-comedy film *Hampstead* (Joel Hopkins, 2017), spends the first five paragraphs of the article describing Keaton's fashion style and attributing it to *Annie Hall*. There are the visual allusions to the character, the male-inspired baggy clothing and hats that Keaton has seemed to wear non-stop since the film premiered, but also the demeanour of the actress and her specific performance style, evident in many of her films.

Although it is not unusual for a star to be closely identified with a career-defining role where all star and character signs coalesce, there are few stars with such long-lasting careers as Keaton that are rarely recognized outside of the fictional character they portrayed onscreen in one film.[3] This overlap between star (Keaton) and character (Annie) has been noted by many scholars (Jermyn 2014) and in the popular press. While Keaton has produced a diverse portfolio as an actress, writer, producer and director, she is still frequently identified as Annie Hall. This chapter examines why this is the case, focusing on the relationships between star, character, social type and performance style through the Annie/Diane case study. It is my intention to diverge from considerations of the 'real self' and instead examine how factors like social types and genre impress on character types, creating a spectrum of performances, more so than a distilled version of the same character in multiple films.

The relationship between stars and characters is complicated with various levels of recognition transpiring at once. As Richard Dyer noted in *Stars*, 'all fictions have characters' (2004, 90) and stars portray fictional characters. Paul McDonald notes that the 'the relationship of actor to character is fundamental to all film acting and so provides the starting point for any discussion of film acting' (2012, 169). Because characters are constructed versions of people, acting through the voice and body gives substance to a character's actions and characteristics. Furthermore, the star is also an actor, adding another dimension to character-actor-star paradigm. These concepts must be decoupled in order to understand the tangled relationship between a star and character, like Diane Keaton and Annie.

Numerous scholars have indicated how the film text singles stars out through various strategies, including the emphasis on the close-up and the habitual use of stars to portray protagonists in narrative fictions. The star is accentuated within the text, but what is identified is the 'dual presence of actor and character' (McDonald 2012, 171). McDonald argues there are degrees to this balance between the actor and character with a tension between the story (i.e. narrative) and the show (i.e. acting). Additionally, McDonald utilizes Barry King's (1985) assertion that star performances are either a 'personification' or 'impersonation' with the former type of performance adhering with the personality of the star and the later indicating stars transforming themselves in order to portray a character. These types of star performances exist in opposition to each other with one indicating a discontinuity (impersonation) and the other sameness (personification). According to Richard Dyer, sameness is one of the principles of star acting: 'because stars are always appearing in different stories and settings, *they* must stay broadly the same in order to permit recognition and identification' (2004, 98). McDonald proposes that instead of viewing these as 'opposed principles', they should be understood as 'poles on a continuum across which any film performance may be positioned' (2012, 173). This is an especially useful distinction in regard to Keaton, who has appeared in romantic comedies, thrillers, animated family films, and historical dramas.

It would be reductive and false to insinuate that she is always portraying a version of Annie Hall. However, there is evidently a spectrum between the characters that appear to be more Annie-like than others and it is possible to read these relationships as folding into one another, as opposed to collapsing character into actor (Smith 2019, xiii). This is the tension McDonald indicates when the star can be understood as star *and* character, arising from the recognition of the star *and* a fictional character. Ted Nannicelli (2019) argues that the 'paradox about star acting in screen fictions' is a puzzle that can be experienced as a twofoldness where the audience's 'seeing-as' character or 'seeing-as' star may be blocked or collapsed. There are some stars, as Nannicelli suggests, that have such an outsized star persona that it impedes 'the viewer's ability to simultaneously see the actor and imagine the character – that is, it can block seeing-as' (2019, 26). Diane Keaton does not possess such an outsized star persona; however, the replication of certain gestures and behaviours, in addition to her fashion style, could be said to close the gap between star and a specific character type.

According to Dyer, 'star images are constructed personages in media texts' with these personages embodied through the fictional character who may be both 'normative with respect to social types and individuated' (2004, 97). Sameness and individuality bookend the star acting continuum with these two poles also informing the star image. Stars are both unique and alike, ordinary and extraordinary (Dyer 2004), and this is also illustrated through the characters they portray onscreen. Stars and characters may be linked to particular social types with audiences identifying with stars through the star's relation to a social type (Dyer 2004, 99). Dyer argues that 'great' stars 'transcend the type to which they belong and become "utterly" individual' (2004, 99). Thus, the brightest stars may be associated with a particular type, but they surpass type to become extraordinarily individual.

Brianne Jewett Brenneman maintains that while the films Keaton made with Woody Allen in the 1970s (specifically, *Play it Again Sam* (Herbert Ross, 1972), *Love and Death* (Woody Allen, 1975), *Annie Hall* and *Manhattan* (Woody Allen, 1979)) illuminated her range as an actress, these films still limited her to 'common stereotypes' that helped illustrate the likeability of the male lead and elicit sympathy from the audience (2016, 24). Brenneman located three main types within these films: 'Mrs. Uptight' ('The Good Woman'), 'Sexual Woman' and 'Manic Pixie-Dream Girl'. The descriptions of these types coincide with the characters Keaton portrayed in these films, and in many of her later films with other writers and directors, especially 'Mrs. Uptight' who 'seems really well adjusted and in control of her life [...] balancing her life makes her tense and insecure, and at times irritable' (Brenneman 2016, 26). Types are 'constructed representations of people' (Dyer 2004, 89), acknowledged as belonging to a specific group whereby their behaviours are, as explained by O. E. Klapp, 'an idealized concept of how people are expected to be or to act' (cited in Dyer 2004, 47). While all fictional characters are typified, an interplay through typification and individuality occurs even in real life, as Henry Bacon notes: 'all encounters with real people as well as fictional characters begins with rough classifications and, depending on circumstances, may or may not then proceed through recognition of more refined traits toward appreciation of individuality' (2019, 78). The same can be said about differentiating between type and star whereby the star may become recognized for a particular character type, but it is the distinctiveness of the star that advances individual identification. While there are many examples to choose from (such as Marilyn Monroe, who epitomizes the ability of a star to transcend type by both embodying the 'pin-up' type and representing the singular Monroe star image), Keaton is an excellent illustration of this conundrum.

Before outlining the Keaton-type, it is important to establish industrial contexts that have led to star types. Pamela Robertson Wojcik suggests that typecasting is 'part and parcel' of the Hollywood institution, due to its emphasis on 'recognizability, marketability, and the necessity for known commodities' (2004, 170). These commodities not only are related to typecasting but filter through to stars and genres, all working to ensure that success can be easily replicated. The notion of the star vehicle is applicable as films that were built around a specific star image by 'exploiting the popularity of a particular performer [...] reworking and advancing aspects of their previous work that had already proven popular with an audience' (Shingler 2012, 111–12). Wojcik and Shingler both situate these frameworks in the Classical Hollywood era when studios employed an institutional system to ensure success, often through repetition and novelty (Shingler 2012, 112). However, Shingler notes that even in Post-Classical Hollywood, 'successive generations of audiences revealed a distinct preference for stars being used consistently to play a particular type or, at least, set of types' (2012, 110). In the contemporary era, stars still appear in vehicles or films that generally attempt to balance this tension between originality and familiarity through various pathways, including genre and character type. Therefore, in the star-led Nancy Myers romantic comedy, *Something's Gotta Give* (2003), the marketing of the film[4] featured prominent displays of the faces of the two stars under their first names, 'Jack and Diane', signifying the two stars and the celebrated connotations associated with their star images, but also distinctive through the pairing of the two in a romantic comedy film. It is rare, even in Hollywood, for stars to be identified by purely a first name. Cine-literate audiences familiar with *Annie Hall*, as many viewers of this film will be, will catch an allusion to Tony Lacey's (Paul Simon) invitation to Alvy and Annie to go back to a hotel to meet 'Jack and Angelica [Houston]', illustrating that Nicholson was already on a first name basis in 1977.

Deborah Jermyn claims that Keaton has a 'particularly heightened sense of "history"' as an actress who is familiar to us. She goes on to say there is nostalgia for 'young Keaton' and because of *Annie Hall*, she is 'inextricably tied to the history of romantic comedy,' a 'genre in which a sense of nostalgia is deeply embedded' (2017, 174). Nostalgia is linked to the type of music that appears in rom-coms, such as traditional pop ballads and popular Jazz standards like 'It Had to Be You' which became the theme of *When Harry Met Sally* (Rob Reiner, 1989) and was sung by Diane Keaton in *Annie Hall*;[5] references to filmic representations of romance, such as the narrative overlap between *An Affair to Remember* (Leo McCarey, 1957) and *Sleepless in Seattle* (Nora Ephron, 1993); and the continued use of specific locations and iconography like New York, a sign that the genre may have, according to Tamar Jeffers McDonald, 'exhausted its inspirations' (2007, 90).⁶ It is notable that all three examples given relate to *Annie Hall*, and if not to that particular film, elements of these contexts of nostalgia appear in all the four films Brenneman utilized as her corpus of Allen films.⁷ Bacon underscores the importance of classification of films in terms of genre because it is 'highly likely to guide our recognition of types and their narrative-cum-thematic functions within situations typical of the genre in question' (2019, 79). Genre is significant in relation to the continuum between star and character type. Perceiving Keaton as Annie Hall only takes place in romantic comedies because the character's signs intersect with the themes and situations imbedded in the genre.

When decoding a film in relation to character, Dyer indicates the 'signs of character' include audience foreknowledge, name, appearance, objective correlatives, speech of character, gesture, action, structure and mise en scène (2004, 107). There are obvious correlations that can be made between Keaton and Annie, such as their names, which are WASP in origin and the fact that Keaton's real name is Diane Hall. We can further connect the actress to the character through the awareness of Allen and Keaton's off-screen relationship and the belief that Allen and co-writer Marshall Brickman wrote the film about Allen and Keaton's relationship (this has been denied and confirmed ad nauseam for over forty years).⁸ The visual image of Keaton in *Annie Hall* is also momentous through her signature menswear-as-womenswear clothing style that debuted in the film and became incorporated into her off-screen appearances. When Keaton won her Academy Award for Best Actress in 1978 for *Annie Hall*, she wore a Ruth Morley outfit that consisted of a baggy blazer, button-up shirt, scarf and long peasant skirt, similar to a costume she wore in the film (sans trademark hat) that was featured in many of the film's posters. This is an example of life imitating art, but even Keaton's fashion style is more diverse than she is given credit for, further illustrating there are fissures on the Diane-as-Annie spectrum.⁹ This kind of extra-textual information supports the blending of Diane and Annie, but according to Nannicelli, the audience's appreciation of a screen character depends on setting aside some of the star persona to become 'absorbed in the story' (2019, 21).

Returning to McDonald's contention that a spectrum exists in relation to star acting, *Annie Hall* is the starting point. Although Keaton had appeared in multiple Allen films leading up to her role as Annie, the overwhelming critical and commercial success of the film, her performance in it – earning the actress her only Academy Award – and the perception of *Annie Hall* as a 'landmark in the genre' (Grindon 2011, 54), all position her performance as the foundation for the slippages that have occurred throughout her career. In addition, as Jermyn notes, the blurred biography, on/off-screen foreknowledge and the film's romantic comedy traditions add to the sense that when Keaton appears in a romantic comedy, the audience is watching 'what Annie did next' (2014, 41). I will now focus on three signs of character – speech, gesture and action – to investigate the star/character overlaps between Keaton and Annie, facilitating a definition of the Keaton character type.

One of the most noted facets of the Annie character is her temperament, labelled as 'giddy' (Fuller 2007, 33), 'carefree' (Brenneman 2016, 31), 'absent-minded' (Björkman 1995, 85) and quirky, among many other descriptors. Heroines in romantic comedies easily fall into these categories, but the specificity of *Annie Hall* as 'a nervous romance' (the tagline used for the film) further particularizes the Annie character. Frank Krutnik (1990) employed this tagline when analysing the 'comedy of the sexes' cycle of romantic comedies from the mid-1970s through to the late 1980s.[10] Krutnik argues, 'the contemporary strain of Hollywood's comedy of the sexes pulls between a nostalgic yearning for the lost possibility of romance and a more cynical awareness of the difficulty of maintaining an overriding faith in The Couple in the face of the divisions which beset modern life' (62). The nervousness, therefore, emerges from the couple who long for 'the stability of the heterosexual couple', but recognize the 'problems seen to jeopardize it' (63).

In one of the most famous scenes from *Annie Hall*, Annie and Alvy first meet for a game of doubles tennis with friends. Afterwards, Annie has changed from her tennis outfit into her regular clothes (the iconic men's trousers, vest, fedora and 'Granny Hall's' tie), bumping into Alvy when she leaves the club. As Alvy is putting his tennis racket into his bag, Annie nervously says 'hello' and then 'bye' before slowly heading towards the door. Alvy tells her that she 'plays very well' before Annie reciprocates, 'Oh yeah? So do you.' At this point, Annie scrunches her face and states, 'What a dumb thing to say.' What follows is an internal monologue spoken out loud, with Annie giggling, talking under her breath, fidgeting, looking down and ending with a broad smile towards Alvy, muttering, 'lah-di-dah, lah-di-dah, la, la ... yeah' (Figure 8.1). Nervous is the optimum way to describe this exchange, at least from Annie's point of view, but it also uncovers a desire to present a respectable exchange with a possible love interest. Annie immediately recognizes that there was a misstep with her response to Alvy, but instead of correcting it, she then digresses into an edgy ramble. The desire for

Figure 8.1 Annie's internal monologue ('lah-di-dah, lah-di-dah, la, la ... yeah').

the exchange to be perfect is undercut by doubt, prompting Annie to expose her imperfect self underneath any sort of romantic façade. This façade continues to break down as the exchanges become more awkward with confusion about Alvy offering Annie a lift, Annie having a car outside, Alvy going uptown, while Annie is going downtown.

This scene adheres to Krutnik's theories about the 'nervous romances', but it also exposes specific Keaton performance traits, such as the mumbling, the darting eyes and the nervous giggle. These performance cues illustrate that some elements of this character type are present in other Diane Keaton romantic comedies. The genre distinction is important because the signs of performance are not always present in non-rom-coms, such as *The Godfather* trilogy. The nostalgia and history of Keaton in the romantic comedy genre warrant a way of reading these signs as fusing around the Annie Hall-type with 2017's *Hampstead* as a recent example detailed below. As Andrew Klevan argues, details are valuable because by 'attending to the moment-by-moment movement of performers', we also enhance 'our understanding of film characterisation' (2005, 7).

Hampstead centres on Emily Walters (Keaton), a recently widowed American living in Hampstead Heath, who has been saddled with debt from her unfaithful husband. She eventually meets Donald Horner (Brendan Gleeson), who lives in a shack on the Heath, and the two fight his attempted eviction in court. Throughout the film, Emily is headstrong, but neurotic, often presented in contrast to the other ladies in her building who dress more femininely than

Emily in her black blazers, white turtlenecks and trousers. In one scene, Emily goes to the attic of her apartment building to look through an old trunk for items to sell and help alleviate her inherited debt. The scene begins with a close-up of the trunk and Emily muttering, 'sell something? … what am I going to do? … There must be something … no no no no … nah, that's not it …. what?' She eventually picks up binoculars, blows the dust off them, coughs and then walks to the window. After she opens the window, the film cuts to a close-up of Emily, followed by a point-of-view shot, before returning to a medium close-up of Emily with the large binoculars over her eyes. At this point, we see what Emily is viewing through the binoculars, but it is what she says that is crucial. She mumbles, 'let's see how, yeah' before bringing the binoculars up to her glasses, hitting her glasses (with an audible noise) and her exclamation of 'ow'! Although these moments are incidental to the film, the attention to performance illuminates how specific ticks that were presented in *Annie Hall*, such as the exposing of an internal dialogue through an anxious delivery, have carried throughout Keaton's rom-com career, further suggesting that the character type is recognized more so than the star actress.

While *Annie Hall* is a 'nervous romance', it was also inspired by the screwball comedy, connecting the Annie-type to a form of comedy with its own female character conventions. This also places Keaton in 'a tradition of 1930's screwball heroines' from Katherine Hepburn to Carole Lombard (Jermyn 2014, 41). The screwball genre 'favourably portrayed unconventional female behaviour' (Landay 1998, 104) through working women who often pursued men. The women are eccentric, energetic and gutsy with the films teetering on the edge of chaos through the spontaneity of the couple and their sense of play (Glitre 2006, 26). The lobster scene from *Annie Hall* exhibits some of the hallmarks of the screwball comedy, with Alvy and Annie joking while they try to get multiple live lobsters into a boiling pot. The scene is clearly scripted with Allen's character delivering joke after joke about calling the 'Lobster Squad' for assistance and luring lobsters from behind the refrigerator with a 'little dish of butter'. Keaton is also performing in this scene, but her laughs and giggles appear more spontaneous, sometimes even interrupting the dialogue she is expected to deliver. These character signs indicate Annie's gaiety and vivaciousness, but this is also countered throughout the film with her self-doubt (especially after her debut as a singer), insecurities about her intelligence (one of the couple's first fights is about this issue) and her general 'moods and hang-ups' (a description she uses when the couple are separating their book collection).

It is also notable that the lobster scene is recreated in *Annie Hall* after Alvy and Annie decide to parts ways. Taking place in the same kitchen as the earlier scene, Alvy states, 'this always happens to me' as he attempts to pick lobsters off the ground and asks his date to get a broom. The woman finishes lighting her cigarette and calmly asks Alvy, 'What are you making such a big deal about? They're only lobsters. You're a grown man. You know how to pick up a lobster.' This woman is the opposite of a screwball heroine; there is no amusement or diversions (in fact, she proceeds to misunderstand a joke Alvy makes). She is unruffled and still, acting as the complete opposite of Annie's excitable nature. This date has more in common with Alvy's other partners/dates, such as Pam (Shelley Duvall), Allison (Carol Kane) and Robin (Janet Margolin), the 'New York girls' (as Annie calls them) that fit the 'intellectual "urban neurotic" type' (Krutnik 1990, 64) that often appear in Allen's films. The principal difference between the 'New York girls' and Annie is the sense of play, further aligning her with the screwball tradition.

Keaton's most recent critical and commercial success was in *Something's Gotta Give*, a film that, according to Kelli Marshall, 'imitates the central conventions, characterization, and narrative structure of classical screwball comedies' (2009, 9). The role of Erica Berry, lovelorn divorced playwright living in the Hamptons, could be viewed as Annie in fifties or Annie 'all grown up' (Jermyn 2017, 174), having given up on her dream to be a singer or actress, parlaying her keen intellect into a career as a playwright, resigned to live her life without the love of a man. Keaton received an Academy Award nomination for the film. Remarkably, it was only her fourth nomination in her career and the second for a performance in a romantic comedy, a genre that is notoriously taken less seriously at the Academy Awards than various drama permutations. One of the most memorable moments in *Something's Gotta Give* takes place after Erica finds her lover, Harry, out to dinner in the city with a younger woman, leading her to say she is 'heartbroken' whereupon she returns to her home in the Hamptons. After Harry's return to the Emergency Room with chest pains, the film cuts to Erica hysterically crying on the edge of her bed as she checks her phone messages. The following montage shows Erica sobbing as she writes a new play based on this failed romance,[11] interspersed with her crying in the shower, on the beach and in bed. This scene adheres to the screwball comedies' aspiration to celebrate 'difficult and anarchic love', 'favouring movement over stasis, and speech and argument over silent compliance' (Haskell 2016, 126). In *Annie Hall*, Annie and Alvy fight and eventually break up because their relationship is not progressing, but it is worth pointing out that the fights are driven by Annie's emotion – her frustration – in contrast to Alvy's neuroses. When the couple fight about Annie's relationship with her college professor, Annie points out that Alvy wanted a 'flexible' relationship and now appears jealous. Annie raises her voice, punches out her words and illustrates exasperation through her voice and body. This is distinct to other moments in the film when Annie's voice is calm, her face is soft and her body is relaxed. Alvy, on the other hand, is always agitated, slumping his body and using his hands as an extension of his speech. I note these differences because emotion is part of the Annie-type, taken to the extreme in *Something's Gotta Give*, emerging from Annie's intelligence and her desire to 'enjoy life',[12] even though there are often roadblocks towards her happiness.

The 'outburst' has come to define Keaton's performances in romantic comedies with these expressions of emotion interconnected with the genre's repression (frequently through the concealment of feelings) and the sparring that takes place between the couple (sometimes referred to as a 'battle of the sexes'[13]). There is, also, the context of Annie as a second-wave feminist character that informs these emotional eruptions.[14] The focus of Annie's life is not on marriage but to become a more rounded, cultured and interesting person. In many of the romantic comedies that follow *Annie Hall*, the 'outburst' scene takes place during a moment of weakness when the woman is irritable, frequently because men are conspiring against her. This is where the 'Mrs. Uptight' type (Brenneman 2016) is exposed as a woman who seems well adjusted, but can lose control of her life, coercing her to act out. Thus, in *Something's Gotta Give*, Erica weeps uncontrollably after Harry, the first man she has allowed herself to love in decades, breaks her heart, something she has written about in her plays, but never actually experienced in real life.

In *The First Wives Club*, Annie MacDuggan suffers from low self-esteem, a controlling mother and a self-absorbed estranged husband (Aaron). After the estranged couple meets for a night of dinner and dancing, ending with them having sex in a hotel room, Aaron blind-sides Annie asking her for a divorce. Annie begins to scream, confusingly walking around the hotel room, asking why he made love to her if he wants a divorce. The therapist they are both seeing, Dr Rosen (Marcia Gay Harden), walks in, confirming that she and Aaron are having an affair. Annie lets her anger out, frenetically shouting at Dr Rosen and Aaron stating she is sorry she ever met either of them. The scene ends with a close-up of Keaton's manic face as she screams at the top of her lungs, 'I'm sorry', before wildly opening the door and letting out multiple tempestuous exclamations.

While this Annie is nowhere near as liberated as Annie Hall, this moment sets in motion her journey towards emotional and financial independence. Annie MacDuggan is an example of a second-wave feminist who was, most likely, presented with the diametrically opposed options of marriage and family *or* a career, opting for the former. However, by the end of the film, she illustrates her business acumen by buying out the majority holders in her husband's advertising company, essentially becoming his boss.

Baby Boom (1987) exists, thematically, between *Annie Hall* and *The First Wives Club*, with Keaton's emotional release acting as a symbol of the impossibility of women 'having it all'.[15] J. C. Wiatt begins the film as a driven Manhattan executive, before she 'inherits' a toddler from a long-lost family member. She attempts to balance her non-stop work life with the new baby, but eventually finds herself pushed from working with prime accounts, ultimately quitting her job and moving to a 200-year-old house on a farm in Vermont. After encountering multiple issues with the house and missing her high-powered lifestyle in the city, she explodes in frustration when she learns that her well is dried up and she has no access to water. The scene is mainly filmed in a long shot, with Keaton pacing in the snow in boots and a large winter coat that dwarfs her body. Her excited demeanour is heard in her shrieking voice as she tells the plumber that she can't live in this place anymore, while the oversized coat emphasizes her uncontrollable gestures (Figure 8.2). The camera slowly zooms in as the actress continues to rant, but the words become more jumbled to the point where the screams overwhelm the dialogue. Again, this performance style is indicative of Keaton in romantic comedies, especially the vocal utterances and body language that 'always speaks volumes' about characters (Fuller 2007, 35). J. C. eventually strikes a work/life balance in Vermont by starting her own gourmet baby food line and begins a relationship with Dr Copper (Sam Shepard). The film presented a second-wave feminist achieving career success and contentment in a non-traditional homelife (as a single mother).

It is not uncommon for audiences to 'only know a star through a string of performances' (McDonald 2012, 180). For many audiences, their knowledge of Diane Keaton may be confined to a few of her romantic comedy performances, some mentioned in this chapter. The success of *Annie Hall*, its place in film history, and within popular culture, will forever bind Keaton with the title character. Furthermore, the off-screen displays of 'Annie' in Keaton's interviews, red carpet events and her own memoirs[16] intensify the union of Annie and Diane. As noted

Figure 8.2 Diane Keaton as J. C. Wiatt in *Baby Boom* (1987).

from the onset, there are issues with the collapse between star and character through the figure of Woody Allen. Keaton is enormously proud of the film, dismissing anyone that may suggest she has been typecast as 'Annie', musing, 'How could I ever regret the fame that came from *Annie Hall* since that gave me every professional opportunity that I've ever had?' (Smith 2006, 131). She remains incredibly complimentary towards Allen, a position that upsets many of his detractors (evidenced by the response to her acceptance of his lifetime achievement award at the 2014 Golden Globes). This adds another evolving part in the tangled web of Annie and Diane.

Diane Keaton is a star who is both entwined with the Annie Hall-type and distinct from it, with a wider continuum of performances than she is generally given credit for. There is an argument to be made that audiences prefer Keaton in rom-coms, especially those that evoke nostalgia for *Annie Hall*. Her greatest box office successes have been in rom-coms (outside of *The Godfather* trilogy), and while she has received critical acclaim for dramatic roles, such as *Looking for Mr. Goodbar* (Richard Brooks, 1977) and *Marvin's Room* (Jerry Zaks, 1996), the rom-coms are the most admired and referenced, evident on the countless film posters that feature Keaton in masculine clothing and smiling (*5 Flights Up* (Richard Loncraine, 2014) is a recent example), similar to her bemused look on the *Annie Hall* poster. It is also possible to read some of these film roles and performances as leaning in to this desire audiences have to see her as Annie. As she stated in 2017, 'I'm not haunted by *Annie Hall*. I'm happy to be Annie Hall' (Dougary). Audiences are just as happy.

Notes

1. Allen has been accused of sexual molestation by Dylan (who has privately changed their name), one of Allen and Farrow's adopted children.
2. Keaton's 2011 memoir, *Then Again*, and follow-up, *Let's Just Say It Wasn't Pretty* (2014), never mention these personal issues.
3. It would be a different argument if the star portrayed the same character in various films, such as Vin Diesel (as Dominic 'Dom' Toretto) in the *Fast & Furious* franchise.
4. See Jermyn (2017).
5. Harry Connick Jr.'s soundtrack for *When Harry Met Sally* (Rob Reiner, 1989), featuring traditional pop and jazz standards, is a good example of this.
6. See Jeffers McDonald (2007) and her chapter on 'Neo-Traditional Romantic Comedy' for other examples of nostalgia in this type of romantic comedy.
7. This is especially true with *Play It Again, Sam*, whose narrative is focused on down-on-his-luck Allan Felix (Allen) who gets back into the dating scene with the help of a ghost-like Humphrey Bogart who gives Allan love advice for wooing Linda (Keaton).
8. The off-screen romantic relationship between Allen and Keaton, which ended long before the filming of *Annie Hall*, at the very least, threads the needle between Allen and Keaton as a pair.
9. Keaton has tended to favour masculine clothing since *Annie Hall*; however, these can vary from a men's tuxedo with tails that she wore to the 2004 Academy Awards to the black leather blazer, truncate belt, leather pencil skirt and beret she wore when receiving the Lifetime Achievement Award at the Goldene Kamera awards in 2014, and the white oversized shirt dress with black voluminous skirt underneath and bowler hat worn at the American Film Institute tribute to the star in 2017.
10. Jeffers McDonald deems these films, from *Annie Hall* to *When Harry Met Sally*, 'neo-traditional romantic comedies', emerging from romantic dramas with an emphasis on tears (2007, 85).
11. *Annie Hall* features a reversal of the real-life relationship inspiring a play that also takes place in *Something's Gotta Give*. While the couple end up together in Alvy's play, they do not in Erica's play. Alvy and Annie do not end *Annie Hall* as a couple, while Erica and Harry do eventually marry (off-screen).
12. On one of the last occasions Annie sees Alvy in Los Angeles, she argues that he is 'incapable of enjoying life'.

13 Glitre refers to the 'battle of the sexes' as the 'most common Hollywood romantic comedy plot' (2006, 19).
14 Brenneman argues that while Allen's films with Keaton (excepting *Radio Days* in 1987 and *Manhattan Murder Mystery* in 1993) were made during second-wave feminism, the female roles perpetuated earlier stereotypes and the women were primarily written to make Allen's male characters appear noble and mature (2016, 33).
15 Virginia Haussegger includes a chapter in her book, *Wonder Woman: The Myth of Having It All*, titled, '"Having it all"- a *f*.....up feminist fantasy' (2005).
16 *Then Again* features diary passages from Diane's mother, Dorothy, often commenting on how much she sees of Diane in film performances and TV appearances. One example from 5 September 1969: 'Diane was on Merv Griffin tonight. She was Diane. Her walk, her laugh, her jumble of words' (Keaton 2011, 72).

Works cited

Bacon, Henry. 2019. 'Being Typical and Being Individual', in *Screening Characters: Theories of Character in Film, Television, and Interactive Media*, ed. Johannes Riis and Aaron Taylor, 77–92. London and New York: Routledge.

Björkman, Stig. 1995. *Woody Allen on Woody Allen*. London and Boston: Faber and Faber.

Brenneman, Brianne Jewett. 2016. 'Play It Again, Diane', *Film International* 14 (1): 24–34.

Dougary, Ginny. 2017. 'Diane Keaton: 'If You're Happy, You're Mentally Ill', *Radio Times*, 23 June. https://www.radiotimes.com/news/2017-06-23/diane-keaton-if-youre-happy-youre-mentally-ill/.

Dyer, Richard. 2004. *Stars*. London: British Film Institute.

Freeman, Hadley. 2014. 'Were the Golden Globes Right to Celebrate Woody Allen?' *The Guardian*, 14 January. https://www.theguardian.com/commentisfree/2014/jan/14/golden-globes-woody-allen-lifetime-achievement-mia-ronan-farrow.

Fuller, Graham. 2007. 'Breaking Away: Iconic Free Spirit, Dramatic Powerhouse, and Of Course, Comedienne Extraordinaire: Dianne Keaton Unbound', *Film Comment* 43 (2): 32–6.

Glitre, Kathrina. 2006. *Hollywood Romantic Comedy: States of the Union, 1934–65*. Manchester and New York: Manchester University Press.

Grindon, Leger. 2011. *The Hollywood Romantic Comedy*. Oxford and Malden, MA: Wiley-Blackwell.

Haskell, Molly. 2016. *From Reverence to Rape: The Treatment of Women in the Movies* (3rd edition). Chicago and London: University of Chicago Press.

Haussegger, Virginia. 2005. *Wonder Woman: The Myth of 'Having It All'*. Crows Nest, NSW: Allen & Unwin.
Jeffers McDonald, Tamar. 2007. *Romantic Comedy: Boy Meets Girl Meets Genre*. New York and Chichester, UK: Wallflower.
Jermyn, Deborah. 2014. '"Glorious, Glamorous and That Old Standby, Amorous": The Late Blossoming of Diane Keaton's Romantic Comedy Career', in *Female Celebrity and Ageing: Back in the Spotlight*, ed. Deborah Jermyn, 39–53. London and New York: Routledge.
Jermyn, Deborah. 2017. *Nancy Meyers*. New York and London: Bloomsbury.
Keaton, Diane. 2011. *Then Again*. London: Fourth Estate.
Keaton, Diane. 2014. *Let's Just Say It Wasn't Pretty*. New York: Random House.
King, Barry. 1985. 'Articulating Stardom', *Screen* 26 (5): 27–51.
Klevan, Andrew. 2005. *Film Performance: From Achievement to Appreciation*. New York and Chichester, UK: Wallflower.
Krutnik, Frank. 1990. 'The Faint Aroma of Performing Seals: The "Nervous" Romance and the Comedy of the Sexes', *The Velvet Light Trap* 26: 57–72.
Landay, Lori. 1998. *Madcaps, Screwballs, and Con Women: The Female Trickster in American Culture*. Philadelphia: University of Pennsylvania Press.
Marshall, Kelli. 2009. *Something's Gotta Give* and the Classical Screwball Comedy', *Journal of Popular Film and Television* 37 (1): 9–15.
McDonald, Paul. 2012. 'Story and Show: The Basic Contradiction of Film Star Acting', in *Theorizing Film Acting*, ed. Aaron Taylor, 169–83. London and New York: Routledge.
Nannicelli, Ted. 2019. 'Seeing and Hearing Screen Characters: Stars, Twofoldness, and the Imagination', in *Screening Characters: Theories of Character in Film, Television, and Interactive Media*, ed. Johannes Riis and Aaron Taylor, 19–36. London and New York: Routledge.
Shingler, Martin. 2012. *Star Studies: A Critical Guide*. London: BFI.
Smith, Liz. 2006. 'At Lunch with Liz', *Good Housekeeping* 242 (3): 131. March. Nexis Uni.
Smith, Murray. 2019. 'Forward: Consorting with Characters', in *Screening Characters: Theories of Character in Film, Television, and Interactive Media*, ed. Johannes Riis and Aaron Taylor, xi–xviii. London and New York: Routledge.
Wojcik, Pamela Robertson. 2004. 'Typecasting', in *Movie Acting: The Film Reader*, ed. Pamela Robertson Wojcik, 169–90. London and New York: Routledge.

Filmography

5 Flights Up. Film. Directed by Richard Loncraine. Universal City: Focus Features, 2014.
An Affair to Remember. Film. Directed by Leo McCarey. Twentieth Century Fox: Los Angeles, 1957.

Annie Hall. Film. Directed by Woody Allen. Hollywood: United Artists, 1977.
Baby Boom. Film. Directed by Charles Shyer. Beverly Hills: MGM/UA Communications Co., 1987.
The Godfather. Film. Directed by Francis Ford Coppola. Hollywood: Paramount, 1972.
The Godfather Part II. Film. Directed by Francis Ford Coppola. Hollywood: Paramount, 1974.
Hampstead. Film. Directed by Joel Hopkins. Entertainment One: Toronto, 2017.
Looking for Mr. Goodbar. Film. Directed by Richard Brooks. Hollywood: Paramount, 1977.
Love and Death. Film. Directed by Woody Allen. Hollywood: United Artist, 1975.
Magic in the Moonlight. Film. Directed by Woody Allen. New York: Sony Pictures Classics, 2014.
Manhattan. Film. Directed by Woody Allen. Hollywood: United Artists, 1979.
Manhattan Murder Mystery. Film. Directed by Woody Allen. Culver City: Tri-Star, 1993.
Play It Again Sam. Film. Directed by Herbert Ross. Hollywood: Paramount, 1972.
Radio Days. Film. Directed by Woody Allen. Los Angeles: Orion, 1987.
Sleepless in Seattle. Film. Directed by Nora Ephron. Culver City: Tri-Star, 1993.
Something's Gotta Give. Film. Directed by Nancy Meyers. Culver City: Sony Pictures, 2003.
When Harry Met Sally. Film. Directed by Rob Reiner. Culver City: Columbia, 1989.

9

The Spanish Annie Hall: Pedro Almodóvar's *Mujeres al borde de un ataque de nervios*

Ana María Sánchez-Arce

Pepa overuses high heels and miniskirts.[1] The truth is that they become her, but force her to walk in a way that Sontag […] considers inappropriate for an independent, modern woman. I understand and agree with Sontag when she objects to the polarisation of the sexes, but this is not Pepa's concern. A woman must be free even to choose her outfits. I respect the imitator of Barbie dolls as much as the woman who dresses like Charlie Chaplin, such as Sontag's compatriot Annie Hall.

(n.p.; my translation)[2]

In the pressbook for *Mujeres al borde de un ataque de nervios* (*Women on the Verge of a Nervous Breakdown*, 1988), Pedro Almodóvar alludes directly to Woody Allen's *Annie Hall* (1977), specifically the character of Annie (Diane Keaton). Almodóvar's allusion speaks to the international impact of *Annie Hall*, released eleven years before *Mujeres ...* and the conflation of Annie the character with Keaton the actor. The link between public and private selves is also reinforced by the fact that, as I discuss later, Annie is styled like Keaton.[3] Keaton is famous for wearing masculine clothes and her performance as Annie Hall has been credited with 'turn[ing] the trouser-suit into a high fashion item' (O'Toole 2007). Annie/Keaton's costumes became an international referent in terms of Anglo-American Women's Liberation as a (sometimes) political fashion statement. By mentioning Annie, Almodóvar invites a comparison between this character and Pepa (Carmen Maura), not simply in terms of clothing but also in terms of whether the trouser suit and the miniskirt are relevant to their position and function within the films' structures.

The characterizations of Annie and Pepa reflect their different personalities and cultural contexts, but not a difference in their relationships with their respective partners: Alvy (Woody Allen) in *Annie Hall* and Iván (Fernando Guillén) in *Mujeres* .... Annie's characterization could not be more dissimilar to Pepa's in *Mujeres* .... Pepa changes outfit eight times in two days and except for pyjamas and a cardigan, all of the outfits are suits, most of them including tight miniskirts and matching jacket and blouse. These are 1980s skirt suits suitable for a 1980s Spanish career woman in media.

Like Annie, Pepa dresses the part she wants to play, and the skirt suits with matching blouses and shoes signal her professional status and how well off she is. Unlike Annie, Pepa has not been born middle class and her use of clothing for self-confidence and to project her new status is an important part of her characterization.

This chapter undertakes a comparative analysis of both films' gender politics in the light of the different times (late 1970s and late 1980s) and contexts (the height of women's liberation in the United States in the late 1970s and the diffused and incipient nature of feminism and women's liberation struggles in post-dictatorship Spain in the late 1980s) in which they were produced. Despite Annie and Pepa's strikingly different characterizations, there is a close affinity between characters and films and a more complex relationship between costume and women characters' plights than it seems. I argue that Pepa is in fact a Spanish Annie Hall of the 1980s. *Mujeres* ... may look more conservative in terms of costume but is progressive in its analysis of gender and in how women characters

Figure 9.1 Pepa dons one of her skirt suits (designed by José María Cossío) as she disposes of Iván's things; Iván is in a phone booth calling her.

are situated within the film's symbolic structures. *Annie Hall*, on the other hand, seems outwardly progressive, but is in fact quite conservative despite containing enough material for a more ambivalent interpretation.

The spat

Almodóvar's reference to Annie comes in response to Susan Sontag's criticism of Pepa's characterization following her visit to the film set in 1988.[4] She says of Almodóvar: 'I was teasing him, but I meant it [...]. Here's this guy who's supposed to be a new breeze from Spain, iconoclastic and irreverent, reproducing this musty, old-fashioned image of women in high heels with their rears sticking out' (qtd. Lida 1988, 80).[5] Sontag and Almodóvar's spat in print shows the impact of second-wave feminist thinking – specifically the sociological approach dominant in the United States – in critiques of film representation of women. This approach to 'women's image in film' is summed up by Sue Thornham as 'a simple matter of "misrepresentation", to be corrected by more "realistic" portrayals' (1999, 1). Writing in 1999, Thornham explains that we can no longer 'envisage a utopian moment when "images of women" will "reflect" the realities of women's lives: cinematic representations are far more complex than this' (1). More than a decade earlier, this utopian goal seems to be what Sontag was hoping for.

Almodóvar, clearly piqued by Sontag's criticism, agrees with her feminist agenda, but also states that this has nothing to do with his character. His response takes up a whole page of the pressbook, a section titled 'tacones y falda tubo' (high heels and miniskirt). This page is split in two equally sized halves: on the right, the riposte to Sontag, and on the left, an illustration of the back of a woman's legs walking wearing high heels.

The illustration is a sketch in grey which recalls the 1950s American women's fashion magazine look of the film's stylized opening credits by Juan Gatti, credits that Gwynne Edwards has cleverly linked to how the film highlights the fragmentation and dehumanization of women (2001, 92). The legs are completely uncovered, provocatively ending in the outline of the woman's backside. The title is cleverly positioned across the sketch, with the letter 'y' suggesting the groin and pubic area were the woman to be facing rather than walking away from the viewer. The absence of the miniskirt draws attention to the fetishizing function of the heels in fashion. Additionally, the focus on heels and legs links fashion to one of the film's most iconic scenes, an extreme close-up of Pepa's feet wearing black high heels as she paces her apartment impatiently waiting for a call from her ex-lover, Iván. Contrary to the sketch in the pressbook and the credits, this scene does not fetishize the woman's body. Instead, the fast pacing and extreme close-up combine to create a sense of growing impatience and urgency as befits a comedy, as well as showing that despite Iván leaving Pepa, she is not going to crumble like the character who inspired her character, Jean Cocteau's abandoned woman in *La voix humaine* (*The Human Voice*, Jean Cocteau, 1930).

This use of shoes and clothes are remarked upon by Carmen Maura, also in this section of the pressbook, as Almodóvar re-produces a conversation with the actor who plays Pepa:

> I [Almodóvar] mentioned this to Carmen Maura.
> – With so much action, won't these heels and tight skirt be uncomfortable?
>
> Carmen replied:
> – Of course they'll be uncomfortable, but I will pretend that they're not. For a character like Pepa high heels are the best way of enduring her anxiety. If Pepa neglects her appearance, her courage will take a tumble. Coquetry is a discipline which represents her main strength. It means that her problems have not destroyed her yet.
>
> (1988, n.p.; my translation)

Maura's comments about her character development are crucial here for two reasons. First, it provides a first-hand idea of Pepa's choice of clothing. Second, it shows Maura's role in character development, with Pepa described as a woman in a particular context with a specific psychology. Interestingly, Pepa can let go of her coquetry when required, such as at the end of the film when her anxiety to talk to Iván has been replaced by calm acceptance of the end of the relationship.

The pressbook glosses Sontag's words to Lida, explaining that Sontag considers that 'high heels' and 'miniskirts' force Pepa to walk in a way that is 'inappropriate for an independent, modern woman' (n.p.; my translation), short for sexualized. Almodóvar's comment that 'this is not Pepa's concern' opens the door for a more nuanced analysis of the context behind Pepa's characterization through clothing. This context includes, for example, Spanish sociopolitical circumstances at the end of the 1980s, just after the Spanish transition from dictatorship to democracy, during which time slow changes in women's roles were taking place from the predominant conservative ideology to an incipient capitalist yet still mostly conservative society. Class is also extremely relevant to an analysis of Pepa. Almodóvar is right in saying that Sontag's political agenda has nothing to do with Pepa, whose outfits are appropriate to how she is characterized as an upwardly mobile Spanish woman in late 1980s Spain who is nevertheless going to find out the hard way the difference between financial and emotional independence.

Despite Almodóvar's proto post-feminist views in the pressbook, costume choices for Pepa and other women characters in *Mujeres ...* show that these women characters in late 1980s Spain are certainly not in a post-feminist world. The film's ensemble women characters dress in a variety of ways, from conservative skirt suits – not fitted like those of lawyer Paulina Morales (Kity Mánver) or fitted like Pepa's – to the hyper-sexualized outfits worn by Pepa's model friend Candela (María Barranco). Regardless of their outfits, these women are shown to be emotionally dependent on the men in their lives, and whereas some will overcome this despite their upbringings, others will not. Characters' choice of clothing is part of their subjection to patriarchal and capitalist ideologies in Spain's newly democratic (and newly open to capitalism) society, whether we like what it says about the characters' ideology or not.

Sontag's label of Pepa's costumes as 'old-fashioned' points to a backwards sense of fashion inflected through second-wave feminist politics and the US context. Skirt suits were incredibly popular with working women in the 1980s in the United States and were popularized even more by TV series such as *Dynasty* (1981–9) and films such as *Working Girl* (Mike Nichols, 1988). The skirt-suit combination of feminine (the skirt and tailored jacket) and masculine (shoulder pads, business attire, block colours adapting the trouser suit's way of blending in) signals a development in women's work attire during their substantial incorporation to the business world in the United States.

In Spain, the skirt suit was not as widespread. The incorporation of women to the business world and professional jobs was behind that of women in the United States. Women had been joining the workforce during the 1960s and 1970s, but most women who worked were young and single, taking low qualification posts with low pay and responsibility. During the Transition from dictatorship to democracy (1975–82) many of the legal barriers to women entering the workforce were removed. For example, it was not until 1975 that married women were allowed to work without the consent of their husbands (*licencia marital*, marital license). It would take time until women entered the workforce in substantial numbers and even more until there were significant increases in the professions and management. Thus, Pepa's outfits are in fact aspirational for her personally and for most Spanish women at the time, who could only dream of Pepa's financial freedom, professional success and wardrobe; they are not old-fashioned in the context of Spanish women's rights.[6] On the contrary, most Spanish women were not in jobs that allowed them to dress in a skirt suit; most of them worked in agriculture, factories and retail. Sontag's critique of traditional, patriarchal 'misrepresentation' of women shows Sontag's wishful thinking in terms of 'the realities of women's lives' (a political aim that as a feminist I share), but it misses the specificity of women's lives in Spain.

It is surprising to see the author of 'Notes on "Camp"' (1964), following a 'traditional sex-role stereotyping analysis' typical of American feminist film theory in the 1970s which, as Thornham explains, 'does not work' (2003, 10). Sontag is taking the lead from American second-wave feminist film criticism that conflated representation of women with the plight of real women. Whereas there is value in considering costume and characterization more generally as part of a film's textuality, the 'tube skirts and high heels' prevented Sontag from considering not only how these are part of Almodóvar's camp aesthetic with 'its love of the unnatural: of artifice and exaggeration' (1964, 515) but also how clothing functions to structure and prompt meaning within the culturally specific context of newly democratic Spain. Sontag berates Almodóvar for doing precisely what she described more than twenty years earlier. Admittedly, she only visited the film set briefly so would have had little opportunity to consider the film as a whole. Almodóvar's camp aesthetic is coupled with a film structure that invites a critique of Spain's patriarchal society and reflection on how even the newly developing demographic of professional Spanish women was bound by patriarchal ideas on femininity and psychologically dependent on men and the discourse romantic love after decades under a fascist, ultra-Catholic dictatorship.

Skirt suits like the ones Pepa wears were mostly seen in American TV programmes and films such as *Dynasty* and *Falcon Crest* (1982–90). Popular Spanish television series of the time featuring professional women (lawyers) such as *Anillos de oro* (Wedding Rings, 1984) and *Turno de oficio* (Public Defender, 1986–7) adopted a realist aesthetic and did not commonly feature skirt suits, with the lawyer in *Anillos de oro* wearing high-neck blouses and below the knee flared skirts in muted colours, and the explicitly labelled 'feminist lawyer' in *Turno de Oficio* sporting a muted wardrobe of high-neck blouses and dresses as well as masculine-looking shirts and jackets.[7] Pepa's skirt suits are part of the artificial aesthetic of *Mujeres* .... This 'emphasis on artificiality' is seen both in film sets and in the costumes' indebtedness to screwball comedy and Hollywood melodramas, which draw attention to the problematic nature of gender constraints and construction. In this context, it is not conceivable that an upwardly mobile professional woman in a Spain where feminism aligned with left-leaning parties in the 1970s and became greatly diffused in the 1980s would dress in any other way than a series of figure-enhancing suits and heels. The number of outfits draws attention to newly discovered consumerism.

Almodóvar's reluctance in the 1980s to align politically to any one movement (cf. Sánchez-Arce 2020) would have precluded a more feminist card-carrying character. However, *Mujeres* ... is clearly concerned with gender, particularly the process of women's emotional emancipation from men and romantic cisgender, heterosexual love. Departing from *La voix humaine*, *Mujeres* ... features four women who are abandoned by their male lovers and two men – father and son Iván and Carlos (Antonio Banderas) – who represent how male (mis)use of women is entrenched across generations.

Does characterization (costume in particular) in film result in better representations of independent, autonomous women? Does Pepa's characterization set *Mujeres* ... up to fail at progressiveness? Conversely, does Annie's characterization in *Annie Hall* signal a more progressive politics? Whereas critique of representation and calls for awareness of what representation may signal are always welcome, focusing only on costume can miss other, less obvious ways in which films may subject female characters to patriarchal discourses.

Because clothing is a big part of femininity – what Joan Riviere termed 'womanliness as a masquerade' in her 1929 essay[8] and thus constitutes gender performativity (cf. Butler 1990) – a narrow focus on costume can mislead viewers into assuming a more ground-breaking, gender-challenging attire corresponds to a more autonomous woman character. Thus, Annie's tailored trouser suits could be seen as a sign of the character's thoughtful statement on gender construction, and her tunics and kaftans may be interpreted as an indication of her liberation from patriarchal structures in line with the 1970s American women's lib movement. Notwithstanding, Annie is still in a coercive relationship with Alvy for most of the film, breaking up with him to move in with her producer Tony Lacey (Paul Simon) and glimpsed at the end of the film with a new boyfriend in New York. On the other hand, Pepa's late 1980s skirt suits and heels may signal (following Sontag) a sexualized woman who is the object of the male gaze despite being a financially independent professional. As I have said elsewhere:

> Pepa is a woman in a society that values women's appearances and puts a great deal of pressure on women who are in the limelight as she is due to her media job. Her characterisation as a woman who despite her financial independence still depends emotionally on her ex-partner Iván […] would not be believable without her desperate desire to look good.
>
> (2020, 101)

Indeed, Pepa only breaks free at the end of the film when she refuses to talk things over with him. Her newfound independence is not reliant on the matching outfit. Her tightly tailored miniskirt suit is stained with *gazpacho* as are her hair and face, destroying her make-up and hairdo. Her shoes are lost, and her tights are riddled with holes.

The ending affirms Pepa's newfound independence. After leaving Iván at the airport on her own terms and not telling him about her pregnancy, she claims her apartment as fully her own, 'Home at last!', and not the place she shared with Iván and which two days before she had considered too big for her. She does not discard the outfit, still wearing it as she settles down for a quiet chat with Marisa (Rossy de Palma). In fact, during her final monologue (which looks like a voiced interior monologue), she explains why she decides to put on her shoes as a practical issue: 'I'd better put on my shoes with this mess. I don't know which would be better, slipping on gazpacho or cutting myself on the glass.' This is followed by another pragmatic decision, this time about a possible relationship with the telephone repairman: 'The repairman is cute, but I'd better leave him for Marisa.'

Pepa's financial independence is reasserted as she mentions calling the cleaner. As she shares the news of her pregnancy with someone for the first time (this is also the first time that the audience hear of Pepa's pregnancy, which was only referred to obliquely at the beginning of the film), she explains her decision not to let the flat out. This decision reinforces her strength and independence, obliquely commenting on her much more important decision to bring her child up alone. The comedic ending, with Marisa confiding in Pepa that she has had an erotic dream and has lost her virginity while dreaming, further reinforces the theme of women's ability to do anything without (male, in this heterosexually-oriented film) assistance. However, the ending is more complex than it first appears because Pepa has resigned herself to living without Iván and bringing up their child by herself in 1980s Spain, where single mothers were stigmatized.

In addition to the disparity between outfit and autonomy at the end of the film, *Mujeres* ... makes the point about women's emotional dependence being unrelated to their use of sexually alluring clothing. There is another character who wears skirt suits, the so-called 'feminist lawyer' who is Iván's latest conquest, Paulina Morales (Kity Mánver). Paulina always wears skirt suits with hemlines beneath the knee and blazers that are not tightly fitted. Her outfits are closer to the power suit, but with a skirt and block colour. These more standard work clothes do not make as much a statement as Pepa's, signalling Paulina's 'womanliness' – necessary for a woman in the very masculine legal profession in 1980s Spain – without encouraging Paulina's sexualization. Despite Paulina's less sexualized outfits as a professional woman, she has also fallen for Iván's tricks and is already losing patience with Iván's outward passivity.

As Florence Redding Jessup states, *Mujeres* ... is 'a story about emancipation from machismo' (1994, 300) through the means of comedy. Jessup makes an eloquent argument in favour of *Mujeres* ... 's underlying feminist politics and its matter-of-fact take on the pervasiveness of patriarchal structures and ideology in 1980s Spain: 'Almodóvar's humour in this funny film renders machismo absurd. Yet our laughter has undertones of frustration as well as optimism. Pepa overcomes her subordination to the macho; the macho continues with someone else. Machismo roves around society throughout this film; the final scenes indicate that mañana it will go away' (302). Among Jessup's many insights is her awareness of Almodóvar's nod in the film to the newly established Instituto de la Mujer (The Women's Institute), founded in 1983 (309). Iván's estranged wife Lucía lives next to the Instituto de la Mujer. This juxtaposition of new institutions and agencies devoted to work against gender discrimination and equality with the story of a woman who is irretrievably wedded to the ideology that makes discrimination possible shows Almodóvar's awareness that Spanish society still had work to do to shed its subjection to strict patriarchal ideology as promoted for more than forty years during the dictatorship.

Annie, a 'post-feminist torch-bearer'?

Almodóvar relates Annie's costumes to Charles Chaplin's formal suit attire when playing The Tramp. The trouser suit in *Annie Hall* bends gender expectations in fashion. It is both aspirational *and* a sign of Annie's adherence to masculine looks to succeed. Bruce Babington and Peter William Evans skilfully analyse

Annie's changing outfits in relation to the character's transformation into an 'assertive, post-feminist torch-bearer of the career woman's cause' (1989, 173). As they explain, 'the Annie Hall Look that [...] so dominated women's fashions after the film's release, is based on the clothes Annie wears in her as yet unreconstructed, empty-headed identity of her first appearances in the film', a look that disappears, 'giving way to a much more liberated outfit' consisting of more skirts and tunics, and overgrown jumpers (173).

While it is true that Annie becomes more assertive, and that her costumes change as Babington and Evans explain, I remain unconvinced that she has become a 'post-feminist torch-bearer', a label that perhaps fits Alvy's first wife Alison Portchnik better. Annie's clothes may be a sign of her individuation process, but she breaks-up with Alvy to move to California with her producer, adopting New Age fashion, which can be seen in the proposal scene: light flowing kaftan, neutral scarf and ombre, neutral sunglasses. She has kept her New York straw bag. This 'new' Annie has left behind the trouser suit and is dressing more similarly to her middle-class mother's style, the style she also nods to when Alvy and Annie visit the Halls in Chippewa Falls, Wisconsin. For this reason, I believe that Annie's outfits are more about fitting in and career aspiration than they are about a feminist agenda.[9]

Mujeres ... occupies a position in Pedro Almodóvar's career like *Annie Hall*'s in the career of Woody Allen.[10] Both films were highly successful and were quickly considered classics, winning numerous awards and nominations. Both marked a jump to mainstream filmmaking for Allen and Almodóvar. More importantly, both films are problematic comedies that develop against the generic grain. *Annie Hall* blends comedian comedy[11] with romantic comedy, ending in a reverse melodrama with the male character, Alvy, suffering despite his attempts at being funny. This can be seen in the use of the chicken joke at the very end where it becomes a poignant reflection on relationships:

> ALVY: It was great seeing Annie again. I realised what a terrific person she was and how much fun it was just knowing her and ... I thought of that old joke, you know ... This guy goes to a psychiatrist and says 'Doc, my brother's crazy. He thinks he's a chicken.' And the doctor says, 'Well, why don't you turn him in?' and the guy says, 'I would, but I need the eggs.' Well, I guess that's pretty much now how I feel about relationships. You know, they're totally irrational, and crazy, and absurd and ... but I guess we keep going through it because most of us need the eggs.

Alvy's statement that romantic relationships are 'totally irrational, and crazy, and absurd' but ultimately necessary closes the film in a would-be comic yet philosophical acceptance of painful feelings surrounding his break-up with Annie. Alvy bookends the film with jokes as a frame for his reflection on 'what went wrong' (note the passive construction devoid of a subject responsible for the failure of the relationship) and, later, as a way of acknowledging that despite 'our' awareness that romantic love is a ruse, we cannot help ourselves from falling for it. *Annie Hall* thus cleverly combines comedian comedy with thoughtful reflection on traditional discourses of love and how they influence behaviour. Alvy's joke is the equivalent of a stage bow, but this is followed by a puncture of his comic persona and return to the painful feelings he sketched in a more comic mode at the beginning of the film. This volte-face shifts the film from comedy to male melodrama as Alvy succeeds in affirming his suffering. The link between male suffering and comedy as described by Kathleen Rowe is thus blurred, a blurring that is perhaps more easily achieved due to Alvy's schlemiel status, a role that already departs from traditional masculinity.

Alvy has managed to hide from himself how much he is to blame for the end of the relationship. Nevertheless, he provides many leads to viewers of his attempts to shape Annie as an intellectually aware, successful woman as well as to control Annie when she becomes just that. His stance is one of reluctant resignation to fate, just like his attitude to life. Alvy's comedic front is not quite what it seems, as seen from the opening scene. As Jason Bailey states, 'his gags aren't greeted with reassuring laughter from a delighted audience […], only the rather eerie silence that accompanies the opening credits. It's a striking choice […] in the opening scene, and throughout *Annie Hall*, he's not performing for us; he's talking to us, sharing of himself, making a personal connection' (2014, 31).

The film casts spectators as detectives piecing together Annie and Alvy's relationship and, like him, searching for a reason for their break-up. It shows Alvy revelling in the past, hence the 'jumbling up the [narrative] pieces so that the audience is lulled out of the complacency of preconceived notions [about a boy-meets-girl narrative]' (Bailey 2014, 32). This retrospection increases the perception of the pain Alvy suffers at the end. This genre blending may be related to Allen's original idea for *Annie Hall*: 'I wanted to do a realistic comedy, where I can speak to the audience and bare my soul. Maybe there'd be fewer laughs, but hopefully the characters will be engaging and their lives will be interesting, even if they're not always speaking in joke' (2020, 189). The working title of the film, *Anhedonia*, about a man who cannot experience pleasure (Allen 2020, 190;

Cowie 1998, 15), also points to the blending of melodrama and comedy, as well as providing a lead as to the reason for the break-up from Annie's perspective.

As Annie exclaims in exasperation during the proposal scene: 'Alvy you're incapable of enjoying life, you know that?' Annie's comment contradicts Alvy's statement in the opening scene: 'I'm not a morose type. I'm not a depressive character.' This is one of many instances where Alvy's self-centredness and the film's use of his point of view/gaze is subverted, allowing a glimpse of Annie's point of view. Other punctures of Alvy's point of view include the split-screen parallel therapy sessions, the fights over Alvy's spying on Annie and, less obviously, Annie's out-of-body experience while having dissociated sex with Alvy or her facial expressions when, for example, Alvy presents her with sexy underwear.

The emphasis on Alvy's failed introspection and the narrative's prevailing use of his point of view colours much of the criticism of *Annie Hall* and Allen more generally as 'operating in the service of sexism and as perpetuating patriarchy' (Girgus 2002, 48). For example, Richard Feldstein explains how *Annie Hall* is, despite its title, not about Annie but about Alvy: 'Trace its code of narrative arrangement and you will find that *Annie Hall* is not about its namesake, because the primary sequence of events depicts Alvy's life, not Annie's. Although Annie is a historical subject who progresses through perceptible transformations, each passage is supervised by Alvy as part of his tutorial' (1989, 74). However, the film's use of metacinematic techniques – including referentiality and self-reflexivity (cf. Schatz 1982), fragmentation, breaking the fourth wall, use of split screen, use of media such as the comic and footage of television programmes and so on (cf. Schwanebeck 2015; Szlezák and Wynter 2015) – encourage distance and, together with the instances where we are provided with opposing points of view as seen above, can be the source of a deconstruction of Alvy's dominant gaze.

I have always interpreted *Annie Hall* against the grain, disliking Alvy intensely and cheering when Annie stands up for herself. This is not simply a matter of feminist politics; the film itself offers enough rope, so to speak, to hang Alvy, who comes across as a patronising, controlling, would-be Pygmalion.[12] Despite most of *Annie Hall* not being 'about its namesake', as Feldstein says, with Annie presented as Alvy's object of desire, we also glimpse another Annie, the character who 'progresses through perceptible transformations', a person who manages to break free from Alvy's control, leaving him only with narrative to pursue his dreams of possession. Alvy's narrative, his play as well as the film, signifies his failure.

'Nearly' a love story: The importance of genre

Mujeres ... blends (particularly screwball) comedy with melodrama (cf. Evans 1996), starting melodramatically with the song 'Soy infeliz' (I am unhappy), reflecting Pepa's feelings on being abandoned by Iván and ending the otherwise frantic story with a quiet scene where female friendship and motherhood substitute the traditional romantic ending. *Mujeres* ... is an anti-romantic comedy, much like *The Women* (1939), 'in which matrimony is undone and men remain a structural absence superfluous to the film's pleasures' (Rowe 1995, 51). The final song of *Mujeres* ..., 'Puro Teatro' (Pure Theatre; La Lupe, 1969), underscores the film's deconstruction of the misleading discourse of romantic love, men's abuse of it and women's subjection to it. *Annie Hall* also deconstructs romantic love but pulls back from this repeatedly to uphold it. Remarkably, whereas *Mujeres* ... lays the blame squarely on the nearly absent male character who refuses to be tied to convention by committing to any one woman, *Annie Hall* presents us with a male comedian who is ready to commit and a female character, also in show business and played by a comic actor in her own right, who refuses to. This reverses comedian comedy in which women 'tend to signify the demands of integration and responsibility for the male' (Krutnik 1990, 37). As Joanna E. Rapf explains, 'with *Annie Hall* in 1977, after he met Diane Keaton, [Allen] did begin dealing with this existential angst and darkness from a woman's point of view. [...] He was able to get away from [Steve] Seidman's misogynistic comedian-centred comedy and, indeed, to laugh at it' (2013, 274). Both films end with Annie and Pepa's rejection of their male counterparts.

Annie Hall was marketed as 'a nervous romance' (see 1977 poster) and, as has been pointed out, marks a development in romantic comedy in its use of an unhappy ending (Bailey 2014, 32). In Spain, the tagline of the poster was '"casi" una historia de amor' ('almost' a love story), which reflects the film's challenge to the genre of romantic comedy whilst still adhering to some of its characteristics, not least the exploration of the tensions in a heterosexual couple.

Traditionally, these tensions are driven by 'the "excessive" woman who "desires too much"' (Rowe 1995, 41). One could say that Annie's desire to learn (going to college) and advance in her music career (moving to LA) causes most of the tensions in her relationship with Alvy. However, the film also allows the opposite, placing Alvy as the excessive character who desires too much, in this case an

Figure 9.2 Spanish poster for *Annie Hall* (1977).

intellectual, independent partner who nevertheless remains compliant and in awe of him. Despite Alvy's initial encouragement, he is not keen on his Galatea striking out on her own (cf. Knight 2004). This is obvious in the way he talks to Annie when he realizes that he wants to get back together with her: 'Listen,

I … I want you to come back here. Then I'm gonna go out and get you.' Not only is Alvy demanding that Annie becomes his girlfriend again, she has to sacrifice her career and move back to New York with him.

Annie Hall's multiple endings reflect the film's uneasy blend of comedian and romantic comedy. After the second break-up, Alvy is back in New York and tries dating other women. He tries to replicate the lobster scene, but his date does not find him funny or even realise he is joking. Alvy's comedy act is dependent on a receptive, comic sidekick, Annie. Alvy tries to get Annie back, flying to Los Angeles and proposing, but Annie rejects him, saying 'No' twice and leaving. On his return to New York, Alvy writes a play about his relationship with Annie, changing the ending of the proposal scene to an acceptance by Sunny/Annie. Alvy breaks the fourth wall to comment upon this trite ending and continues narrating his later encounter with Annie and final lunch when (he says) they 'kick around old times'. There is a montage of scenes from happier times to the song 'Seems Like Old Times'.

Because the end credits are silent, the last aural impression is of Annie singing 'Seems Like Old Times', bringing back memories of the selective montage about the relationship, all of it positive. The ending is quiet and nostalgic, enabling both the construction of an idealized relationship and revelling in the knowledge that it has ended. This, of course, is from Alvy's perspective as he is narrating and most of the film is focalized through him. This is a comedy that ends as a male melodrama with the main character, comedian Alvy, mired in his painful feelings and accepting that he must move on. At this point, the film's structure has put autonomous Annie back in the place Alvy would have liked her to end, back with him in New York and pining for their lost relationship as described in the song. Nostalgia encourages viewers to yearn for the relationship to have worked, regardless of the film's techniques to enable a deconstruction of Alvy's point of view as outlined above.

Annie Hall's ending is remarkably different from that of *Mujeres …*, where nostalgia had briefly made an appearance during the film but ends by looking to the future as Pepa discusses her pregnancy and decision not to let out her apartment. The end credits song, 'Puro Teatro', also extends the main character's perspective. This is a song about a woman seeing through her ex-lover's lies and refusing to accept him back after he broke her heart. The singer uses a theatre metaphor, the 'final curtain', to refer to the definitive ending of the relationship. This is a far cry from *Annie Hall*'s nostalgic revision; Pepa's point of view continues to be privileged and Iván's actions are not excused. He is not allowed to reframe the events to suit himself, as Alvy does.

Conclusion: Keaton and Maura, Annie and Pepa

Annie and Pepa are watershed roles in their respective national cinemas, both characters being shaped by and shaping their stars' personas. As well as Keaton being a comedian and singer in her own right, her wardrobe was mostly used to characterize Annie, as Allen explains:

> [Keaton] came in, and the costume lady on the picture, Ruth Morley, said, 'Tell her not to wear that. She can't wear that. It's so crazy.' And I said, 'Leave her. She's a genius. Let's just leave her alone, let her wear what she wants. If I really hate something, I'll tell her. Otherwise she can choose for herself.'
>
> (2004, 83–5)

Nevertheless, as Claire Mortimer explains, 'Keaton's contribution to *Annie Hall* has been sidelined – not only by critics and scholars but also by Keaton herself, whose generosity and humility serve to eclipse her creative contribution and shore up the status of Allen as auteur' (2022, 244). Similarly, Maura had an established star persona by the time *Mujeres …* was made from multiple credits and, most importantly, her hosting of *Esta noche* (*Tonight*, 1981–2, Fernando García Tola), a TV variety show where she performed the role of candid presenter whose weekly tagline was the comment a supposed producer had made to her: 'Nena, tu vales mucho' (Babe, you're worth a lot). Maura's star image is referenced in her role as Pepa. It is important to look beyond the auteur framework to consider how women collaborators shape these projects. Mortimer's essay on the Keaton/Allen collaboration does just this. There is no equivalent for Maura/Almodóvar so far.

The films portray similar struggles and victories by their women characters as they become autonomous beings despite the filmic and social structures that are stacked against them. As Ernesto Acevedo-Muñoz states, 'Pepa's dramatic arc leads her from drug-induced incoherence, heartbreak and desperation to redemption, regeneration, the assertion of her subjectivity and desire, and the satisfying closure of her unresolved narrative' (2007, 114). Likewise, Annie's development (which from Alvy's perspective seems to be all down to his mentoring) leads to her breaking away from his controlling grip. As Sam B. Girgus explains: 'Annie does learn to use language more effectively, at least in terms of achieving her independence and advancing her career. Annie's acquisition of more developed and coherent speech often evidences itself in rebellious exchanges with Alvy, a psychologically accurate way of relating her growth and her independence from Alvy' (2002, 56).

Both the two films' are comedies with the heterosexual break-up as main the theme. There the similarities seem to end. *Annie Hall* uses a documentary style and overt metacinematic techniques to puncture realism and emphasize representation; *Mujeres ...* is a camp pop comedy indebted to screwball comedy and melodrama. The former is dominated by the male character – Alvy – whose point-of-view viewers are almost exclusively shown and whose voice over opens and intrudes upon the film repeatedly; the latter begins with a voiceover from the female protagonist, Pepa, and offers her point of view nearly exclusively, even during the few times her ex-partner speaks, speech that is nearly always mediated by technology (answering machine, dubbing studio recording, Pepa re-reading an old postcard of his). In *Annie Hall*, we get Alvy's personal history of desire and are shown how he returns to Annie as nostalgic object of desire periodically and, most importantly, at the end; *Mujeres ...* shows us how Iván's personal history of desire impacts on the women he uses and the child he fathers, but this is secondary to Pepa's journey to emotional independence from him and her decision not to tell him that she is pregnant by him.

In conclusion, this comparative analysis of the two films' gender politics within their specific cultural contexts has highlighted the international impact of *Annie Hall* and the many points of contact between these seemingly disparate films. The analysis of costume and characters' plights is used to explore how a critique of film representation can move beyond comparing cinematic representations of women, what Thornham calls 'a utopian moment when "images of women" will "reflect" the realities of women's lives'. To do this, one must consider filmic structures in relation to genre, style and other formal matters alongside cultural contexts. Paying close attention to these has shown that both films portray similar struggles and victories by their women characters as they become autonomous beings (Pepa even more than Annie) despite the social and filmic structures that are stacked against them. In addition to this, the analysis of the spat between Almodóvar and Sontag in relation to representation reveals the need to revise first impressions based on characterization. As we know, an outfit that breaks canons of femininity is not a safeguard against more psychological structural patriarchal oppression of women or guarantee of film's pushback against structural oppression. Alternatively, a character dressed in a way that upholds these same canons of femininity may not in itself account for the film's overall politics.

Pepa's accidental burning of her double bed at the beginning of *Mujeres ...*, the bed she used to share with Iván, anticipates the burning of the whole set representing the marital home by Tilda Swinton in Almodóvar's latest return to Cocteau's play *La voz humana* (*The Human Voice*, 2020). The accidental burning in the 1980s, which is followed by Pepa destroying and disposing of mementos of her life with Iván, is followed by Swinton's deliberate burning of the props and set to the life she has been pining for, a life that we are shown to be a play/masquerade. Both Annie and Pepa masquerade. Both become aware of the strictures of these roles. Both achieve small victories in worlds that are shown to be hostile to women. Despite (possibly because of) the heels and miniskirt, Pepa's journey seems to be the most remarkable. She is truly a Spanish Annie Hall.

Notes

1. The literal translation is 'high heels and tube skirt'. However, Pepa is seen mostly in miniskirts rather than tube skirts, hence my translation of 'falda tubo' as miniskirt throughout. The use of 'falda tubo' seems a direct allusion to Susan Sontag's use of 'tube skirt' (qtd. Lida 1988, 80), a comment that this section of the pressbook responds to.
2. Many thanks to the Filmoteca Española (Spanish Film Archives) for providing access to this pressbook.
3. See also Peter Krämer's chapter in this collection.
4. Many thanks to Professor Kathy A. Parsons (Iowa State University) for invaluable help in tracking down Sontag's comments for *Elle*.
5. As I have said elsewhere, 'Almodóvar's defence sounds a little dated and not particularly progressive. […] Almodóvar plays down the fact that Pepa's choice of clothes reveals a patriarchal culture at work, even in a woman who on the surface appears to be independent' (2020, 101).
6. For insightful analyses of costume and the construction of the female body, see Gaines and Herzog.
7. For a discussion of the construction of national identity through television in Spain and representations of women, see Louis (2020).
8. 'Womanliness therefore could be assumed and worn as a mask, both to hide the possession of masculinity and to avert the reprisals expected if she was found to possess it – much as a thief will turn out his pockets and ask to be searched to prove that he has not the stolen goods. The reader may now ask how I define womanliness or where I draw the line between genuine womanliness and the "masquerade". My suggestion is not, however, that there is any such difference; whether radical or superficial, they are the same thing' (Riviere 1986, 38).

For an analysis of masquerade and the construction of femininity in *Women ...*, see Girelli 2006.
9   Diane Keaton's outfits are also not necessarily feminist statements. In a 2014 interview, she was asked about her trademark look, replying thus: 'Clothing that actually hides the body. There's a lot to hide in my case' (Siegel 2014).
10 See Krämer's chapter in this collection and Symons for the importance of *Annie Hall* in Woody Allen's career, also Smith (2014) and Sánchez-Arce (2020) for the centrality of *Mujeres ...* to the career of Pedro Almodóvar.
11 Frank Krutnik analyses the genealogy and development of comedian or comedian-centred comedy, explaining that it 'differed from mainstream fiction films in one important respect: comedian-centred films were not organized simply in accordance with the narrative-based aesthetic of classical cinema. They exhibit, instead, a combination of fiction-making and performative entertainment spectacle' (1990, 17). This creates a tension between the fiction-making and comedian performance: '[t]he comedian figure deforms familiar conventions of film heroism, unified identity and mature sexuality. [...] At such moments, the comedian's performance intrudes into the fictional masquerade. [...] Through the intrusion, the comedian figure demonstrates that unified character identity is a fictional mask' (29).
12 For an analysis of *Annie Hall* and the Pygmalion myth, see Knight (2004).

Works cited

Acevedo-Muñoz, Ernesto. 2007. *Pedro Almodóvar*. British Film Institute. London: Palgrave Macmillan.

Allen, Woody. 2004. *Woody Allen on Woody Allen*. Edited by Stig Björkman (Revised edition). London and New York: Faber and Faber.

Allen, Woody. 2020. *Apropos of Nothing*. New York: Arcade Publishing.

Babington, Bruce and Peter William Evans. 1989. *Affairs to Remember: The Hollywood Comedy of the Sexes*. Manchester and New York: Manchester University Press.

Bailey, Jason. 2014. *The Ultimate Woody Allen Film Companion*. Minneapolis: Voyageur Press.

Butler, Judith. 1990. *Gender Trouble. Feminism and the Subversion of Identity*. New York and London: Routledge.

Cowie, Peter. 1998. *Annie Hall*. BFI Film Classics. London: British Film Institute.

Edwards, Gwynne. 2001. *Almodóvar: Labyrinths of Passion*. London and Chester Springs: Peter Owen.

Evans, Peter William. 1996. *Women on the Verge of a Nervous Breakdown*. London: British Film Institute.

Feldstein, Richard. 1989. 'Displaced Feminine Representation in Woody Allen's Cinema', in *Discontented Discourses: Feminism/Textual Intervention/Psychoanalysis*, ed. M. S. Barr and R. Feldstein, 68–83. Urbana: University of Illinois Press.

Gaines, Jane and Charlotte Herzog, eds. 1990. *Fabrications: Costume and the Female Body*. New York and London: Routledge.

Girelli, Elisabetta. 2006. 'The Power of the Masquerade: *Mujeres al borde de un ataque de nervios* and the Construction of Femininity', *Hispanic Research Journal* 7 (3): 251–8.

Girgus, Sam B. 2002. *The Films of Woody Allen. Second Edition*. Cambridge and New York: Cambridge University Press.

Jessup, Florence Redding. 1994. '*Women on the Verge of a Nervous Breakdown*: Sexism or Emancipation from Machismo?' in *Gender and Comedy*, ed. G. Finney, 299–314. Amsterdam, Reading and Langhorne: Gordon and Breach.

Knight, Christopher. 2004. 'Woody Allen's *Annie Hall*: Galatea's Triumph over Pygmalion', *Literature/Film Quarterly* 32 (3): 213–21.

Krutnik, Frank. 1990. 'The Faint Aroma of Performing Seals: The 'Nervous' Romance and the Comedy of the Sexes', *The Velvet Light Trap* 26 (26): 57–72.

Lida, David. 1988. 'Cinematador: Spanish Film Director Pedro Almodóvar's Fresh Style Wakes Up American Audiences', *Elle* 4 (4), December: 80–2.

Louis, Anja. 2020. 'Television, Justice and National Identity in Spain', *Entertainment and Sports Law Journal* 18 (1), doi: https://doi.org/10.16997/eslj.259

Mortimer, Claire. 2022. 'Keaton and Allen: Collaboration and the Screwball Couple in *Annie Hall* and *Manhattan Murder Mystery*', in *Women in the Work of Woody Allen*, ed. Martin R. Hall, 243–61. Amsterdam: Amsterdam University Press.

Mujeres al borde de un ataque de nervios [Women on the Verge of a Nervous Breakdown]. 1988. Pressbook. El Deseo, S.A.: n.p.

O'Toole, Lesley. 2007. 'Diane Keaton: She Wears the Trousers', *The Independent*, Friday 9 February. https://www.independent.co.uk/arts-entertainment/films/features/diane-keaton-she-wears-the-trousers-435571.html

Rapf, Joanna E. 2013. '"It's Complicated, Really": Women in the Films of Woody Allen', in *A Companion to Woody Allen*, ed. Peter Bailey and Sam B. Girgus, 257–76. Somerset: John Wiley & Sons, Inc.

Riviere, Joan. 1986. 'Womanliness as a Masquerade', in *Formations of Fantasy*, ed. Victor Burgin, James Donald and Cora Kaplan, 35–44. London and New York: Methuen.

Rowe, Kathleen. 1995. 'Comedy, Melodrama and Gender: Theorizing the Genres of Laughter', in *Classical Hollywood Comedy*, ed. Kristine Brunovska Karnick and Henry Jenkins, 39–59. New York and London: Routledge.

Sánchez-Arce, Ana María. 2020. *The Cinema of Pedro Almodóvar*. Manchester: Manchester University Press.

Schatz, Thomas. 1982. '"*Annie Hall*" and the Issue of Modernism', *Literature/Film Quarterly* 10 (3): 180–7.

Schwanebeck, Wieland. 2015. 'Woody and "Woody": The Making of a Persona', in *Referentiality and the Films of Woody Allen*, ed. Klara Stephanie Szlezák and D. E. Wynter, 193–209. Houndmills: Palgrave Macmillan.

Siegel, Robert. 2014. 'A Film and Fashion Icon on Aging, And the Power of Turtlenecks', *NPR*, 5 May. https://www.npr.org/transcripts/308346882?t=1656065631087 (accessed 24 June 2022).

Smith, Paul Julian. 2014. *Desire Unlimited: The Cinema of Pedro Almodóvar*. London and New York: Verso.

Sontag, Susan. 1964. 'Notes on "Camp"', *Partisan Review* 31: 515–30.

Symons, Alex. 2013. 'The Problem of "High Culture" Comedy: How *Annie Hall* (1977) Complicated Woody Allen's Reputation', *Journal of Popular Film and Television* 41 (3): 18–127.

Szlezák, Klara Stephanie and D. E. Wynter, eds. 2015. *Referentiality and the Films of Woody Allen*. Houndmills: Palgrave Macmillan.

Thornham, Sue, ed. 2003. *Feminist Film Theory. A Reader*. Edinburgh: Edinburgh University Press.

Filmography

Anillos de oro (*Wedding Rings*). TV. Directed by Pedro Masó. Spain: Pedro Masó Producciones Cinematográficas, 1984.

Annie Hall. Film. Directed by Woody Allen. Hollywood: United Artists, 1977.

Dynasty. TV. Created by Esther Shapiro and Richard Shapiro. USA: Aaron Spelling Productions, 1981–9.

Esta noche (*Tonight*). TV Talkshow. Directed by Fernando García Tola. Spain: Televisión Española (TVE), 1981–2.

Falcon Crest. TV. Created by Earl Hamner, Jr. USA: Amanda & MF, Lorimar Television, 1982–90.

La voz humana (*The Human Voice*). Film. Directed by Pedro Almodóvar. Spain: El Deseo, S.A., 2020.

Matador. Film. Directed by Pedro Almodóvar. Spain: Iberoamericana with Televisión Española (TVE), 1986.

Mujeres al borde de un ataque de nervios (*Women on the Verge of a Nervous Breakdown*). Film. Directed by Pedro Almodóvar. Spain: El Deseo, S.A. with Lauren Film, 1988.

Turno de oficio (*Public Defender*). TV. Directed by Antonio Mercero. Spain: Alma Ata International Pictures S.L., 1986–7.

The Women. Film. Directed by George Cuckor. USA: Metro-Goldwyn-Mayer (MGM), 1939.

Working Girl. Film. Directed by Mike Nichols. USA: Twentieth Century Fox, 1988.

10

'Don't look back': The relationship between Richard Linklater's *Before ...* trilogy and *Annie Hall*

Jonathan Ellis

The Woody Allen genome

Before Sunrise (1995) was not the first romantic comedy I saw at the cinema, but it was undoubtedly one of the most influential films on my development as both a critic and a person, alongside, you will not be surprised to hear given the focus of this book, *Annie Hall* (1977). I went to see the film with my best friend at the time, a fellow English literature undergraduate called Rob whose favourite film was *When Harry Met Sally* (1989), a film, like *Before Sunrise*, that is clearly inspired by *Annie Hall*. My relationship with Rob was similar to Alvy's friendship with another Rob in *Annie Hall*. We talked a lot of rubbish about women, none of it based on experience. The year after *Before Sunrise*'s release, I bought a EuroRail ticket to Italy, ostensibly to visit a university friend in Bergamo, but with the not so secret desire to meet an Italian Celine somewhere between Venice and Rome. Rob flew to a summer camp in the United States looking for Sally. Neither of us were in luck. At the time of *Before Sunrise*'s release in 1995, Celine and Jesse felt a lot older than I did, even though the actors playing them, Julie Delpy and Ethan Hawke, were only six and five years older than me. As the second and third films in the trilogy were released, *Before Sunset* in 2004 and *Before Midnight* in 2013, the age gap did not feel like much of a gap anymore. In an essay on the trilogy, Dennis Lim reflects on the very personal relationship people have with these films:

> Especially for those who have aged with them, these films ask to be read reflexively, which is to say personally. Watching them entails a very particular

form of viewer participation: as Celine and Jesse openly wrestle with the transience of love, the deceptions of time, and the specter of mortality, we are obliged to do so as well, in ways that relate to our own lives.

(2017, 10)

The trilogy also asks to be read in dialogue with other romantic comedies, not just those directed by Woody Allen of course, though for the purposes of this chapter I am going to limit myself to the ways in which Richard Linklater's work flirts with and at the same time distances itself from the type of cinema popularized by Allen in what I am going to characterize as his middle-not-so-funny-period, roughly the long decade between the release of *Annie Hall* in 1977 and the release of *Husbands and Wives* in 1992.

One of the curious effects of teaching *Annie Hall* for more than a decade has been the realization that most of my students have already seen numerous versions of the film even if they have never watched *Annie Hall* itself. By this, I mean they have probably all seen at least one film or TV series influenced by *Annie Hall*. In 2014 Manohla Dargis and A. O. Scott published 'Woody's Other Family Tree' in *The New York Times*, a visual map of what they described as 'the Allen genome'. In addition to Allen's comic, intellectual and literary influences, they also list some of his cinematic heirs, including writer-directors like Nanni Moretti, Wes Anderson, Noah Baumbach, Greta Gerwig and Lena Dunham. Dargis and Scott's family tree is not meant to be definitive. Re-watching *Gilmore Girls* recently, I was struck by the constant stream of references to Allen's life and work and simultaneously by the thought that this would no longer be possible if the series were airing now. Lauren Graham's Lorelei Gilmore has many cinematic antecedents, particularly in Classic Hollywood, one of Lorelei's favorite film genres. At the same time, her character also acts and sounds a lot like the type of middle-aged commitment-phobe played by Allen in numerous films over the past fifty years. Confident about her taste in books, films and food but jittery about love and marriage, Lorelei behaves a lot like Alvy. *Talking as Fast as I Can* (2016), the title of her first collection of essays, applies equally to Allen's delivery of lines as her own. In her book *A Theory of Adaptation*, Linda Hutcheon reflects on the frequency with which we read or see a so-called 'original' text '*after* we have experienced the adaptation, thereby challenging the authority of any notion of priority. Multiple versions exist laterally, not vertically' (2006, xiii). Helpfully for my consideration of how influence might be present in terms of acting styles and verbal delivery, she also discusses how character can be 'transported from one text to another' (11), an example of which would be Graham's presumably unconscious channelling of 'the Woody Allen character' in *Gilmore Girls*. Influence of this kind is present even when filmmakers are pushing against it, as I think is the case with Linklater, who in interviews hardly ever mentions Allen, a squeamishness not shared by one of *Before Sunrise*'s co-stars and co-writers Julie Delpy, who has repeatedly described herself as a Woody Allen fan and made at least two films – *2 Days in Paris* (2007) and *2 Days in New York* (2012) – that are as close to fan fiction of Allen's back catalogue as cinema gets without the element that makes Allen's influence so difficult to acknowledge nowadays, never mind address, Allen himself.

Passing through

I want to think now about the specific influence of *Annie Hall* on the *Before* trilogy, focusing initially on the character of Celine played by Julie Delpy and her relationship to Annie Hall played by Diane Keaton. In the first film, Celine is dressed a lot like Annie, though she is less hesitant than Annie is about sharing her feelings and opinions. It is not the case, I want to make clear, that Annie does not feel or think as much as Celine, more the fact that Annie begins the relationship intimidated by Alvy, who is happy to over-share his opinions when almost anybody else is in earshot. Alvy and Annie meet for the first time playing tennis before a hilariously awkward drink on Annie's terrace during which the audience learn what the characters actually think of each other via subtitles that reveal their unspoken feelings. The cinematic joke has a serious edge: Allen does not appear to have much faith in words as an effective means of communication. Celine and Jesse meet in a similar social occasion on a train, but with the significant difference that both are reading a book: Celine shares the cover of Georges Bataille's *Story of the Eye*, and Jesse shares Klaus Kinski's *All I Need Is Love*. From the outset, both characters are introduced to the audience and to each other as literate, perhaps even over-earnest readers, an impression confirmed when we spend more time in their company. Annie, we suspect, reads just as much as Alvy, but she does not have the confidence or discourse to compete with him when the conversation turns to literature. He famously dismisses her reading of Sylvia Plath and continually makes fun of her mannerisms and phrasing. For somebody who believes he is in love, Alvy has a funny way of showing it. Does he love Annie as she is when he meets her or the idea of a mature Annie sometime in the future once she has been transformed by his teaching? As many Allen critics have observed, there is a Pygmalion element to Alvy's 'romantic' behaviour. For Foster Hirsch: 'Their relationship is based on the premise that Annie is an idiot; and once she begins to question that, once she begins, however tentatively, to strike out on her own, cultivating friends and developing interests, the affair is doomed' (1981, 86). Christopher J. Knight is just as critical of Alvy's intentions, but more optimistic about Annie's escape, summarizing the film hopefully as 'Galatea's triumph over Pygmalion'.

Celine and Jesse are artists *and* muses. It is difficult to make the case that one dominates over the other. They exchange roles like exchanging hats. *Before Sunrise* is not immune to gender politics or to men talking over women. Celine's pent-up frustration at Jesse for turning her into his muse explodes in the third film in the trilogy, but is present as a warning note in the first film too. She gently makes fun of his desire to kiss her on the Ferris wheel, and is suspicious of romantic gestures like sleeping together on their first night, worried, with good reason as it turns out, that he might transform their time together into a romantic story for other people. In terms of the film's dialogue, they have an equal number of lines. They also actively enjoy listening to each other. Screenshots from the film create the mistaken impression that they fall in love with each other via looking. Consider the images in context and it is clear they primarily fall in love through listening. Alvy and Annie constantly talk at cross-purposes. When Annie, reflecting on her first session in analysis, means to say, 'Will it change my life?' but instead says, 'Will it change my wife?' we see how language creates disharmony rather than intimacy in their relationship. Do they ever really hear what the other is saying?

According to Rob Stone, 'walking and talking is what characters in the cinema of Richard Linklater do best' (2013, 105). As Stone later points out, the subject of death utterly dominates Celine and Jesse's conversation, more than love, certainly more than sex. So far, so Allenesque. Yet once again there are differences as David Denby picks up in his 2013 review of *Before Midnight*: 'Woody Allen, repeating Godard's audacity in *Breathless*, created walking-and-talking sequences in *Annie Hall* and *Manhattan*, but not with the kind of sustained takes that Linklater pulls off, some of which go on for five or six minutes, the camera steadily receding before the actors as they stroll through city streets and gardens.' The walking-and-talking sequences in Linklater's films are not just longer than Allen's. They appear a crucial element of being alive, connecting couples with each other and with the wider networks of friends and strangers of which they are a part. In *Before Sunrise*, for example, almost every conversation involves somebody other than Celine or Jesse: two actors on a bridge, a palm reader, a street poet, a bartender. The audience arguably resents these interruptions more than the main characters who incorporate these other lives into their developing love story. A cameo, in other words, is more than a cameo in Linklater's world. It is an important reminder of our interconnectedness to and with each other, a reminder, too, that every person is unique. In Allen's films, there are one or two unique people at best; everybody else are making up the numbers. Intelligence rather than kindness is equated with specialness. Stupid people may be happier than Alvy, but he is not particularly interested to know why. Celine and Jesse's story, for all its intimacy, is always in dialogue with other people.

Other people do not need to be physically present in Linklater's films to be important. Celine's relationship with her grandmother, who dies between the first and second film and is the reason Celine misses their planned reunion in Vienna six months after the first meeting, is as important to her as Annie's relationship with her grandmother (the famous Grammy Hall). In fact, grandmothers are important to both characters at different points in the trilogy. One of Jesse's first childhood memories is connected to his great-grandmother. His memory of seeing her ghost is one of one of the most affecting stories in *Before Sunrise* and crucial to Celine trusting him. In the third film, Jesse learns of his grandmother's death and wonders whether to attend the funeral. Linklater even dedicated the first film to his grandparents. Allen is not interested in older people in this way, even as he has become old himself. His films are mainly about mid-life crises even if they involve younger or indeed older actors.

As Celine and Jesse age throughout the trilogy, their life experiences become closer to Alvy and Annie's. This does not become apparent until the second and third films in the trilogy where we learn that Celine, like Annie, is a singer, and that Jesse, like Alvy, is a writer. If Alvy falls in love with Annie when he hears her sing, perhaps Jesse does the same in *Before Sunset*. 'I fucked up my entire life because of the way you sing', he says, only half-jokingly, in *Before Midnight*. Might Alvy be thinking the same? Rob Stone describes *Before Sunrise* as a 'musical without singing or dancing' (2013, 120). The 'music' in this film, he states, 'is the dialogue' (120). *Annie Hall* fit this description too. A duet of sorts between two singers: Alvy by name and Annie by vocation. *Annie Hall* is not a conventional musical any more than *Before Sunset* is (in fact, it probably contains less incidental music than any other Woody Allen film), but both films share a conception of music as significant sound that we might fall in love to and also with, conversation and silence being forms of music too.

Before Sunset, like *Annie Hall*, begins with a break-up or at least what sounds like a serious argument: a couple arguing in German that Linklater does not subtitle. Celine and Jesse break the ice by discussing the failure or perhaps even the inability of old people to listen to each other. Do young people love differently than the old?, the film asks. Alternatively, do all relationships turn sour, however and wherever they begin? In Allen's film, we know Alvy and Annie have broken up. Watching the film we assess Alvy's memories to see what happened and what went wrong. In Alvy's words: 'I keep sifting the pieces of the relationship through my mind and examining my life and trying to figure out where did the screw up come' (4). In Linklater's trilogy, we watch memories as they are happening: time, as it were, before it has the chance to become memorable. For me, this is the main difference between a film like *Annie Hall* and a film like *Before Sunrise* and more generally between the philosophy of a director like Allen and the philosophy of a director like Linklater. Alvy mourns Annie, even as he lets her go. It is not that he is incapable of pleasure, as the original title of the film (*Anhedronia*) has it, but that he is incapable of enjoying new pleasure in the present, knowing, even as he is experiencing it, that such pleasure is temporary. His remembering is thus always a form of anticipatory mourning, even if the memories themselves are positive. Linklater, it seems to me, has far more in common with what Yiyun Li calls an artist's responsibility *not* 'to manipulate the memories of my characters' (2017, 65). 'Memory', Li writes, 'is a collection of moments rearranged – recollected – to create a narrative. Moments, defined by a tangible space, are like sculptures and paintings. But moments are always individual notes of music; none will hold still forever. In the instant they are swept up in time – in that shift from space to time, memory is melodrama' (58). Allen has fun rearranging moments as memory; Linklater attempts to intervene as little as possible.

The lobster scene in *Annie Hall* is a good example of this. For me it is the most magical scene in the entire film because it seems as if Allen and Keaton are not really acting, as if we have caught them goofing around before the camera rolls, messing up lines and walking into the camera. It has the unscripted bumpiness and business of experience rather than the rehearsed sheen of memory. It is, of course, a moment that Alvy, and by extension Allen, keeps recollecting and reshooting. After breaking up with Annie the first time, Alvy returns to the house with a new girlfriend. The dialogue and props are the same, including the lobsters, but without Annie there to laugh at Alvy's jokes the scene falls flat. Alvy is not the only person to do this. Annie does so too, photographing the scene as it is happening and producing black-and-white still images of the scene to decorate her apartment. The lobster scene generates at least several lobster scenes, as single moments always become multiple on being remembered, whether fondly or sadly. Does the second lobster scene lessen the emotional effect of the first scene or make it more perfect?

Linklater's take on the lobster scene occurs in the Allen-esque space of a record store, specifically in a listening booth, where Celine and Jesse listen to a folk song by Kath Bloom, glancing at each other as they do, each looking away when they sense the other's gaze on them (Figure 10.1). Robin Wood, in his essay 'Rethinking Romantic Love', admitted to being caught by and caught out by the scene, an experience I can relate to:

> Even on first viewing I told myself that I would 'one day' analyze in detail the scene in the listening booth of the record store, in which nothing happens except that Ethan Hawke and Julie Delpy either do or don't look at each other, their eyes never quite meeting. After a dozen viewings I abandoned the project. … With no camera movement, no editing, no movement within the frame except for the slight movement of the actors' heads, nothing on the soundtrack but a not-very-distinguished song that may vaguely suggest what is going on in the characters' minds and seems sometimes to motivate their 'looks' … it completely resists analysis, defies verbal description. All one can say is that it is the cinema's most perfect depiction, in just over one minute of 'real' time, at once concrete and intangible, of two people beginning to realize that they are falling in love.
>
> (1998, 330–1)

Figure 10.1 Celine and Jesse falling in love in a record store: *Before Sunrise* (1995).

'The cinema's most perfect depiction [...] of two people beginning to realise they are falling in love.' Isn't this the lobster scene as well, its magic emphasized by the realism of Alvy's attempt to recreate it?

If it is tempting for Celine and Jesse to revisit this moment, it must be equally tempting for the filmmaker. Jesse presumably remembers listening to Bloom's song with Celine in *This Time*, his novel about their affair. It is the book that he reads from in Shakespeare & Co when they meet again in Paris nine years after their initial night in Vienna. But our cinematic encounter, *our* moment, is not spoiled by Linklater revisiting the places again, or at least not revisiting them with Celine and Jesse present. At the end of the first film, he collects images of nearly all of the places that they have passed through during their time together in Vienna. But he shows them as they are *now* not as they were *then*, in the cold light of dawn without the people that made them special. This idea of 'passing through' is picked up in the first film – both Celine and Jesse are literally 'passing through' Vienna on their way home – and in the latest film, *Before Midnight*, when a widow uses the phrase about the death of her husband: 'We're just passing through.' Allen gives us a similar montage of places towards the conclusion of *Annie Hall* with the significant difference that his slide show is a repetition of earlier scenes with Alvy and Annie together again. Allen, like Alvy, cannot help turning moments into memories, something live into something almost live. Linklater keeps the film running, life turning. One looks back, the other at least sideways.

The sideways glance is everywhere in Linklater's work (Figure 10.2). In part, this is a formal necessity. If you want to keep two characters in the same shot,

Figure 10.2 Looking sideways: *Before Midnight* (2013).

particularly if they are walking towards the camera, the main way the actor can acknowledge what the other person is doing or saying is by turning their face. Such gestures are noticed by the camera – indeed, the camera is there to record them – but not always or even very often by the other person. It is a gestural rather than a spoken aside to the cinema audience. Two of my favourite gestural but crucially unseen and thus non-reciprocated asides happen in the first and second films in the trilogy. In *Before Sunrise*, on their first tram ride together, Jesse reaches out to touch Celine's hair but withdraws his hand before she can notice. Celine repeats the gesture in a taxi-ride in *Before Sunset*, almost but not quite touching Jesse without him ever realizing. The filmmakers, by this point Delpy and Hawke are credited as joint scriptwriters, are conscious of returning to the past and repeating a moment that has already happened. But, unlike in *Annie Hall*, nostalgia is resisted. Jesse is conscious of his desire to touch Celine on the tram, but Celine is not. The same happens in reverse nine years later in Paris. Audience members of the film, not the characters in the film, notice the repetition of gestures. The repetition of moments is moving because we notice them. Without us there, the meaning of each gesture and its eventual success is lost. Celine is precociously aware of the importance of meaning being generated by more than one or two people, even when thinking about a romantic couple. 'If there's any God', she suggests, 'he wouldn't be in any one of us, not you, not me, but just this space in between'. In cinematic terms, mise en scène is 'this space in between' where extra-diegetic spectators (you and I) get the chance both to eavesdrop on two people falling in love and notice the non-verbal gestures that at different times both Celine and Jesse miss by looking the wrong way. Eugenie Brinkema calls this 'the spacing that is the measure of love' (2022, 328). In Linklater's trilogy, love occurs between characters and also in our love for the film.

I do not find this spacing in Allen's films, or if there is space for us to interpret gestures, it is always from the male character's perspective. There is hardly a single scene in which Annie does or says something that Alvy does not notice. For this reason, we are always more involved in what Alvy feels about Annie than what Annie feels about Alvy. We get one side of the story, not both.

Don't look back

Let me pursue this idea about looking a little further in relation to a scene from Linklater's 2014 film, *Boyhood*. It is probably the most dramatic scene in the entire film. The mother, played by Patricia Arquette, arrives to rescue her children, Mason and Samantha, from their alcoholic stepfather's house. Mason and Samantha both look back at crucial moments in the scene: Mason at his stepbrother and stepsister, presumably for the last time, Samantha at the house itself and all it has represented. Most films would allow its characters a longer look back. In Terrence Malick's *The Tree of Life* (2011), Malick allows the characters a long farewell when they leave their childhood home behind. Peculiarly, the house returns their gaze, as if it, too, were a character in the film. Olivia (Mason and Samantha's mother) prevents any kind of formal goodbye. 'Don't look back', she tells them, breaking her own advice to look back one last time herself before returning to focus on the road ahead. This is clearly a significant moment in the characters' lives – for Olivia, it represents a second marriage breaking down, for her children, yet another uprooting – but what interests me here is its significance for cinema history and its break with making moments like this one melodramatic. Linklater places his faith in a relatively new form of storytelling for fictional cinema, what I am going to call, borrowing the title of Sarah Manguso's book, ongoingness.

Manguso explores this idea in a non-fiction book called *Ongoingness: The End of a Diary* (2015), in which she reflects on different forms of record keeping through her own decision to keep a diary for the last twenty-five years. Interestingly, Manguso does not include a single diary entry in the book. 'I decided', she writes, 'that the only way to represent the diary in this book would be either to include the entire thing untouched – which would have required an additional eight thousand pages – or to include none of it' (94). The book is less about her individual diary, then, and more about what we choose to remember and whether forgetting might be a more healthy way to live. Manguso is particularly compelling on our attraction to the idea of life as a series of vivid moments. 'I tried to record each moment', she admits, 'but time isn't made of moments; it contains moments. There is more to it than moments' (5). 'I started keeping a diary in earnest', she explains, 'when I started finding myself in moments that were too full' (11):

> At an art opening in the late eighties, I held a plastic cup of wine and stood in front of a painting next to a friend I loved. It was all too much. I stayed partly contained in the moment until that night, when I wrote down everything that had happened and everything I remembered thinking while it had happened and everything I thought while recording what I remembered had happened.
>
> (11)

The problem is not 'today', she suggests, 'it's tomorrow. I'd be able to recover from today if it weren't for tomorrow. There should be extra days, buffer days, between the real days' (11). Manguso's solution to this dilemma is not to abandon diary writing but to abandon the notion that we can contain time in writing. 'Perhaps all anxiety might derive from a fixation on moments', she concludes, 'an inability to accept life as ongoing' (79).

Ongoingness allows her to 'contemplate time as that very time, that very subject of one's contemplation, disappears' (72). It is a form of radical forgetting. This is not necessarily sad, at least in Manguso's version of events:

> The best thing about time passing is the privilege of running out of it, of watching the wave of mortality break over me and everyone I know. No more time, no more potential. The privilege of ruling things out. Finishing. Knowing I'm finished. And knowing time will go on without me. [...] I came to understand that the forgotten moments are the price of continued participation in life, a force indifferent to time.
>
> (83, 85)

There is much to absorb here, not least Manguso's belief that remembering may not necessarily be good for us, that we need to structure our lives not in relation to what has come before or what might happen tomorrow but what is happening now, here. How, she asks, do we 'inhabit time' in a way that is not 'a character flaw'? 'Remember the lessons of the past. Imagine the possibilities of the future. And attend to the present, the only part of time that doesn't require the use of memory' (27). *Boyhood* was twelve years in the making. Linklater cast four actors in the role of a family, gathering them together each year to continue the story. This is, of course, not the first time he had observed the effect of a relationship over time. *Before Sunrise*, *Before Sunset* and *Before Midnight* were filmed over the course of eighteen years with a nine-year gap between each film. If Linklater continues the story, we are overdue a fourth film. There are significant ellipses both in each film and between films. In *Before Sunrise*, Linklater chooses not to include the sex scene the film has been building towards up to this point. Between *Before Sunrise* and *Before Sunset*, Jesse becomes a father and finishes his first novel. Between *Before Sunset* and *Before Midnight*, Celine and Jesse have finally become a couple and had children. As Manguso advises, the characters in these films certainly 'attend to the present'. Dead time is not edited out, nor are awkward silences. Time, in other words, 'isn't made of moments; it contains moments'.

This is even clearer in *Boyhood*. As Linklater explains, he wanted the film to seem 'like the memory of a young life, just rolling through time':

> So a movie of memories, but which ones exactly? With such a vast twelve-year canvas spread out before us, the question was what exactly to fill it with. There could be all the big events and 'firsts' of a maturing person, but why were so many of those moments for me now residing in some dusty file with a label reading 'yes, I remember, but kind of boring and not very original.' And why were so many random, seemingly inconsequential moments having such extended long runs in my memory? Why could I still feel and see certain things from several decades before as if they were ever-present? The looks on people's faces, the conversations, the exact lighting, tone, and energy of a day.
>
> (2014, 8)

It is difficult to explain the cumulative emotional effect of the film on the viewer. Isn't it just a relatively simple presentation of moments, one after the other? As Linklater points out, none of them is particularly memorable in the traditional sense. There are few if any 'big events' or 'firsts'. Indeed, for the majority of the film they are the type of moments we probably want to forget or are surprised that we remember. As Manguso admits with a degree of frustration: 'I can't seem to forget what I want to forget' (2015, 32). This is also the case with Mason, whose most vivid memories are not necessarily those moments in which he or his family are close or particularly happy. Indeed, many of the scenes we remember most depict arguments and breakdowns of one variety or another: Mason and his sister Samantha quarrelling in the car, the mother's rescue of her two children from the house of their drunken stepfather already mentioned, Mason's break-up with his high school sweetheart. If Mason is haunted by any of these experiences, he does not let on. He appears, like Manguso, 'to accept life as ongoing'.

One of my favourite sequences in the film occurs approximately halfway in when, after yet another house move, Mason is befriended by a girl from school. The sequence is in three parts: Mason being briefly roughed up in the toilet, his long walk home with a girl he does not appear to know very well, and his arrival at the end of his mother's psychology class where she has been discussing John Bowlby's attachment theory. In nearly every coming-of-age film I can think of the first scene would have some kind of echo or follow-up later on in the story, but not here. The two boys have no more than a small walk-on role. It is not that Mason shrugs off the bullies completely. He does remember the moment, after all. But in giving it so little screen time, Linklater suggests that it is just another part of the day, another part of growing up. The scene that follows is mostly a long single take of Mason and Jill walking and talking as they move down an alleyway, past various houses and parking lots. Mason is hoping to catch a lift home with his mother, and Jill is simply hanging out. They discuss books, his impressions of the city and whether he is going to a party later. Nothing really happens. The two teenagers are passing the time as teenagers everywhere pass the time. References to reading *Twilight* give it a specific timeframe, but this is not about late Noughties America so much as it about the beauty and strangeness of daily living, what Linklater calls the 'energy of a day', what Manguso calls 'ongoingness'.

I have seen *Boyhood* many times now, first at the cinema, several times at home. My love for it has if anything deepened. Perhaps *Boyhood* caught me at a vulnerable time when my own son was about to start primary school? Perhaps being a similar age to Ethan Hawke was like watching myself grow up? Peter Bradshaw, in his 2014 review for *The Guardian*, admitted to loving the film 'more than I can say. And there is hardly a better, or nobler thing a film can do than inspire love'. 'In some ways', he goes on,

> the movie invites us to see Mason from an estranged-dad's-eye-view, alert to sudden little changes and leaps in height. As an unestranged dad myself, I scrutinised Coltrane at the beginning of each scene, fascinated and weirdly anxious to see if and how he'd grown. But the point is that all parents are estranged, continually and suddenly waking up to how their children are growing, progressively assuming the separateness and privacy of adulthood.

If the film is, as Bradshaw observes, partly imagined from the father's mainly absent perspective, it is just as astute on the mother's mainly present perspective. The father's absence allows him to see Mason grow up, but the mother's closeness makes this almost impossible. This is why in one of the film's most shattering scenes, she finds his departure for college so emotionally shattering. 'I knew this day was coming', she says. 'I just didn't know you were going to be so fucking happy to be leaving.' (The film is not just about boyhood either. The story of Mason's sister, Samantha, played by Linklater's own daughter, Lorelei Linklater, is just as bewitching.)

Ongoingness is more than simply a formal decision to avoid flashback, though this is its most obvious feature. It is more than a love of long takes and tracking shots, though this, too, is something we note in all of Linklater's films. Rather it places the viewer with Celine and Jesse, or perhaps more accurately somewhere between them, in the privileged position of seeing two people fall in love or attempt to remain in love, as in the listening booth in the first film, or in the car journey from the airport in the third film. 'I like the idea', Linklater admitted, of being 'able to look at either Jesse or Celine – of not letting film syntax lead you toward either one of them' (qtd. in Horne 2013, 33). Allen's camera leads and points; Linklater's lingers.

'Don't look back.' Three words of advice that most of us fail to follow. Does a day or even an hour pass by when we are not looking back? At what we looked like last year. At what we thought or felt this morning. At who we loved when we were teenagers. At who loved us when we were children. To look back is to remember but also to mourn, for others and for our own younger selves or for the selves we might have been. These activities are part of being human, but perhaps there are implicit time limits on mourning that do not apply to remembering? John Donne's seventeenth-century poem 'A Valediction: forbidding Mourning' still feels relevant on this subject. Donne implores the reader to 'make no noise / No tear-floods, nor sigh-tempests move' (1990, 120). Emotion, or rather the signs of emotion, the 'tear-floods' and 'sigh-tempests', are strictly banned, not to be seen or heard in polite company. If this sounds like ancient history, the words of a seventeenth-century poet that have no place in our share-all-and-share-immediately twenty-first-century culture, we do not have to look very far to find contemporary reiterations of the same idea. That it is basically fine to mourn as long as you do not do it for too long or around too many people.

Time travel

Films, like people, are often anxious to return to the land of the living, to make new memories as opposed to reworking old ones. One of my favourite conclusions to any film is the ending of *Annie Hall* where after watching Alvy and Annie say goodbye from outside the café, we then go inside to watch them part for good. Allen keeps the intimate details of what we presume to be one of their last conversations private. We can only imagine what they are saying. He thus keeps nostalgia and sentimentality, particularly about romantic love, at arm's length. Note not just the glass screen that prevents us from listening in but also the stark window frame that separates Alvy on the left of the screen from Annie on the right. It is a two-shot that stresses division. Alvy has overcome his phobia of both flying and Los Angeles to attempt to win Annie back. When this fails, he rewrites the conclusion to his first play to perfect in art what he cannot get right in life. The film we are watching is another piece of art that Allen as opposed to Alvy perfects, but he perfects it by showing most Hollywood endings to be fake. Alvy and Annie are more than just friends, but they are no more than friends. The former couple remains uncoupled.

It would be easy to end here, contemplating Alvy and Annie in relative close-up, but Allen instead finishes on a New York street. In doing so, he places the spectator back in the café as if occupying the table Alvy and Annie have just vacated, too late to hear what they had to say. We are on the wrong side of the glass window, prevented from listening in. Instead, we watch Alvy and Annie go their separate ways once the flashing signal gives them permission to go. Don't walk. Walk. The decision to end on the street, on people carrying on their lives indifferent to Alvy and Annie's existence, is for me an important questioning of nostalgia, of dwelling on memories that are simply that, memories. Allen does not prevent us looking back on the film we have just seen – the flashback structure of the film is to some extent the very essence of nostalgia – but he does prevent us remaining there. It is odd to be sitting at Alvy and Annie's table at the end of the film. Revisiting old haunts from movies is what we tend to do after the film has finished, not in the very last frames of the film. The ending encapsulates the feeling we often have at the end of a film we have loved. Sitting in the dark, looking up at the screen, we do not want to leave yet. And so we sit through the credits until the film definitively concludes. Allen includes this dead time before the credits roll. It gives us time to adjust to time continuing, to the present beginning again.

Dead time is how most of us experience time. We have relatively few moments that we might describe as 'magical'. *Annie Hall* collects them, remembers them, but struggles to let them go. The ending of the film is the only time that Allen lets time pass without interrupting it, whether by breaking the fourth wall, splitting the screen in two, or turning the relationship between Alvy and Annie into a cartoon. Every character in *Annie Hall* exists in relation to Alvy. Even strangers on the street have an opinion on his affairs. This is partly true of Linklater's first film in the trilogy where nearly everybody Celine and Jesse meet is in a mood to help them, from the palm reader in the café to the barman who gifts them a free bottle of wine. Over the course of the trilogy, however, Linklater increasingly resists this temptation to see one's own life as any more representative or significant than anybody else's. As Celine and Jesse mature, Linklater's understanding of the genre of romantic comedy matures too.

'Think of this as time travel', Jesse says to Celine in the first film, a motif that is picked up on in all three films. Jesse, like Alvy, also has a problem distinguishing between 'fantasy and reality'. In the original script, his attempt to kiss Celine on the Ferris wheel borrows Alvy's similar argument in *Annie Hall*: 'I propose we jump in time to that moment when we would naturally do that, probably a couple of hours from now after a certain amount of awkwardness and stuff.' Celine, unlike Annie, resists this line: 'How come every time you want me to do something, you start talking about time.' It is a conversation they revisit in *Before Midnight* where Jesse apologizes to Celine by pretending to write her a letter from the future. In *Annie Hall*, characters *do* time travel, from Alvy's childhood classroom to Annie's high school dates. In the *Before* trilogy, time travel can only be imagined and talked about. The past cannot be revisited.

Both experiences of time are real, of course. We move, like Alvy, forwards and backwards continually in memory, but we are also stuck, like Celine and Jesse, in the bodies and lives we exist in from day to day.

Works cited

Allen, Woody and Marshall Brickman. 2000 (first published in 1982). *Annie Hall*. London: Faber and Faber.
Bradshaw, Peter. 2014. *'Boyhood'*, *The Guardian*, 10 July. https://www.theguardian.com/film/2014/jul/10/boyhood-review-richard-linklater-film
Brinkema, Eugenie. 2022. *Life-Destroying Diagrams*. Durham and London: Duke University Press.
Dargis, Manohla, A. O. Scott, Alicia DeSantis and Jennifer Daniel. 2014. 'The Woody Allen Genome', *The New York Times*, 5 January. https://www.nytimes.com/2014/01/05/movies/awardsseason/the-woody-allen-genome.html
Denby, David. 2013. 'Couples', *The New Yorker*, 20 May. https://www.newyorker.com/magazine/2013/05/27/couples-4
Donne, John. 1990. *John Donne: A Critical Edition of the Major Works*. Edited by John Carey. Oxford and New York: Oxford University Press.
Hirsch, Foster. 1981. *Love, Sex, Death and the Meaning of Life*. New York: McGraw.
Horne, Philip. 2013. 'Passing Through', *Sight & Sound*, July: 30–4.
Hutcheon, Linda. 2006. *A Theory of Adaptation*. New York: Routledge.
Knight, Christopher J. 2004. 'Woody Allen's *Annie Hall*: Galatea's Triumph Over Pygmalion', *Literature/Film Quarterly* 32 (3): 213–21.
Li, Yiyun. 2017. *Dear Friend, from My Life I Write to You in Your Life*. London: Hamish Hamilton.

Lim, Denis. 2017. 'Time Regained', in *The Before Trilogy*, 9–27. New York: Criterion Collection.

Linklater, Richard. 2014. 'Memories of the Present', in *Boyhood: Twelve Years on Film*, 8. Austin: University of Texas Press.

Manguso, Sarah. 2015. *Ongoingness: The End of a Diary*. Minneapolis: Graywolf Press.

Stone, Rob. 2013. *The Cinema of Richard Linklater: Walk, Don't Run*. London and New York: Wallflower Press.

Wood, Robin. 1998. *Sexual Politics and Narrative Film: Hollywood and Beyond*. New York: Columbia University Press.

Filmography

2 Days in New York. Film. Directed by Julie Delpy. USA: Magnolia Pictures, 2012.
2 Days in Paris. Film. Directed by Julie Delpy. USA: Samuel Goldwyn Film, 2007.
Annie Hall. Film. Directed by Woody Allen. Hollywood: United Artists, 1977.
Before Midnight. Film. Directed by Richard Linklater. USA: Sony Pictures Classics, 2013.
Before Sunrise. Film. Directed by Richard Linklater. USA: Columbia Pictures, 1995.
Before Sunset. Film. Directed by Richard Linklater. USA: Warner Bros, 2004.
Boyhood. Film. Directed by Richard Linklater. USA: IFC Films, 2014.
Gilmore Girls. TV series. Created by Amy Sherman-Palladino. USA. 2000–2007.
The Tree of Life. Film. Directed by Terrence Malick. USA: Twentieth Century Fox, 2011.
When Harry Met Sally. Film. Directed by Rob Reiner. USA: Columbia Pictures, 1989.

11

Dancing and falling: *Annie Hall*'s influence on *Frances Ha*

Jessica Hannington

Woody Allen's influence on Noah Baumbach and Greta Gerwig's film *Frances Ha* (2012) is clear from the very first shots. The New York streets are cast in nostalgic monochrome, recalling Allen's films *Manhattan* (1979) and *Celebrity* (1999), as best friends Frances (Greta Gerwig) and Sophie (Mickey Sumner) walk around the city. It is the influence of *Annie Hall* (1977) on the film, however, that is most keenly felt, especially in its exploration of a break-up. While in *Annie Hall* the break-up is between the romantic, heterosexual couple Annie (Diane Keaton) and Alvy (Woody Allen), *Frances Ha* explores the break-up of two platonic female friends. *Annie Hall*'s greatest influence on the film is thus paradoxically a point of deviation: *Frances Ha*'s focus on a break-up recalls *Annie Hall*, but the lack of a heterosexual love story in the film marks a split from Allen's work, which so often centres on these stories.

Frances's main concern is always Sophie, never romantic love with a man. In fact, the film begins with her breaking up with her boyfriend so she can carry on living with Sophie. But Sophie decides to move to Japan with her fiancé, leaving Frances angry, unmoored, bereft and longing for reconciliation. Consequently, Frances is forced to crash at friends' apartments, including rich-kid slackers Benji (Michael Zegen) and Lev (Adam Driver), both of whom show a romantic interest in her, an interest that she does not share. Frances has a brief visit to Paris and to her home in Sacramento for Christmas, all confirming her rootless state. Frances equally cannot quite succeed in her professional life as a dancer. Ultimately, this failure leads Frances to choreograph her own show, in essence writing her own work in an *Annie Hall*-like moment of talent realized. By the end of *Annie Hall*, Annie has embraced her creative talent as a singer, leaving behind Alvy and singing as an amateur in bars in New York. At the end of

Frances Ha, Frances, too, commits to her talent as a choreographer. Poignantly, Sophie attends the event. Their friendship has shifted dramatically, as Sophie now lives in Japan with her husband, but her presence at the show is the moment Frances has been dreaming of for the entire film. They smile at each other from across the room in a look that conveys affection, mutual understanding and the memory of their intimacy and devotion. They are remembering a time when their closeness was essential but are now content in their own space.

Failure defines Frances's most transformative and important actions. Instead of being a regressive phenomenon, failure prompts a movement towards creativity and independence. Thus, *Frances Ha* fails to repeat *Annie Hall* and is more subversive for it. This chapter argues that both Allen's influence on *Frances Ha* and the film's step away from his work are characterized by failure. I will look at the use of dancing and falling in *Frances Ha*, two acts that signal failure in the films in different ways. These acts will be analysed using dance theory which will be underpinned by Jack Halberstam's *The Queer Art of Failure* (2011). This will reveal failure to be a present theme in *Annie Hall* manifested most clearly in its exploration of a failed romantic relationship. But failure is also crucial in some of the most memorable scenes of the film, like Annie's bad driving, her playing tennis poorly and the couple's failed attempt at making a lobster dinner. These moments, not coincidentally, are remembered by Alvy at the end of the film, as failure is presented as something of a trademark for Annie. However, we must remember that the Annie we see in *Annie Hall* is the creation of Alvy's memories. Perhaps Annie's failures make her less intimidating to Alvy, and so he sabotages her through his memories, to render her safe, less threatening and ultimately able to be left behind. To Alvy, she is less appealing when she is successful at the end of the film, somehow disappointing him in her decision to leave New York.

Failure is a creative act that defines *Frances Ha*'s relationship with Allen's influence. Through the focus on Frances's heterosexual failure, the film dances and stumbles away from Allen's influence, creating a new space for itself among the plethora of films inspired by Allen, and one which has a decidedly less androcentric focus. For Halberstam, failure has always accompanied feminism, often a better option when 'feminine success is always measured by male standards, and gender failure is often being relieved of the pressure to measure up to patriarchal ideals', because 'not succeeding at womanhood can offer unexpected pleasures' (2011, 4). *Frances Ha*'s playful avoidance of masculine ideals, heteronormativity and a distinct focus on female friendship mark its deviation from Allen's cinema. All this springs from Frances's failures: her lack of heterosexual romantic success means that she can side-step the heteronormative storyline that she clearly does not want just as her career failures allow her to experiment creatively.

The female-focus in *Frances Ha* enables a more nuanced understanding of the character of Frances who, like Annie in *Annie Hall*, could be viewed as not taking her life or herself seriously. In forgetting some aspects of Allen's film, a new vantage point is established. After all, in *Annie Hall,* Annie is only ever shown through Alvy's eyes, and the male perspective inevitably conceals her. This is, after all, a man who is also trying to forget her. How can we trust the memories of somebody who is trying his best to move on from Annie and onto his next relationship?

Frances Ha's conscious forgetting of the masculine perspective of *Annie Hall* connects to Halberstam's argument that 'forgetting becomes a way of resisting the heroic and grand logics of recall and unleashes new forms of memory' (2011, 15). The act of forgetting is necessarily a resistance against traditional masculine ideas of hard evidence which has relegated spectrality and lost genealogies (2011, 12). These traditional ideas are, perhaps surprisingly, upheld by Alvy. In one scene in *Annie Hall,* Alvy seeks to quantify and qualify Annie's pleasure, insisting she give up the marijuana she likes to smoke before they have sex. For Alvy, Annie's pleasure cannot be taken as genuine, as he sees her induced state as a cheat and not an authentic reaction to her experience with him. But for Annie, pleasure is pleasure, and Alvy's reliance on evidence and fact eventually kills the pleasure they share.

Frances's career as a dancer is another way in which patriarchal norms are queried. Dance destabilizes Laura Mulvey's theory of the male gaze in so much as it complicates the apparent binary upon which the theory rests. According to Mulvey, woman 'stands in patriarchal culture as a signifier for the male other' (1999, 59). In doing so the woman 'always threatens to evoke the anxiety it originally signified', namely the threat of castration that is implied in the otherness of the woman (1999, 65). As Jessica Benjamin attests, Mulvey's theory proposed that to overcome this a woman's 'alien otherness is either assimilated or controlled, that her own subjectivity nowhere asserts itself in a way that could make his dependency upon her a conscious insult to his sense of freedom' (1986, 80). This is seen in *Annie Hall* via Alvy's visual control of Annie's image: Annie is only ever figured through Alvy's memory, as he controls and manipulates the image of her to rectify the threat she poses to his psyche after their break-up. As Mulvey's gaze theory suggests, the assimilation and control of the woman is manifested in a rendering of her as an image, a site upon which the man 'projects its fantasy onto the female figure' who are 'simultaneously looked at and displayed, with their appearance coded for strong visual and erotic impact so that they can be said to connote to-be-looked-at-ness' (1999, 65). Through the apparently unmovable binaries of gaze theory (male/female, object/subject), Mulvey's theory cements woman in a state of stasis: unable to progress politically, the spectatorship of women on screen is stuck in the unrelenting grasp of male desire. Through Alvy's memories, Annie is similarly locked in the male protagonist's perspective – that is, until Alvy works through his break-up by investigating these memories, allowing Annie finally to walk away.

Mulvey's gaze theory has been frequently critiqued and revisited, including by Mulvey herself in 1987. She acknowledged that her initial theory of the gaze 'hinders the possibility of change and remains caught ultimately within its own dualistic terms', a restriction that is particularly problematic for a theory centred on the repositioning and progression of feminist thinking (1987, 6). For Ann Daly, another troubling problem is the type of analyses Mulvey's theory inspired. Daly notes the 'then flourishing "success-or-failure" brand of feminist criticism, whose brittle, reductive analyses were not only unconvincing scholarship but problematic politics as well' (2000, 39). For Daly, Mulvey's theory precipitated a win-or-lose mentality when it came to female representation on film, and the inescapability of the gaze meant an inflexibility of the theory which only ever ended in failure. Mulvey's gaze theory therefore proved to be a site of contention, and its apparently rigid binaries and boundaries provided an irresistible temptation for some feminist theorists (such as those working on dance theory) to test, puncture and manipulate.

Daly is critical of the use of Mulvey's theory when it comes to dance (2002, 335). According to her, the theorizing of the male gaze as unmoveable leaves no room for the dance scholar and choreographer, as we expect them to 'topple a power structure that we have theorized as monolithic' (2002, 307). Mulvey's binaries position dance, therefore, in a realm of success or failure, trapped by the omnipresence of the patriarchy which is, by its definition, a loaded dice. Dance as a means of feminist expression can never succeed in overcoming these odds and is therefore always destined to fail. Some dance theorists have challenged this binary, aiming to find a breathing space between such extremes.

Carrie Lambert-Beatty suggests that Mulvey's gaze theory cannot work because dance ultimately does not subscribe to its notions of seeing: 'as a temporal art, disappearing even as it comes into being, dance resists vision' (2008, 1). The dancer, therefore, avoids the male gaze by resisting being captured in sight for too long, dancing around the scopophilic gaze that would render the dancer 'as bearer, not maker, of meaning' (2008, 59). Similarly, Adrienne L. McLean argues that the dancing body is a knowing party in the spectacle and therefore cannot be the body upon which the man projects his fantasy: 'A dancing body is not only the object of the gaze but also a subject who participates and presents chosen aspects of herself to that gaze, willingly and consciously' (2008, 16). Agency is therefore restored to the female figure through dance, something that is often theorized as impossible in Mulvey's gaze theory.

Sally Banes takes this argument a little further by positioning dance as an art that complicates the binary of man and woman, action and inaction, as 'the distinction between doing versus being looked at is a category error, since with dance doing and being the object of the gaze are not opposites' (2007, 327). For Banes, the dancing body is looked at precisely because it dances, and dances because it is being looked at. This different perspective on spectacle shows how dance can offer an imaginative and compelling way into the discussion of feminist film theory, stretching the binaries that can at times seem dishearteningly immoveable. Dance offers a playful and creative means by which to, if not completely avoid the male gaze, at the very least restore agency to the dancer, and therefore offer new ways of talking about feminist film theory. That being said, important work is being undertaken by queer and disabled scholarship, noting the inaccessibility of some forms of dance and the way it is spoken of as the key to female representation on screen (Whatley, Kafer). While many disabled people do dance, there are many architectural and sociological barriers to this form of expression that able-bodied people do not face (Whatley 2007, 5). It is impossible for dance theory, therefore, to hold the key to all female representation on screen. However, the focus on dancing in *Frances Ha* offers one way rather than *the* way of expressing female desire that is neither shackled to traditional patriarchal norms nor Mulvey's theory of the gaze.

In one scene, Baumbach employs a long shot that displays Frances's entire form as she dances, framed by the angular architecture of the dance studio and the intersecting straight lines of the dancing bar (Figure 11.1). Frances's body echoes the straightness of the mise en scène, as her extended arms and stretched legs transform her shape into angles, points, and edges. Her angles, however, are not perpendicular like the architecture that surrounds her, and, while they are an aspect of the beauty of the composition on screen, she is clearly separate, distinctly a moving body, a combination of straightness and bends. As she spins,

Figure 11.1 In the dance studio: *Frances Ha* (2012).

she critiques herself in the mirror and adjusts her form, and in doing so, Frances retains her look and her vision that exerts power over the body: we are simply witnessing it. We see the transformative power of looking when it is held by the subject as well as the object, as Frances can adjust her body to how she wants it to be viewed. It is not the gaze that transforms Frances into art, but rather Frances's art that is transformed by her own gaze.

Even though Annie is always seen through Alvy's point of view in *Annie Hall*, there are moments when Annie, too, retains (or perhaps regains) the gaze that holds power in the film. Annie's photography enables her to capture moments in time as she sees them, moments that hold significance for her, and memories that are outside of Alvy's control. The lobster scene is remembered by Alvy through a combination of flashback and re-enactment with another date. Annie, however, remembers through photography. Like Frances, who uses her own gaze to transform her art, so Annie uses her look through the camera to transform memories into art, and in turn, breaks through Alvy's one-sided version of the events of their relationship. We can glimpse Annie's gaze in *Annie Hall* if we look hard enough.

Throughout Frances's self-critiquing process, she learns from her actions, changing and evolving. She must remember where she has been in order to develop. Lambert-Beatty considers memory to play an important role in dance spectatorship itself: 'All dance spectatorship relies on memory' (2008, 53). Dance relies on the spectator's ability to 'hold the just-past in mind long enough to make connections across the ephemeral art form's temporal unfurling' (Lambert-Beatty 2008, 56). Remembering is therefore pivotal in both the theory and the praxis of dance.

In another scene, Frances attends dance class, copying the movements of her dance teacher. She is clearly struggling to keep up. Frances's identity as the perpetual understudy is marked both by her position behind Rachel and her partner-less state. While Rachel practices with her male dance partner, Frances is forced to imagine the male presence. We are reminded of Frances's lack of interest in men as she dances by herself with her eyes fixed on her female teacher who is the guiding, nurturing presence that offers so much more. In the close-up shot, Baumbach prioritizes Frances's face and facial gestures over her dancing body. In the scene, dance is presented as being about more than the body. It is through Frances's grimaces, exasperated puffed out cheeks and intense, concentrated stare that we understand Frances to be trying hard, but not quite getting it. Her failure is cemented with her dance teacher's words – 'Understudies out!' – and Frances's reluctant exit from the studio. Frances's inability to participate in the hetero-choreography is symbolic of her being a perpetual understudy of accessible femininity.

Instead of making Frances 'fit', the film never punishes Frances's metaphorical wrong turns. Her lack of romantic and professional linearity is mirrored in Frances's movements across the city, which are sometimes aimless, sometimes disobedient and sometimes just fun. The subway becomes a make-shift toilet as Frances publicly urinates on the subway tracks, and the streets where people walk to work becomes Sophie and Frances's stage and playground. In failing to abide by the rules of the city, new possibilities are created. These city-based disobediences recall Michel de Certeau, who outlines the 'multiform, resistance, tricky and stubborn procedures that elude discipline', acts which promote transgression from commonly assumed rules of everyday life (1988, 96). The city is the place where the masses are expected to operate according to established rules and norms but where, in fact, the individual wanderers make decisions that rupture these supposed boundaries.

More recently, Lauren Elkin focuses on the female flâneur (here named the flâneuse), explaining that she engages with the city in a very different way from her male counterpart. For Elkin, 'Space is not neutral. Space is a feminist issue. The space we occupy – here, in the city, we city dwellers – is constantly remade and unmade, constructed and wondered at' (2016, 11). One way that the space can be made and unmade is through this walking figure, through the paths she chooses (or doesn't choose) to walk on. The flâneuse doesn't always take the path laid out for her, but sometimes explores outside its well-worn edges. The pleasures and creative potential of getting lost and taking the long way around is also supported by *Frances Ha*. Alternatives are generated constantly by the city wanderer as she navigates her way by ignoring maps and signs, just as Frances's often aimless meanderings around the city, as in many of Allen's films, are a moment of pleasure for both the character and the audience. Allen's urban films include scenes where characters walk and talk as they make their way along the streets. Many of the dates depicted feature a walk in the city, for example after Annie's first performance in *Annie Hall*, or Mary and Isaac's iconic streetlamp-lit walk in *Manhattan*. The result is to weave the narrative of the characters into the city space itself, to complicate the relationship between the residents, visitors or inhibitors of the city and the space in which they wander.

In *Frances Ha*, these steps contain memorable falls. Frances's falls and silent movie-esque vignettes draw a comparison between Charlie Chaplin and Frances. This influence is made through a detour via Allen and *Annie Hall*. Annie's costume imitates Chaplin's Little Tramp, a costume that is recalled in Frances's somewhat shabby shirts and oversized layers of clothing. Of course, many critics have noted the influence of Chaplin on Allen's cinema, so much so that it is now a commonly held understanding of his oeuvre that Chaplin's presence (alongside Buster Keaton and the Marx Brothers) is felt in his silent movie-like comedic sequences (see *Sleeper* (1973) and *Love and Death* (1975) for example), and that Allen is a sort of urban successor of Chaplin (Fox 1996, 11). Chaplin's clownishness chimes with many of Allen's characters. This is illuminated by Dymphna Callery's words on failure as the marker a truly great clown:

> The art of clowning is to realise that the vulnerability of the clown is what draws the audience. The clown wants to please, but rather than getting things right, gets them wrong. However, the clown tries very hard and very seriously to get things right, as Laurel and Hardy, and Charlie Chaplin demonstrate. It is the clown's failure, despite hard work, which seduces the audience into laughter.
>
> (2001, 109)

This is certainly true of Annie for a time, as she tries hard to impress both Alvy and her audiences when singing. Alvy, however, becomes the more clownish figure when he attempts to get Annie back, desperately trying to do the right thing and failing: his attempts to drive to her are disastrous, and the resultant encounter with the police sees him behave so nervously and clownishly he is put behind bars. The art of clowning is therefore an expression of failure, and one of the characteristic tricks up the clown's sleeve is surely the fall, a physical expression of failure, and something that became ubiquitous in Chaplin's routines. But according to Alison Kafer, to fall as a disabled person is to fulfil a societal norm: it 'lives up to expectations about what disability does', even as it 'fails expectations about what the body does' (2013, 36). For Kafer, 'failure and success thus coincide in the moment of falling' (2013, 36). Here, the apparent rigidity of the success and failure binary of falling and not falling is complicated, exposing the mutability of the action.

It is true that falling has had something of a bad reputation, synonymous with a loss of control and a stumble in moving forward. Friends fall out, and one falls sick. Success and pride come before the fall, as does a fall from grace. Those that are lost fall through the cracks or fall behind. But falling also evokes ideas of liberation, of letting go. We fall in love, fall for someone, fall asleep. For Frances, falling proves to be something other than a failure to remain upright. She stumbles on to the road less travelled and pursues different professional fulfilments. She fumbles in heteronormative relationships, instead focusing on her more nourishing love for Sophie. And Alvy fails to see Annie for what she is all along, a brilliantly talented photographer and singer. Allen, at least, does not fail to see this, and *Annie Hall* is in many ways a celebration of Keaton-as-Annie's talents as comedian, singer, photographer and actor.

At the end of the film, Frances's choreography reflects this relationship with falling. The piece begins with two dancers meeting in an embrace, only for them to separate and the attention to be focused on another set of dancers, of which there are three. The duo has now become a trio, reminiscent of the addition of Sophie's fiancé Patch (Patrick Heusinger) to Sophie and Frances's partnership. The next movement involves a collision, an almost-wrestle, between a pair of dancers, representing the violence of Sophie and Frances's break-up (and at the same time remembering the play fighting that is a motif of their relationship in the film). Frances's romantic failures are shown when a dancer walks towards the sole male dancer in the troupe, only to turn abruptly to walk in the opposite direction. Not only does the dancing remember Frances's failures but the very movements of the dancers embody and physicalize failure. The playful and surprising nature of Frances's choreography comes from the fact that at any moment a dancer could end up on the ground.

Frances's choreography at the end of the film reflects Alvy's play at the end of *Annie Hall*: both detail the protagonists' failures and mark the point that both are ready to move on and embrace a new type of art. Frances moves away from Sophie and into the world of choreography, and Alvy lets Annie go through remembering his relationship failure, embracing theatre as a new artform. The multiple endings of *Annie Hall* are also implied in the conclusion to *Frances Ha*. Annie and Alvy's final break-up in Los Angeles, Alvy's montage sequence, his play and finally their chance meeting in New York, all move towards without reaching a definitive conclusion of the film, suggesting that they may well meet again, or that at least love stories like theirs will continue in the memory of both participants (as well as its audience). In *Frances Ha*, the dance mirrors the events of the film, but its ending does not mark the film's conclusion. The film continues, with *Frances Ha*'s final image being her name written on a post box. Even though the previous shot saw Frances spreading her arms in a new apartment with her own space, her name, Frances Halliday, doesn't quite fit, and instead only 'Frances Ha' is visible, referring to the opening credits. The implication is that Frances, like Alvy, will repeat some of these same failures. Just as Alvy will continue to search for romantic love (he needs the eggs), so Frances will continue to not quite fit in, to trip and to stumble in her effort to do so. And, of course, the name that connects the 'Ha' to the 'Halliday' is arguably 'Hall', once again invoking Annie, in both the eponymous title of the films and their protagonists.

The subversive power of falling is shown in one scene where Frances trips over while on a date with Lev. The fall is a manifestation of Frances's failure to conform to the smooth, massive force of heteronormativity, and thus acts as a bug in the system of heterosexual progression. As Halberstam attests, failure is an act which privileges the voices of women and queer people and 'can be a useful tool for jamming the smooth operations of the normal and the ordinary' (2011, 12). Frances's forgetfulness jars the mechanics of patriarchal trajectories in *Frances Ha*, specifically the unspoken and gendered rituals of heterosexuality. After receiving a tax rebate, Frances takes Lev out for dinner. Frances's disorganization means that her card is declined, and she runs to the nearest ATM. The tracking shot follows her in a mid-shot as she darts down the street, but she trips and falls on the ground. Despite her heroic attempts to carry on as normal, the smoothness of Lev and Frances's interaction is shattered upon her return to the restaurant, symbolized by her bleeding arm. The presence of blood deters Lev from pursuing her as a viable love object.

Lev's repulsion at the sight of Frances's blood taps into long-held misogynistic notions of menstruation and heterosexuality, and of the disruptive presence of menstrual blood in relation to sex. This is based on historical, religious and scientific texts that have peddled the notion of menstrual blood as contaminating. Religious writings during the Middle Ages decried intercourse during menstruation as both immoral and a potential health risk for men (Freidenfelds 2009, 27). By the twentieth century, while some of these concerns were allayed and rejected scientifically, many of these notions remained. Sex education literature still cautioned against sex during menstruation, specifically due to its believed risk to sexual health, as the likelihood of the transmission of sexually spread diseases was believed to be linked to the proximity to menstrual blood (Freidenfelds 2009, 28).

The power of this blood in a patriarchal world does, however, offer some opportunities for those who bleed. In keeping with the spirit of this chapter, the ostensible failure to understand menstruation creates a space through which opportunistic people who menstruate can grasp control. Male revulsion at the sight of menstrual blood allows an abstinence from sex that is unquestioned, something that can be a useful tool for some parties (Freidenfelds 2009, 29). For Frances, the presence of blood is useful during her meeting with Lev, as his repulsion consequently curbs his advances for a time. Frances's awkwardness back at Lev's flat continues their bumpy interaction, a potholed version of the heterosexual story Lev is trying to engineer. The pair stand in a two-shot in front of a wall of framed photographs that Lev reveals are not of his family or even people he knows (Figure 11.2).

Chosen for their aesthetic values, they promote the heteronormativity of the conventional family. In between the pair, a photograph of a man, woman and child looms, a visual reminder of heteronormative time and the pressure and expectation of a fulfilment of this narrative. In the scene, Frances holds a camera, at once recalling Annie's love for photography in *Annie Hall* and acting as a barrier between herself and Lev.

The camera Frances holds is a tool for surveillance and recording. When Lev places his arm on Frances's shoulder, she jerks it upwards mechanically, letting out a squeak of awkwardness and discomfort. This movement is a reminder of her position as a stick in the mud, a bug in the system that halts the progression of heteronormative romance. Lev removes his hand, and the pair remain friends. The mise en scène in this scene is a persistent reminder of the rupture of time: the photographs that form the backdrop of the shot recall Annie's house in

Figure 11.2 Lev's photographic studio.

Annie Hall and the photographs of her brother Dwayne, other family members and, of course, Alvy with the lobsters (Figure 11.3). Annie's clothing is also recalled in Lev's as well as Frances's outfits. Lev's Jewishness recalls Allen too, especially in his attempted wooing of Frances, the Californian, the state where Annie finds temporary refuge.

The photographs also call attention to Baumbach's use of black and white, and recall Allen's own black-and-white films like *Manhattan* (1979) and *Celebrity*

Figure 11.3 Annie's lobster photos.

(1998) which depict the city in the nostalgic light of the Classical Hollywood era. As Leonard Quart writes of Allen's black-and-white films:

> These are contemporary, familiar New York images, shot in dazzling high contrast black and white rather than color, which Allen utilizes to project the city's continuity with, from his perspective, its more elegant and civilized past. These fabulistic images also act as a self-conscious reminder of the way many old Hollywood films once projected a portrait of a city that gleamed and soared.
> (2006, 17–18)

In many ways, *Frances Ha* is a film in conversation with the cinematic memories of its creators Baumbach and Gerwig, both Allen acolytes who, through their remembering of him, tap into the wider cinematic memory of Allen himself, too.

This repetition of Allen's world, however, comes with dangers. Frances's privilege as a white middle-class woman, like Annie, means that nothing ever truly feels risked in the film. Frances's economic and professional concerns are never critical. Even after losing her already paltry wage working as a dance apprentice, her devoted and distinctly middle-class family back in Sacramento act as a perpetual economic and emotional safety net. Class privilege is manifested as a safety net in *Annie Hall* too. In the scene where Annie moves in with Alvy, the pair begin to argue after Alvy suggests they keep Annie's apartment, just in case. For Annie, the suggestion is an example of Alvy not taking her seriously as a legitimate romantic partner, an exposure of Alvy's dismissal of her. For Alvy, the apartment acted as a 'free-floating life raft' that reminded them both that they weren't married. Alvy is so certain of the need for this safety net that he offers to pay for it, proposing to write it off as a tax deduction. As in *Frances Ha*, the presence of this safety net belies Alvy's economic privilege, something Allen cements in the next scene depicting Annie and Alvy's visit to his house in The Hamptons. The 'bad plumbing and bugs' become a hot pot of water and live lobsters. Perhaps this is made all the more clear from Annie's own specific class privilege as a WASP fully upper-middle-class person, in comparison to Alvy as a Jewish person who has worked to achieve economic privilege from his decidedly working-class background. The scene in which the couple's families sit side by side in a split-screen roast dinner highlights, among other things, the respective families' class and racial differences. Seemingly from a different time altogether (most likely Alvy's childhood), the Singers display their working-class, Jewish heritage, while the Halls, commented upon by Alvy, are figures of WASP privilege.

Frances Ha's focus on the experience of a middle-class woman is not itself concerning, but the film's notable lack of people of colour in such a racially diverse setting as New York City shows a compulsion to repeat the white middle-class New York featured in Allen's films. *Frances Ha* takes place in Allen's fantasy version of a white washed New York, a New York that is inherently nostalgic. Allen is not a filmmaker dedicated to presenting the realism of life in America, and his version of New York is a hermetically sealed world that ignores the racial tension and social sores of the city. The whiteness of Allen's New York has been picked up on by some Allen critics, including Renée R. Curry:

> Allen's eye dominates, and Allen's eye envisions whiteness. For this filmmaker, the grand schematic landscape of these cities is a white landscape that dominates, threatens, and ultimately obliterates any existence he deems not pertinent to his worldview.
>
> (2013, 291)

Of course, Allen's films are often concerned with antisemitism, a frequent source of comedy. In *Annie Hall*, Alvy is obsessed with antisemitism, and sees it everywhere. At the beginning of the film, Alvy is sure he heard someone refer to him as 'Jew', while Rob is sure he misheard, and he repeatedly drags Annie to see *The Sorrow and the Pity* (1969), a film about the Holocaust, even when she's had enough of watching films about Nazis. Allen's critical eye is present when discussing concerns of assimilation, tradition, theism and atheism within New York Jewish culture, but he overwhelmingly selects white actors to do it.

In remembering Allen's New York, *Frances Ha*'s version of the city is equally selective. There are only two people of colour in the entire film: Frances's friend from Sacramento, who remains silent, and a Black woman who shows Frances around a theatre and has one, very short, line. Their time on screen is less than ten seconds combined. Their presentation on screen is one of passivity and their presence only serves to highlight the ostentatious absence of non-white people in the film. As bell hooks writes, 'If the many non-black people who produce images or critical narratives about blackness and black people do not interrogate their perspective, then they may simply recreate the imperial gaze – the look that seeks to dominate, subjugate, and colonize' (2015, 7). Baumbach and Gerwig's version of the city repeats Allen's depiction of New York. It is a nostalgic memory of a nostalgic memory, resulting in a crystallization of the city as middle class and distinctly white. The repetition of Allen's portrayal of a largely white New

York shows the shortcomings of its progression from Allen's cinema, including those elements that are more than a little troubling.

The repetition of Allen's New York in *Frances Ha* is made ostentatious through an explicit reworking of an iconic scene from *Manhattan*, where Isaac (Woody Allen) runs to meet Tracy (Mariel Hemingway) before she leaves for London at the end of the film. Allen's scene is itself a reworking of Antoine's 'escape' at the end of *The 400 Blows* (*Les quatre cents coups*, 1959). While in Allen's film, the run is entirely filled with purpose and masculine drive to fulfil his Oedipal trajectory, namely the heterosexual romance that will stabilize the plot, Frances's run is empty of any real purpose, propelled by the fun and thrill of being in New York. This is a loving homage to Allen's cinema, but a defiant step away that separates itself from his work.

In *Manhattan*, Isaac runs from left to right, following the Western practice of reading in this direction, intimating the idea of progression. Isaac runs with his face set forward with complete purpose and determination. Unlike Frances, who twirls and dances through the streets, Isaac's steady pace expresses a certainty of intent rarely seen from such an indecisive character. The tracking shot in *Frances Ha* strains to retain her in the shot, often behind or in front of her (Figure 11.4). She is like Elkin's flâneuse who walks across the city for the sake of it, and not in any need to get somewhere. But the largely perpendicular-angled camera in *Manhattan* works with Isaac. The similarity but clear differences of these scenes show the deviation of *Frances Ha* from Allen. Frances darts around lampposts

Figure 11.4 Frances running home.

and pedestrians seemingly in a rush to get somewhere. But as the montage progresses, Frances begins to weave dancing into her movement. Smiling broadly, she twirls and leaps along the sidewalks, and it becomes clear that she runs for the fun of it. The next shots are of Frances returning home to her new flat with Benji and Lev, and of her asleep in bed. Frances's run through the streets is therefore revealed to be propelled by play rather than urgency. She acts, as Halberstam advocates, dancing down the road less travelled and disregarding the conventions of walking through the city.

Isaac's run towards Tracy in Manhattan reflects the so-called Oedipal trajectory, wherein the male child moves to complete his trajectory by identifying with the father and finding a woman representing his mother. According to Freud, the 'liberation of an individual, as he grows up, from the authority of his parents is one of the most necessary though one of the most painful results brought about by the course of his development' (1977, 221). The Oedipal complex is articulated in film through the male protagonist's overcoming of a crisis which usually culminates in a union with a woman who represents his stabilization. This trajectory is by its very nature a propulsion forward. Isaac's run from left to right echoes this motion, especially as his movement is directed towards Tracy, a symbol of safe femininity as opposed to the destabilizing figure of Mary (Diane Keaton). The obstacles Isaac needs to overcome are his problems with his ex-wife Jill (Meryl Streep), and crucially her lesbianism, which constantly threatens the heteronormative storyline, as well as his obsession with his age difference with Tracy, and his infatuation with Mary. All are overthrown by his reunion with Tracy at the end of the film, even if she does intend to leave New York for a while.

Frances is not motivated by such Oedipal notions. The small successes gained at the end of the film are all due to her rejection of straightforward progression, acceleration forward and conscious development. The digressions and detours from the social order that are mirrored in her run are never punished, and the stability she enjoys at the end of the film is made through these disobediences and not through a union with a man. Instead of the camera following her patiently as it does Isaac, Baumbach's style emphasizes Frances's nowhere-ness. As she runs into the space in front of her, the camera's position waits there in anticipation, meaning that she runs into a space always made ready for her by the film.

Disrupting our spatial notions, this places the audience in front of her, but distinctly unaware of the diegetic space that we enter. The implication is that Frances isn't carving out a space for herself but rather following a path already forged. Her way of walking that path, however, is distinctly her own. By using the same tools, similar images, themes and aesthetics from *Annie Hall*, *Frances Ha* always returns to Allen but uses those methods to arrive in a different way, be it dancing or falling. Through dance, Baumbach and Gerwig return to Allen's influence, playfully using it (like Frances's own choreography) as an inspiration for their own dance. The focus on failure demonstrates the necessary limits of influence, enabling Baumbach and Gerwig to forget the focus on heteronormative relationships and masculine memory that Allen favours in *Annie Hall*.

It is precisely this focus on failure that allows for a consciously playful handling of Allen's influence. At once paying homage to Allen's cinema, *Frances Ha* also darts away from this influence in its focus on decidedly female desires. In remembering elements of Allen's cinema, however, *Frances Ha* repeats the nostalgic depiction of the New York City of his films: Baumbach and Gerwig erase and forget the presence of people of colour once again. The film's relationship with Allen's influence is a dance characterized by careful, deliberate mirroring and playful leaping away on many (but not all) fronts, a tension that is reverential and deferential, but also mischievous and creative. Through its failing protagonist, *Frances Ha* remembers Allen, but moves away from him too.

Works cited

Banes, Sally. 2007. *Before, Between, and Beyond: Three Decades of Dance Writing*. Wisconsin, USA: University of Wisconsin Press.

Benjamin, Jessica. 1986. 'A Desire of One's Own: Psychoanalytic Feminism and Intersubjective Space', in *Feminist Studies/Critical Studies*, ed. Theresa de Lauretis, 78–101. Hampshire, UK: The Macmillan Press Ltd.

Callery, Dymphna. 2001. *Through the Body: A Practical Guide to Physical Theatre*. London, UK: Nick Hern Books.

Curry, Renée R. 2013. 'Woody Allen's Grand Scheme: The Whitening of Manhattan, London, and Barcelona', in *A Companion to Woody Allen*, ed. Peter J. Bailey and Sam B. Girgus, 277–93. West Sussex, UK: John Wiley & Sons, Inc.

Daly, Ann. 2000. 'Feminist Theory across the Millennial Divide', *Dance Research Journal* 32 (1): 39–42.

Daly, Ann. 2002. *Critical Gestures: Writings on Dance and Culture*. Connecticut, USA: Wesleyan University Press.

De Certeau, Michel. 1988. *The Practice of Everyday Life: Volume One*. London, UK: The University of California Press.

Elkin, Lauren. 2016. *Flâneause: Women Walk in the City in Paris, New York, Tokyo, Venice and London*. London, UK: Chatto & Windus.

Fox, Julian. 1996. *Woody: Movies from Manhattan*. New York, USA: The Overlook Press.

Freidenfelds, Laura. 2009. *The Modern Period: Menstruation in Twentieth-Century America*. Baltimore, USA: University of Pennsylvania Press.

Freud, Sigmund. 1977. *On Sexuality: Three Essays on the Theory of Sexuality and Other Works*. Middlesex, UK: Penguin Books.

Gilmore, David. 2001. *Misogyny: The Male Malady*. Philadelphia, USA: University of Pennsylvania Press.

Halberstam, Judith. 2011. *The Queer Art of Failure*. London, UK: Duke University Press.

hooks, bell. 2015. *Black Looks: Race and Representation*. New York, USA: Routledge.

Kafer, Alison. 2013. *Feminist, Queer, Crip*. Indiana, USA: Indiana University Press.

Lambert-Beatty, Carrie. 2008. *Being Watched: Yvonne Rainer and the 1960s*. Massachusetts, USA: Institute of Technology.

McClean, Adrienne L. 2008. *Dying Swans and Madmen: Ballet, the Body, and Narrative Cinema*. London, UK: Rutgers University Press.

Mulvey, Laura. 1987. 'Changes: Thoughts on Myth, Narrative and Historical Experience', *History Workshop Journal* 23 (1): 3–19.

Mulvey, Laura. 1999. 'Visual Pleasure and Narrative Cinema', in *Feminist Film Theory: A Reader*, ed. Sue Thornham, 58–69. Edinburgh, UK: Edinburgh University Press.

Parsons, Deborah L. 2000. *Streetwalking the Metropolis: Women, the City and Modernity*. Oxford, UK: Oxford University Press.

Quart, Leonard. 2006. 'Woody Allen's New York', in *The Films of Woody Allen: Critical Essays*, ed. Charles L. P. Silet, 13–20. Oxford, UK: Scarecrow Press, Inc.

Rosewarne, Lauren. 2012. *Periods in Pop Culture: Menstruation in Film and Television*. Plymouth, UK: Lexington Books.

Whatley, Sarah. 2007. 'Dance and Disability: The Dancer, the Viewer and the Presumption of Difference', *Dance Education* 8 (1): 5–25.

12

'The sadness of goodbye in a funny movie': Desiree Akhavan's *Appropriate Behavior* and the melancholic legacy of *Annie Hall* in contemporary US film and television break-up narratives

Hannah Hamad

Introduction

In her 2011 autobiography *Then Again*, Diane Keaton, who famously played the title character in *Annie Hall*, encapsulated what she saw as the core theme at the heart of the film: 'However bittersweet, the message was clear. Love fades' (Keaton 2011, 128). She acknowledges that Woody Allen had taken something of a risk in letting 'the audience feel the sadness of goodbye in a funny movie' (128). With these remarks, Keaton pinpoints the essence of *Annie Hall*, its status as melancholic rumination on the sad reality of faded love, and on the disintegration and demise of a once joyful romantic relationship. Indeed, as Wes Gehring writes, *Annie Hall* and the break-up it depicts between Annie and Alvy is 'a comically mundane litany of why most relationships fail' (2016, 171).

The last decade has seen a noticeable cluster of tonally and narratively cognate narratives of failed romance and relationship breakdowns/break-ups emerge in relationship comedy, drama and memoir narratives across the spectrum of American entertainment media, as well as elsewhere in popular culture at a more discursive level. Noteworthy examples of this include, but are not limited to, films such as *Eternal Sunshine of the Spotless Mind* (Michel Gondry, 2004), *Blue Valentine* (Derek Cianfrance, 2010), *Take This Waltz* (Sarah Polley, 2012), *Begin Again* (John Carney, 2013), *What If* (Michael Dowse, 2013), *How to Be Single* (Christian Ditter, 2016) and *Marriage Story* (Noah Baumbach, 2019). It can also be seen in television shows such as the Netflix series *Master of None* (2015–17) and select episodes of the Amazon Video anthology web series *Modern Love* (2019), as well as phenomena such as the entrance of the term 'conscious uncoupling' (Woodward Thomas 2015) into millennial pop culture parlance.

Part of this mid-2010s cluster, and arguably the epitomic and paradigmatic example of the legacy of *Annie Hall* in this respect, is Desiree Akhavan's *Appropriate Behavior* (2014), which adopts a non-linear flashback-oriented structure to chart the demise of the queer intercultural relationship between first-generation Iranian American Shirin (played in the film by Akhavan herself) and her white girlfriend Maxine (Rebecca Henderson). As Maria San Filippo has explored at length, the breakdown and eventual break-up of Shirin and Maxine's relationship is a 'fictional chronicle' of the breakdown and break-up of Akhavan's own relationship with her former partner, the filmmaker, writer and performer Ingrid Jungermann (2019, 991–1008). Comparisons to *Annie Hall* on these grounds and others formed a structuring discourse in how the film was received by industry critics and press reviewers, so much so that the film came to be known and referred to in critical circles as 'the gay *Annie Hall*' (Hair 2017; San Filippo 2019, 1007). Indeed, Akhavan herself has openly and explicitly characterized her film in exactly this way on numerous occasions. For example, as far back as 2012, in an interview with Nick Dawson for *Filmmaker* magazine, Akhavan made reference to a 'big-screen' project she was scripting at that time, explicitly calling it 'a gay *Annie Hall*' (Dawson 2012). Later, upon the film's general release, in a 2015 interview with comedian Scott Rogowsky for an episode of his live talk show *Running Late With Scott Rogowsky*, Akhavan responded to the host's invitation to provide a 'capsule synopsis' of her film with the candid description, again: 'It's a gay *Annie Hall*'. She goes on to nod in agreement with Rogowsky's follow-up description of it as 'A Persian *Annie Hall*'. Thus, a reading of *Appropriate Behavior* as a queer riposte to Allen's film is very easily opened up.

Appropriate Behavior's opening depicts a mournful-looking Shirin as she rides the New York City subway en route to move the paltry remainder of her property out of the Brooklyn apartment that she had formerly shared with Maxine. After a sombre and tense exchange by way of goodbye, the tone shifts to comedy at the conclusion of this sequence, as Shirin thinks better of her decision to toss her meagre collection of possessions into a dumpster and doubles back on herself to retrieve her discarded strap-on – originally gifted to Maxine, but now unceremoniously returned in an unnecessary act of comic but cruel pettiness. The film thus wears its queer credentials on its sleeve from the outset and declares its intention to temper the sadness of goodbye with bittersweet laughs and moments of tragicomedy in what unfolds to be a funny but melancholy rumination on Shirin's experience of mourning the end of her relationship with Maxine. This break-up leaves Shirin feeling lost and purposeless, and we spend much of the ensuing present-day scenes observing her attempts (hindered at first by her insistent attempts to reconcile with a manifestly unwilling Maxine) to move on with her life by forming a new flat share, getting a new job and, eventually, coming out to her family. Many of the ensuing scenes take place in intermittent flashback though, as the lifespan of Shirin and Maxine's relationship is related to us in vignettes that each offer different little insights into their relationship dynamic – how it formed, how it was cemented and how it withered and ultimately came apart. Much of what troubled their relationship, it is revealed over time, stems from Shirin's fearful unwillingness to come out as bisexual to her family and Maxine's impatience and inability to empathize with the cultural specificities attendant to Shirin's experience as a closeted queer first generation immigrant ethnic minority. In the film's final scene, Shirin makes eye contact with Maxine, standing on the platform as she talks on a mobile phone, from her seat in a moving subway car. Shirin raises her hand into a motionless wave and offers a small smile, both of which are eventually reciprocated, just in time for Shirin to see them before her train pulls away. In this way the film is bookended by encounters between the two of them at the beginning and end of Shirin's mourning of their lost love.

This chapter explores the influence of *Annie Hall*'s treatment of the ending and aftermath of (particularly queer intercultural) romantic relationships in contemporary US film and television, culminating in a comparative and contextual interrogation of Akhavan's *Appropriate Behaviour*, including quantitative and qualitative analysis of comparisons to *Annie Hall* made by reviewers during the film's critical reception. It also discusses how contemporary examples like this (and some others) push back against what has heretofore been the compulsory heteronormativity and universal whiteness of the *Annie Hall* break-up narrative paradigm.

Break-up narratives and failed romance in contemporary popular culture

As indicated above, *Appropriate Behavior* is one of the key centrepieces of a cluster of recent and current cultural texts that deal with discourses of modern romance, and which narrate, or otherwise ruminate, on experiences of mourning and melancholia that are attached to the breakdown and dissolution of failed or failing love relationships. Maria San Filippo observes the emergence of this trend in her remarkably astute take on the contemporary cultural discourse of 'uncoupling':

> In the last decade, amid the waning popularity of the neo-traditional rom-com[1] and the genre's migration away from Hollywood and into indie, international and online realms, rom-com revisionism has taken hold and with it an enlivening trend for uncoupling narratives.
>
> (San Filippo 2019, 993)

San Filippo points to the moderately successful mid-noughties American film *The Break-Up* (Peyton Reed, 2006), which narrates the breakdown and dissolution of the romantic relationship between characters played by Vince Vaughn and Jennifer Aniston, as a noteworthy early example of this trend to emerge out of Hollywood (2019, 993). While *Annie Hall* is undoubtedly the ur-text for this narrative paradigm in Anglophone cinema, San Filippo is right to single out *The Break-Up* as an early example of its appearance in the recent cluster. She then situates this 'originary film' (Klein 2011, 4) in relation to a number of subsequent films that likewise follow the pattern of narrating an 'uncoupling' process, including the American independent film *Breaking Upwards* (Zoe Lister-Jones and Daryl Wein, 2009), documentary feature *Flames* (Josephine Decker and Zefrey Throwell, 2017) and French film *In The Move For Love* (Romane Bohringer and Phillippe Rebbot, 2018) (2019, 993). She thus positions this thematic and narrative pattern towards break-ups and 'uncoupling', albeit implicitly, as constituting the emergence of a cycle; or, if not a full-blown 'film cycle' of the kind that scholars like Amanda Ann Klein (2011) and others have theorized and conceptualized, then certainly as a noteworthy cluster of narratively and thematically cognate films.

It is worth noting further that the named examples, with the exception of *The Break-Up*, have had relatively little reach or impact. Elsewhere in film, television and media culture, as highlighted above, there have been a whole slew of more mainstream and higher-profile examples that compound and cement San Filippo's observation of the emergence of this cultural trend. In film culture, for example, Derek Cianfrance's 2010 romantic drama *Blue Valentine* moves backwards and forwards in diegetic time (as do both *Annie Hall* and *Appropriate Behavior*) to narrate the formation, breakdown and ultimate dissolution of the romantic relationship, and then marriage, of the central couple Dean (Ryan Gosling) and Cindy (Michelle Williams). The following year, Sarah Polley's Canadian relationship drama *Take This Waltz* narrated the end of the marriage between Margot (Michelle Williams again) and Lou (Seth Rogen), after Margot begins to experience doubts about the solidity of their marriage and her satisfaction with the relationship, alongside a flirtation and ultimately a burgeoning romance with Daniel (Luke Kirby). In John Carney's 2013 film *Begin Again*, Keira Knightley plays Gretta, an undiscovered musician who must rebuild her life in New York City following her break-up with long-term boyfriend and musical collaborator Dave (Adam Levine). The same year, in Michael Dowse's Canadian film *What If* (aka *The F Word*), the young male protagonist Wallace (Daniel Radcliffe) is processing the double disappointment of a thwarted medical career and a failed love relationship when he begins to realize that he is falling in love with his best friend Chantry (Zoe Kazan) (this one is something of an outlier in that while it begins by privileging the mourning and melancholia that follows a painful break-up, it ends more traditionally with the formation of a new relationship). In 2016, Christian Ditter's *How to Be Single* (adapted from the novel of the same name by Liz Tucillo) resisted the narrative imperative of the 'neo-traditional rom-com' (San Filippo 2019, 993) to hetero-romantically partner the central female protagonist with a suitable man, enabling a narrative conclusion that sees Alice (Dakota Johnson) hiking the Grand Canyon solo, rather than partnered up with any of the romantic prospects the film had earlier placed in front of her. More recently, Noah Baumbach's emotionally charged 2019 family relationship drama *Marriage Story* charts the traumatic process of parenting through a painful divorce while the adult parties in the now divided family, Nicole (Scarlett Johansson) and Charlie (Adam Driver), attempt to manage their working lives at opposite ends of the country, in Los Angeles and New York, respectively.

Centring her discussion on Akhavan's post-*Appropriate Behavior* sit-com charting the aftermath of a break-up between Leila (Akhavan) and Sadie (Maxine Peake), *The Bisexual* (Channel 4/Hulu, 2018), San Filippo argues that television (especially 'Indie TV') is 'proving a more amenable incubator than Hollywood' for break-up narratives and discourses of failed romance and 'uncoupling' (2019, 1002). She does so on the grounds that it 'accommodates a greater degree of departure from the "positivity and palatability" ethos governing legacy television' (something that San Filippo views as particularly germane in the case of shows that depict queer relationships) (2019, 1002). In line with this then, the following television shows represent a range of relatively high-profile examples that likewise form part of this trend, albeit the relationships they depict are, for the most part, hetero ones.

The 2015 first season of the Aziz Ansari-fronted and scripted Netflix series *Master of None* melancholically charts the inception, formation, disintegration and end of a New York City intercultural romance between Ansari's Dev, a thirty-year-old first-generation Indian American, and his white (seemingly WASP) girlfriend Rachel (Noël Wells). The 2017 second season begins with a depiction of the period of mourning that Dev undergoes to get over the end of his relationship with Rachel, which he spends undertaking a pasta-making apprenticeship in a small shop in the town of Modena in Italy. Upon his return to New York, the show proceeds to chart Dev's misadventures in the world of online dating, the perils and pitfalls of which Ansari has written about at length in the book that emerged from his research collaboration with sociologist Eric Klinenberg on the vagaries of 'modern romance', and which was published in the same year that *Master of None* began streaming on Netflix (2015). It then proceeds to provide Dev with yet another failed romance narrative, this time with his friend Francesca (Alessandra Mastronardi), albeit one that ends ambiguously.[2] The two meet and befriend one another in Modena. Francesca is the granddaughter of the proprietor of the pasta shop to which he is apprenticed. Later in the series, Francesca, who is engaged to her childhood sweetheart Pino, visits Dev in New York, and as they spend more and more time together, his feelings for her become romantic, but she does not (or will not) reciprocate them. Dev eventually comes to the conclusion that Francesca has been using him as an escape from her stale, passionless and failing relationship with Pino.

The Amazon Video series *Modern Love*[3] is adapted from stories published in the long-running (since 2004) weekly column, and later podcast, of the same name in the *New York Times*. For the associated podcast, the stories are narrated by prominent actors and performers from US entertainment media, many of whom bring intertextual baggage to their readings from their appearances in other, and sometimes contemporaneous, failed romance and break-up narratives. For example, British actor Ruth Wilson, who is best known to Anglophone media audiences for her starring role in Golden Globe Award–winning Showtime series *The Affair* (2014–19), narrated the December 2019 episode 'Never Tell Our Business to Strangers'. *The Affair* begins by charting the relationship breakdowns of two married couples: Noah and Helen (Dominic West and Maura Tierney) and Alison and Cole (Ruth Wilson and Joshua Jackson), viewing them from the point of view of the love affair that ensues between Noah and Alison. This is offered up in the first instance as a result rather than the cause of the faded love that characterizes the relationship dynamics between the two married couples when we first meet them in the inaugural season.

There are two episodes of *Modern Love*'s inaugural season that stand out in particular for their narrativizations of failed romance and faded love: the second episode, 'When Cupid Is a Prying Journalist', and the fourth episode, 'Rallying to Keep the Game Alive'. In the former episode, Joshua (Dev Patel), a dating app entrepreneur, narrates the tragic story of his former love Emma – lost to him after he ends their relationship when she is unfaithful – to Julie (Catherine Keener), a journalist, who reciprocates by telling him her own tragic story of love in a time before smartphones, lost to circumstances unknown to her at the time, when her lover fails to arrive for a planned rendezvous, and she has no way of contacting him. In the latter episode, married couple and parents Sarah (Tina Fey) and Dennis (John Slattery) attend couples counselling, only to arrive at the conclusion that their relationship has failed, their love no longer exists and their marriage is over. In thus thematizing faded love and failed romance, these episodes can clearly be understood as cognate examples to the aforementioned entries in this patterned cluster. Equally noteworthy, however, is that both episodes ultimately adhere to the hetero-romantic imperative of mainstream romantic storytelling – repairing (and re-pairing) the broken bonds of their respective couples and revivifying their lost loves.

Contemporaneously, the mid-2010s also saw the emergence elsewhere in popular culture and media of the term 'conscious uncoupling'. This arose from the celebrity flashpoint that occurred around a public announcement made by film star Gwyneth Paltrow and rock star Chris Martin of the British band Coldplay. They were ending their romantic relationship, and were doing so performatively amicably. The entrance of this term into the pop-culture lexicon at that time was thus symptomatic of a cultural trend towards what San Filippo has described as 'the destigmatizing of the breakup' (2019, 992).

Critical reception of *Appropriate Behavior* – the 'gay *Annie Hall*'

Imagine, if you will, that Woody Allen, Jerry Seinfeld and Louis CK go together to create a love child who had Lena Dunham as a nanny, and who grew up to become a bisexual Iranian-American woman. Such a person, if they also happened to have become a filmmaker, would probably make something like *Appropriate Behavior*, the wonderful debut feature from writer-director-actor Desiree Akhavan.

(Bourne 2015)

This excerpt from a press review of *Appropriate Behavior* is typical of much about the way the film was talked about by cultural commentators upon its release, in the build-up to its release, and subsequently; it draws the reader's attention to the film's thematic concern with (and Akhavan's) queerness, intercultural identity and intercultural romantic relationships, non-white ethnicity, the influence on Akhavan of revered (albeit in two out of three of the named cases, reverence has turned to disgrace after sexual abuse allegations) white male forebears, a specifically named white female peer (Dunham in this case, although on other occasions the named female peer is Greta Gerwig) and the interaction of all of these things in the context of the film itself and Shirin's melancholic but humorous narrative of faded love and failed romance.

The critical reception of *Appropriate Behavior* was characterized by comparisons of the film to *Annie Hall* and comparisons of Akhavan to Allen.[4] Looking at the corpus of criticism in bald quantitative terms: of the fifty-seven reviews and articles under analysis, twenty-one (37 per cent) of them either make or invoke a straightforwardly direct comparison between *Appropriate Behavior* and *Annie Hall*, while a further four reviews/articles make or invoke a comparison between *Appropriate Behavior* and the cinema of Woody Allen more broadly. For example: 'her [Akhavan's] work also references Woody Allen' (Silvester 2015), the film unfolds 'with a whiff of Woody Allen' (Nixey 2015), and 'It's clear that this is a very personal work for Akhavan – she is Shirin, in the same way that Woody Allen's characters are proxies of himself' (Arnold 2015). Taken together these articles therefore represent 44 per cent – which is not a majority, but is nonetheless a very sizeable proportion – of the total number of reviews and articles included in the corpus.

The size of the proportion is noteworthy in itself, symptomatic as it is – irrespective of the undeniable extent to which *Appropriate Behavior* does indeed lend itself to formal and thematic comparison with *Annie Hall*, as any cursory textual reading would reveal – of the persistence of a problem often faced by women filmmakers. This is a problem whereby their work struggles to be seen or understood on its own terms, independently of comparison with a canonized male filmmaker (all the more noteworthy in this case given that the filmmaker in question is a queer, minority ethnic woman of colour). Akhavan herself is quoted in one of the articles from the corpus reflecting on this issue, albeit she limits the scope of her critique to gender:

> I don't see my male counterparts written about in the same way, as being the new Woody Allen, or the new Noah Baumbach, or Todd Solondz. I think the implication is that there is a limited amount of space for an intelligent, funny woman and right now it's *Lena Dunham*. But there is an infinite pool for men to play in.
>
> (Akhavan quoted in Aftab 2015)

For Akhavan, these comparisons play a part in diminishing the value of her work to film culture. She also positions this in relative terms alongside the way that the work of her male peers has been seen and treated (she is certainly correct that hers is far from the only work to emerge from recent American independent cinema that bears obvious comparison with Allen's). This, Akhavan indicates, is also relative to the way that Dunham was contemporaneously discussed by critics and commentators. Dunham, she suggests, has been singled out and held up as exceptional (for a woman), and that being the case, the work of Dunham's female peers, herself included, is devalued by default.

Continuing to examine this 44 per cent of reviews more qualitatively, a number of noteworthy recurring themes emerge concerning the nature of the comparisons being made, and on what grounds they are made. The thing that rises to discursive prominence above all others, across the surveyed comparisons, is the film's non-linear structure, encompassing the way that flashback is used to depict the coupling and uncoupling of the central duo of Shirin and Maxine in the case of *Appropriate Behavior* and Annie and Alvy in the case of *Annie Hall* (Figure 12.1). Eighteen reviews/articles (81 per cent of all those in the corpus that directly invoke a named comparison with *Annie Hall*) make the comparison by explicitly citing their structural similarity, with particular respect to the use of flashbacks, and the cutting back and forth between flashback and the present of the diegesis. In this way, *Appropriate Behavior* has, to cite just a few examples, 'episodic flashback overtones of *Annie Hall*' (Kermode 2015), is 'structured much like *Annie Hall*' (Barker 2014), and 'borrows the flashback structure of *Annie Hall*' (Kang 2015).[5]

Other points of comparison between the films that are made in the corpus include the city of New York as a setting for a melancholically romantic narrative (Kang 2015; Phelan 2015; Schwartz 2016), the 'bittersweet' tone of the two films (Kang 2015; Phelan 2015) and the obsessive tendencies that Alvy/Shirin respectively manifest in the form of things like 'neuroticism' and 'self-loathing'

Figure 12.1 In one of the many *Annie Hall*-esque flashback vignettes that structure the film's depiction of the doomed relationship of Shirin (Desiree Akhavan) and Maxine (Rebecca Henderson), Shirin's parents occupy the space between them in the frame, representing the barrier created by their ignorance of her bisexuality.

(Hassenger 2015; Hermsmeier 2015). Rarely are individual moments or scenes from either film pointed to as grounds for comparison, but one reviewer invokes what is arguably *Annie Hall*'s most famous scene in highlighting what he views as a divergence in the films' respective depictions of the pre-break-up relationships of the central couples as joyful (Alvy and Annie) versus joyless (Shirin and Maxine): 'Oh, for a lobster-wrangling scene!' (Goldstein 2015).

The next most prominent theme after structure that emerges from the critical discourse comparing the two films is, significantly for the purposes of this chapter, their shared status as films that are principally concerned with the loss of love and the aftermath of romantic relationships. It is more common, of course, in films that have been assigned to a 'rom com' genre classification, as both of these films, to different extents, have been, that it is the beginnings of love and the formation of romantic relationships that is most prominent in the storytelling.[6] For example, the grounds on which Sheila O'Malley offers up her observation that *Annie Hall* was 'a clear influence on "Appropriate Behavior"' is the core subject matter of 'lost love' (2015). Jesse Hassenger compares them on the grounds of their shared status as 'relationship post-mortem[s]' (2015), and Rachel Lubitz on the grounds that they each depict their central characters 'trying to get over the … breakup of a … relationship' (2015). Similarly, Chris O'Falt's comparison highlights the films' shared depiction of 'life after breaking up' (2014).

Several articles go to great lengths to emphasize that in making a comparison with *Annie Hall* they are not minimizing Akhavan's achievements as a filmmaker in her own right, or diminishing the sound of her own authorial voice. In these instances, the reviewers and critics point to divergences between Allen and Akhavan, things they see as individual to her, and to what they see as pathbreaking about her film or her as a filmmaker. In this way, Amanda Waltz writes that 'unlike Woody Allen, Akhavan has no desire to portray her protagonist as the neurotic, but well-meaning good guy. She writes Shirin as an amusing, but ultimately flawed character prone to delusion' (2015). In a similar vein, David Ehrlich states that 'For all of its matter-of-fact modesty [via, for example, textual nods to *Annie Hall*] ... *Appropriate Behavior* comes uniquely into its own as Shirin comes into hers. Akhavan does small wonders with the role she was born to play, and by the time her film gets to its note-perfect conclusion, it's clear that she's nothing less than a true original' (2015).

The remarks, in this regard, of critics like Leslie Coffin and Inkoo Kang further highlight some important aspects of what is ideologically at stake in how Akhavan's film's treatment of the core theme of lost love manifests differently from Allen's in *Annie Hall* (notwithstanding the extent to which Allen's film offers itself up as an intercultural romance due to the Jewish/WASP relationship dynamic between Alvy and Annie). As Kang notes, *Appropriate Behavior* echoes *Annie Hall* in some ways, 'but in service of a startlingly new love story that's ... queer and contemporary' (Kang 2015). And as Coffin writes, '*Appropriate Behavior* is admirable in that it takes elements of the *Annie Hall* genre of romantic comedy or break-up film, and uses them in relation to different ethnicities, genders, and relationships' (Coffin 2015). In this way, both Kang and Coffin signal, to different extents, that for all the obvious comparisons that there are to be made between the two films, one of the key things that sets *Appropriate Behavior* apart from *Annie Hall* is that the former is a queer film, depicting lost love between women in a queer relationship, and that Shirin's gender and sexuality (as well as those of Maxine) change the stakes of the intercultural nature of their relationship. The nature of these stakes manifests in different ways, but most vividly around Shirin's fearful reluctance to come out to her Iranian immigrant parents (as Shirin is at pains to remind Maxine when she gives her a hard time for having thus far remained closeted: Iran is a country in which 'you get stoned to death if you're convicted of being gay'). Hence, this strand of the critical discourse circulating around the release of *Appropriate Behavior* does noteworthy ideological work in communicating the extent to which Akhavan's film makes a needed and long overdue intervention in the status quo of the break-up sub-genre of relationship comedy/drama by depicting that queer minority ethnic women of colour can get their hearts broken too. In this way it pushes back against the compulsory heteronormativity and universal whiteness that has tended to characterize the *Annie Hall*-esque break-up narrative paradigm.

Conclusion

Thus, with *Appropriate Behavior* and its non-linear charting of the lifespan of the queer intercultural relationship between Shirin and Maxine, Akhavan too lets the audience feel 'the sadness of goodbye in a funny movie' (Figure 12.2). Long before audiences had Diane Keaton's words as a go-to for characterizing it, this basic principle was always key to *Annie Hall*'s appeal. In some ways the sadness of goodbye in *Annie Hall* remains as moving as it ever was. But in others it gets harder and harder over time to separate text from context. And in a film where the protagonist is such a clear avatar for the filmmaker himself, the possibility of empathy for Alvy has inevitably become complicated by Allen's extra-textual celebrity persona. And all the more so since the broadcast of the 2021 documentary mini-series *Allen v. Farrow* (HBO, 2021), which goes to lengths to trouble Allen's *onscreen* persona in addition to its more obvious confrontations of the well-known sexual abuse allegations made against the filmmaker.

Perhaps inescapably as a result of its intertextual relationship to *Annie Hall*, *Appropriate Behavior* has become a new touchstone for the sadness of goodbye in a funny movie. But irrespective of the extent to which Akhavan's work bears formal comparison to that of Woody Allen, which in the case of *Appropriate Behavior* it manifestly does, arguably it matters little who or what set the genre precedent for narrating a romantic break-up using a flashback structure. As a film that candidly articulates the graduated experience of a slowly unfolding heartbreak for a queer woman, in the sad aftermath of a failed relationship, with emotional honesty, quick wit, contextually specific humour and endearing flaws, *Appropriate Behavior* sets its own precedent. It is one of the most basic tenets of critical media and cultural studies understandings of the concept of representation that to exist in represented form is to have a form of social power. For queer women of colour in Anglophone nations to experience 'the sadness of goodbye in a funny movie' in anything more than the abstract has required the production of a film like *Appropriate Behavior*. But for all its welcome and

Figure 12.2 Shirin's riposte 'You're ruining my twenties' to Maxine's accusation 'You are ruining my birthday' is her final quip of their relationship before they agree to break up, and is illustrative of the film's depiction of 'the sadness of goodbye in a funny movie.'

worthy intersections and interventions, the extent to which it lends itself so readily to comparisons with *Annie Hall* shines a clear light on the felt need by both reviewers and the filmmaker herself ('It's a gay *Annie Hall*') to translate the queer and minority ethnic character experiences that define the film in ways that are legible, comprehensible and acceptable to white hetero-patriarchy and to masculinist film culture. Specifically, by emphasizing and insisting on (albeit easy) comparisons with the work of a white male auteur long established in the canon of American film history. Akhavan has of course been complicit at times in fostering these comparisons. But as a queer filmmaker operating at the margins of the mainstream for her debut feature, packaging her work in a normatively comprehensible way that presented itself as accessible to (white male) audiences and critics was also a strategy of survival. And especially so in the contexts of a film industry that routinely abuses women (Cobb and Horeck 2018) and a film culture that is rife with what Stefania Marghitu calls 'auteur apologism', which as, she explains it, constitutes arguments that advocate for 'the separation of the art from the artist, underpinned by the claim that a problematic identity is a prerequisite for creative genius' (2018, 491). The applicability of this phenomenon to Woody Allen and his work is noteworthy and striking, and unsurprisingly, Allen is one of the filmmakers specifically singled out by Marghitu as a decades-long beneficiary of such 'auteur apologism'. Debates continue to be heated about the persistence of discourses of 'auteur apologism' and the presence of misogyny (and misogynists) in the film canon (Harrison 2018). I do not advocate the erasure of anything or anyone from film history. I do think we should remember *Annie Hall*, but I also think we should move on from it. Feel the sadness of goodbye if we must. But there is a whole range of emotions to be experienced from engaging with the work of the countless relatively unsung women filmmakers to have been structurally disenfranchised from film industries and left behind by film history, which will allow us to do this, and so much more besides.

Notes

1. Shelley Cobb and Diane Negra correspondingly argue that output of Hollywood films in the so-called 'chick flick' genre has noticeably slowed since peaking in the 1990s (2017).
2. Interestingly, the 2017 second season of *Master of None* seems to textually and thematically anticipate what has quickly become an iconic moment in another narrative of failed romance, Luca Guadagnino's *Call Me By Your Name* (2017). In the same way that Guadagnino's film ends with a long protracted close-up lasting several minutes of Elio's (Timothée Chalamet) face as he experiences a spectrum of emotions, seemingly including mournful melancholia, following a telephone call with his lost love Oliver (Armie Hammer), so the *Master of None* episode 'The Dinner Party' ends in a similar way. As Francesca exits the taxi she has shared with Dev, the camera remains on him alone for several more minutes thereafter as it likewise records the range of emotions on his face as he contemplates her imminent departure from New York (and his life) and comes to terms with the feelings of romantic love that by this point he knows he has for her.
3. It is noteworthy that the creative lead on this television adaptation of *Modern Love* is John Carney, the filmmaker who directed the aforementioned *Begin Again*.
4. Sourcing reviews from online databases Movie Review Query Engine (MRQE) and NexisUK I conducted a basic content analysis to determine what proportion of the articles that comprised the corpus made direct nominal reference to *Annie Hall* as part of a review of *Appropriate Behavior* that was written and published either following a film festival screening, or upon its release in cinemas in 2014 and 2015 (depending on the country), or as part of a profile of Akhavan. MRQE was selected as the starting point for data gathering due to its (self-proclaimed) status as the largest online index of film reviews. However, this yielded only thirty English

language reviews of the film towards the corpus. Data gathered from MRQE was therefore supplemented by further reviews and point of release profiles sourced using the online news archive NexisUK. A search was conducted using the terms 'Appropriate Behavior' *and* 'Desiree Akhavan'. This search yielded a starting corpus of 637 articles, from which 27 were selected for inclusion in the final corpus of 57. Only articles for which full text access was available have been included in the corpus. In addition, reports concerning the film's production or distribution were eliminated from the NexisUK corpus, as were articles which make named reference to *Appropriate Behavior*, but which are more substantively concerned with Akhavan's subsequent output, such as her next film *The Miseducation of Cameron Post* (2018) and her sitcom *The Bisexual*. Reviews of 300 words or shorter were also excluded on the grounds that the principal function of pieces of this length is to provide bald synopsis making for minimal discussion and evaluation, and that there is thus little scope for the pieces in question to engage with the film's relationship to wider film culture, or for the authors to engage with the film's content beyond the succinct reiteration of details of the narrative premise and central characters. Teaser and listings articles were eliminated for similar reasons. Naturally, any reviews that had already been counted and included in the MRQE corpus were disregarded when dealing with the NexisUK corpus, so duplication of entries was avoided. As a result, most of the articles that comprise the final corpus constitute reviews of the film published following its January 2014 premiere at the Sundance Film Festival, those published upon its general release in cinemas later that year and upon its release on DVD and streaming services in 2015, and also promotional pieces and profiles of the filmmaker, generally from the same period (2014–16).

5   According to the critical discourse about *Appropriate Behavior* that comprises the sample, the film has 'episodic flashback overtones of *Annie Hall*' (Kermode 2015); it is 'structured much like *Annie Hall*' (Barker 2014); it 'borrows the flashback structure of *Annie Hall*' (Kang 2015); it is 'a kind of Iranian American-bisexual *Annie Hall* … as we see in a slew of non-linear flashbacks' (Goldstein 2015); it 'will certainly draw comparisons to *Annie Hall*' on account of its 'cuts back and forth between Shirin's present-day transition and key moments from her life with Maxine' (Waltz 2015); 'Shirin and Maxine's relationship is charted through flashbacks inserted between the present-day scenes, a structure borrowed from Woody Allen's *Annie Hall*, as Akhavan herself acknowledges' (Bourne 2015); 'The movie's fractured chronology is so evocative of *Annie Hall*' (Ehrlich 2015); 'The film flips between Shirin's present-day attempts to regain Maxine's affections, and flashbacks that illuminate key moments in their relationship … filching directly from *Annie Hall*' (Erbland 2015); the film 'owes' its 'structure … to *Annie Hall*'

(Hassenger 2015); 'No one has yet compared *Appropriate Behavior* with *Annie Hall* [a ridiculous claim: many critics had in fact already made this comparison, as had Akhavan herself], which, with its relationship-told-in-retrospect structure, clearly inspired Akhavan' (Freeman 2015); 'The flashbacks actually remind [one] of *Annie Hall*' (Hermsmeier 2015); the film has '*Annie Hall*-style flashbacks' (Lubitz 2015); 'The film in its current form is intricately structured with flashbacks, which was influenced by the structure of the classic New York rom com *Annie Hall*' (Walsh 2014); Akhavan is 'cleaving to the classic structure of *Annie Hall*' (The Scotsman 2015); it is 'cut together with flashbacks in the style of *Annie Hall*' (Kachka 2015); 'The film employs an *Annie Hall*-esque structure as it flashes back through the relationship' (Elphick 2015); '*Appropriate Behavior* is more Woody Allen than Lena Dunham [on account of its being] … structured like *Annie Hall*' (O'Falt 2014).

6   Film scholars working in the field of genre studies have long debated the genre status (or not) of *Annie Hall* as a romantic comedy, with others viewing it more contextually in relation to industry culture as part of a historically contingent cycle. I will not restage the debate here. For more on this see, for example, Krutnik (1990), Neale and Krutnik (1990), Neale (1992), Shumway (2003), Jeffers McDonald (2007), Grindon (2011), Gehring (2016) and Jermyn (2017).

Works cited

Aftab, Kaleem. 2015. 'New York State of Mind', *i*, 9 March.
Ansari, Aziz and Eric Klinenberg. 2015. *Modern Romance: An Investigation*. New York and London: Random House/Allen Lane.
Arnold, Brett. 2015. 'This Indie Comedy Is Everything HBO's Girls Wants to Be', *The Business Insider*, 26 January. https://advance.lexis.com/api/permalink/7b30a378-c698-48b5-8a1f-8089946bbd54/?context=1519360.
Barker, Andrew. 2014. 'Sundance Film Review: *Appropriate Behavior*', *Variety*, 18 January. https://variety.com/2014/film/reviews/sundance-film-review-appropriate-behavior-1201063854/.
Bourne, Christopher. 2015. 'Review: *Appropriate Behavior* Marks the Emergence of a Major Comedic Talent', *ScreenAnarchy*, 15 January. https://screenanarchy.com/2015/01/review-appropriate-behavior-marks-the-emergence-of-a-major-comedic-talent.html.
Cobb, Shelley and Diane Negra. 2017. '"I Hate to Be the Feminist Here … ": Reading the Post-Epitaph Chick Flick', *Continuum: Journal of Media & Cultural Studies* 31 (6): 757–76.
Cobb, Shelley and Tanya Horeck. 2018. 'Post Weinstein: Gendered Power and Harassment in the Media Industries', *Feminist Media Studies* 18 (3): 489–91.

Coffin, Leslie. 2015. 'Review: *Appropriate Behavior* Thinks It's Better Than It Actually Is', *The Mary Sue*, 22 January. https://advance.lexis.com/api/permalink/1d6c52a8-e30b-4634-8a69-0d6fcd5f3e53/?context=1519360.

Dawson, Nick. 2012. 'Desiree Akhavan and Ingrid Jungermann', *Filmmaker*. https://filmmakermagazine.com/people/desiree-akhavan-and-ingrid-jungermann/#.XjQH_cj7TIU.

Ehrlich, David. 2015. 'Review/*Little White Lies* Recommends: *Appropriate Behavior*', *Little White Lies*, 5 March. https://lwlies.com/reviews/appropriate-behaviour/.

Elphick, 2015. 'Desiree Akhavan: "I Don't See Bisexuality in Movies ... There's a Discomfort, It's Taboo"', *Yerepouni – Armenian Independent News*, 4 June. https://advance.lexis.com/api/permalink/fa67d4b8-78c1-4c04-a6cc-2db882cbc89d/?context=1519360.

Erbland, Kate. 2015. '*Appropriate Behavior*', *The Dissolve*, 13 January. http://thedissolve.com/reviews/1308-appropriate-behavior/.

'Film Review: *Appropriate Behavior*'. 2015. *The Scotsman*, 7 March. https://advance.lexis.com/api/permalink/68c1e733-5f87-4d75-9ddc-ee7620d18f4f/?context=1519360.

Freeman, Hadley. 2015. 'Desiree Akhavan on *Appropriate Behavior* and Not Being the 'Iranian bisexual Lena Dunham', *The Guardian*, 8 March.

Gehring, Wes. 2016. *Genre-Busting Dark Comedies of the 1970s: Twelve American Films*. Jefferson, North Carolina: McFarland.

Goldstein, Gary. 2015. 'Review: *Appropriate Behavior* an Uneven but Fun Dating Adventure', *Los Angeles Times*, 16 January. https://www.latimes.com/entertainment/movies/la-et-mn-appropriate-behavior-movie-review-20150116-story.html.

Grindon, Leger. 2011. *The Hollywood Romantic Comedy: Conventions, History, Controversies*. Oxford: Wiley-Blackwell.

Hair, Melissa. 2017. '"A Gay *Annie Hall*": Radical Romance and Bisexuality in *Appropriate Behavior*', Presented at Queer Screens, Northumbria University, 2–3 September.

Harrison, Rebecca. 2018. 'Fuck the Canon (Or, How Do You Solve a Problem Like Von Trier?): Teaching, Screening and Writing About Cinema in the Age of #MeToo', *MAI: Feminism & Visual Culture*, 9 November. https://maifeminism.com/fuck-the-canon-or-how-do-you-solve-a-problem-like-von-trier-teaching-screening-and-writing-about-cinema-in-the-age-of-metoo/

Hassenger, Jesse. 2015. '*Appropriate Behavior* Is a Flawed but Promising Debut from a new *Girls* Co-Star', *The AV Club*, 15 January. https://film.avclub.com/appropriate-behavior-is-a-flawed-but-promising-debut-fr-1798182408

Hermsmeier, Lukas. 2015. '*Annie Hall* in Schwul; Vielen gilt die Serie *Appropriate Behavior* von Desiree Akhavan als bisexuelle Antwort auf *Girls*. Sie vergleicht sich lieber mit Woody Allen', *Welt am Sonntag*, May 17. https://advance.lexis.com/api/permalink/6ed66829-c901-4da1-a9d6-c87f0818c386/?context=1519360.

Jeffers McDonald, Tamar. 2007. *Romantic Comedy: Boy Meets Girl Meets Genre*. London: Wallflower.
Jermyn, Deborah. 2017. *Nancy Meyers*. London and New York: Bloomsbury.
Kachka, Boris. 2015. '93 Minutes With … Desiree Akhavan', *New York Magazine*, 12 January.
Kang, Ingoo. 2015. '*Appropriate Behavior* Review: Desiree Akhavan's Hilarious ComedyHeralds an Essential New Voice', *The Wrap*, 14 January. https://www.thewrap.com/appropriate-behavior-review-desiree-akhavan-scott-adsit-girls/.
Keaton, Diane. 2011. *Then Again*. New York: Random House.
Kermode, Mark. 2015. '*Appropriate Behavior* Review: A Razor Sharp Bisexual Rom Com', *The Observer*, 8 March. https://www.theguardian.com/film/2015/mar/08/appropriate-behaviour-review-razor-sharp-rom-com-desiree-akhavan.
Klein, Amanda Ann. 2011. *American Film Cycles: Reframing Genres, Screening Social Problems, & Defining Subcultures*. Austin: University of Texas Press.
Krutnik, Frank. 1990. 'The Faint Aroma of Performing Seals: The Nervous Romance and the Comedy of the Sexes', *Velvet Light Trap* 26: 57–72.
Lubitz, Rachel. 2015. '*Appropriate Behavior*: An Outsider's Perspective on Life', *The Washington Post*, 17 January.
Marghitu, Stefania. 2018. '"It's Just Art": *Auteur* Apologism in the Post-Weinstein Era', *Feminist Media Studies* 18 (3): 491–4.
Neale, Steve. 1992. 'The Big Romance or Something Wild? Romantic Comedy Today', *Screen* 33 (3): 284–99.
Neale, Steve and Frank Krutnik. 1990. *Popular Film and Television Comedy*. London and New York.
Nixey, Catherine. 2015. 'If There's Anything I Can Do, It's a Good Sex Scene', *The Times*, 28 February.
O'Falt, Chris. 2014. 'Check Out the Trailer for Indie Spirit-Nominated *Appropriate Behavior*', *The Hollywood Reporter*, 8 December.
O'Malley, Sheila. 2015. '*Appropriate Behavior*', *RogerEbert.com*, 16 January. https://www.rogerebert.com/reviews/appropriate-behavior-2015.
Phelan, Laurence. 2015. 'Alice Would Be Less Without Moore', *The Independent*.
RunningLateShow. 2017. 'Desiree Akhavan's "Gay *Annie Hall*"' – Running Late with Scott Rogowsky', YouTube Video, 5:14, 15 February.
San Fillippo, Maria. 2019. 'Breaking Upwards: The Creative Uncoupling of Desiree Akhavan and Ingrid Jungermann', *Feminist Media Studies* 19 (7): 991–1008. https://doi.org/10.1080/14680777.2019.1667064.
Schwartz, Dennis. 2016. '*Appropriate Behavior*: Ms Akhavan Shows Promise as an Assured Director, a Talented Writer and an Interesting Actress', *Dennis Schwartz Movie Reviews*, 1 January. https://dennisschwartzreviews.com/appropriatebehavior/.
Shumway, David R. 2003. *Modern Love: Romance, Intimacy, and the Marriage Crisis*. New York: New York University Press.

Silvester, Christopher. 2015. 'I'm not the new Lena Dunham', *London Evening Standard*, 5 May.
Walsh, Katie. 2015. 'Exclusive: Clip from Sundance film *Appropriate Behavior*', *IndieWire*, 15 January.
Waltz, Amanda. 2015. 'Review: *Appropriate Behavior*', *The Film Stage*, 16 January. https://thefilmstage.com/review-appropriate-behavior/.
Woodward Thomas, Katherine. 2015. *Conscious Uncoupling – 5 Steps to Living Happily Even After: How to Break Up in a Whole New Way*. London: Hodder & Stoughton.

Index

Abrams, Nathan 90
absurdism 80, 100, 140–1, 177
Acevedo-Muñoz, Ernesto 184
actor 1, 6, 43–4, 54 n.3, 59, 97, 120, 127, 136, 152–3, 169, 172, 191, 194–5, 197, 199, 201, 222, 232. *See also specific actors*
adaptation 14, 39, 40, 42, 69, 134, 192, 240 n.3
Adorno, Theodor 145
aesthetic criteria 88, 119
aesthetics 12, 59, 71, 96, 102, 114, 133, 138–9, 142, 144–5, 174–5, 187 n.11, 219, 225
The Affair (2014–19) 232
An Affair to Remember (1957) 155
Akerman, Chantal 8, 21, 30–1
Akhavan, Desiree 15–16, 228–9, 231, 234–5, 237–9, 240–1 n.4, 242 n.5
Alfie (1966) 77
Allen v. Farrow (2021) 2, 6, 238
Allen, Woody 1–6, 8–9, 13–16, 22, 28, 33–5, 39–40, 45–7, 53 n.2, 54 n.3, 54 n.10, 57, 60–4, 67, 70–3, 77, 95–6, 98, 110 n.1, 113, 115, 121, 128, 133–4, 136–47, 148 n.2, 151, 154, 156, 163, 164 n.1, 164 n.8, 165 n.14, 178, 187 n.10, 204–5, 209–10, 216–17, 222, 225, 227, 233–4, 237–9, 241–2 n.5
  Apropos of Nothing 6, 70
  career 40–4, 53 n.2
  cinematic art 138
  comi-tragic cosmology 139
  genome 191–3
  'Mechanical Objects' 146
  Mere Anarchy 70
  and New Hollywood 50–3
  Side Effects 70
  Standup Comic: 1964–1968 146
All in the Family (1971–1979) 69

Allio, René 21
Allison Portchnik (fictional character) 12, 124–5, 178
All the President's Men (1976) 71
Almodóvar, Pedro 10, 13, 169, 171–5, 177–8, 185–6, 186 n.5, 187 n.10
Alvy Singer (fictional character) 1, 9, 11–13, 22–5, 27–30, 35, 44, 46–7, 58–60, 61, 69, 77–82, 86, 91–3, 95–7, 99–100, 103, 105, 108–10, 113, 115, 119, 120–3, 125, 134–5, 140, 144–6, 155, 157–8, 160–1, 164 n.11, 170, 175, 178–9, 182–4, 191, 193, 195–6, 199, 204–6, 209–12, 214, 217–18, 221, 227, 235, 238
  adult education courses 82
  aesthetic criteria for photography 88
  birthday gift to Annie 126–7
  classic Jew-hater 84
  domesticity 98
  dynamite ham 89
  intellectual authority 104
  lifestyle of California 101–2, 105
  memory 83–5, 87
  paranoid fears 84
  partiality 84
American arthouse cinema 41
American cinema 1, 7, 41, 230, 235
American Film Institute 41, 164 n.9
Amstell, Simon 77
anaclisis 116
Anderson, Wes 192
androgyny 126
Anhedonia 89, 147, 179
Anillos de oro/Wedding Rings (1984) 174
animation 78. *See also* cartoon character
Aniston, Jennifer 230
Annie Hall (1977) 1–2, 4–6, 10–11, 39, 50, 54 n.13, 57, 60–4, 68–72, 77–8, 90, 95, 99, 105, 113, 118–19, 133, 135, 138–9, 143–4, 148, 152, 155–6,

159–60, 162–4, 164 nn.8–11, 169, 171, 175, 177, 179–81, 187 n.10, 187 n.12, 191–2, 194, 199, 204–6, 209–10, 214, 227–8, 240, 240 n.4, 241 n.5, 242 n.6
 criticism 3, 180
 gay 228, 233–8
 history and reception 12
 the lobster scene 123, 125, 159–60, 183, 196–8, 210, 214, 220–1, 236
 opening titles of 58
 operational aesthetic 139
 production and release 7–8
 Spanish poster for 182
 style flashbacks 242 n.5
 success of 40–4, 162
Annie Hall (fictional character) 9–13, 15, 24–5, 28, 30, 44, 46–9, 58, 68, 78–9, 81–3, 88, 91–3, 97, 99–100, 102, 104–5, 110, 115, 119, 121, 123, 125–6, 134–5, 138, 145–6, 148, 152–3, 155–7, 160–2, 164 n.11, 169–70, 175, 179–80, 182, 184–6, 195–6, 199, 204, 209–12, 214, 216, 221, 227, 235
 as Charlie Chaplin's Tramp 126
 internal monologue 158
 post-feminist torch-bearer 177–80
anti-hero 113, 147
anti-mimetic emblems 138
anti-narrative mode 128
anti-romantic comedy 10, 181. *See also* romantic comedy
antisemitism 120, 222
Appropriate Behavior (2014) 11, 15, 228, 240–1 n.4, 241–2 n.5
 break-up narratives 229–33
 critical reception 233–8
 Maxine (fictional character) 228–9, 235, 237–9, 241 n.5
 Shirin (fictional character) 228–9, 234–9, 241 n.5
Arquette, Patricia 199
arthouse cinema 14, 41, 57, 74
artistic development 20, 47
art nouveau 61, 68
assemblage 139
attachment theory 202

auteur apologism 239–40
auteur film 1, 62, 64, 184, 239
auteur-structuralism 22, 34
auteur theory 9
authorship 8, 20, 22–3, 44, 47, 64, 81
autobiographical reading 1, 9, 35, 47, 96
autofiction 77, 92
'Automatic Suicide Device for Unlucky Stock Speculators' 140
avant-garde film 31
average shot length (ASL) 29

Babington, Bruce 177–8
Baby Boom (1987) 162–3
 J. C. Wiatt (fictional character) 162–3
Bacon, Henry 154, 156
Bailey, Jason 179
Bailey, Peter 138–9
Bananas (1971) 42, 61–2, 141
Bancroft, Anne 40
Banes, Sally 213
Bass, Saul 61
Bataille, Georges, *Story of the Eye* 193
Bates, Sandy 143
battle of the sexes 165 n.13
Battlestar Galactica (1978) 71
Bauer, Dale 146
Baumbach, Noah 192, 209, 213, 215, 220–2, 224–5, 231
Beatty, Warren 49
Beekman Movie Theater 115
Before Midnight (2013) 191, 194–5, 198, 201, 206
Before Sunrise (1995) 14, 191, 193–7, 199, 201, 206
 Celine and Jesse (fictional characters) 193–9, 201, 203–6
Before Sunset (2004) 191, 195–6, 199, 201, 206
Begin Again (2013) 227, 231, 240 n.3
Benguiat, Ed 63, 70–1
Benjamin, Jessica 211
Bergman, Ingmar 62, 81
Berman, Contra 136
Berman, Judy 135
Berry, William Turner, *Encyclopedia of Type Faces* 67
Bersani, Leo 116, 128

248   Index

Between the Lines (1977) 21
Bhabha, Homi 12, 114, 117–18, 121, 126, 128
    iterative process 119
    performativity and doubling 117–18
Biale, David 124
Billy Two Hats (1974) 69
biographical film 9, 98
The Bisexual (2018) 231, 241 n.4
Björkman, Stig 58, 62
black-and-white films 220–1
blackness, representation of 222
Blake, James 66
Bloom, Kath 197
Blue Valentine (2010) 227, 230
Bond, James 42, 61
Boyhood (2014) 199, 201–3
    Mason and Samantha (fictional characters) 200, 202–3
boy-meets-girl narrative 26, 179
Bradshaw, Peter 203
breaking of the fourth wall 77, 180, 183, 205
Breaking Upwards (2009) 230
The Break-Up (2006) 230
break-up narratives 13, 227–33, 238
Breathless 194
Brenneman, Brianne Jewett 154, 156, 165 n.14
Brickman, Marshall 1, 136–7, 156
Bringhurst, Robert, *Elements of Typographical Style* 68
Brinkema, Eugenie 199
British Film Institute 1
Broadway Danny Rose (1984) 64
Butler, Judith 117, 119

Cahiers du cinéma journal 21
Caine, Michael 77
Callery, Dymphna 216
Call Me By Your Name (2017) 240 n.2
cameo 14, 58, 99, 124, 195
camp 125, 174, 191
camp pop comedy 185
canned laughter 13, 122–3. *See also* fake laughter
capsule synopsis 228

Carney, John 231, 240 n.3
Carroll, Kathleen 48
cartoon 61, 119, 141, 143, 205
cartoon character 119, 205. *See also* animation
Casablanca (1942) 42, 45
Casino Royale (1967) 42
Cavell, Stanley 12, 95–6, 103–6, 108
Celebrity (1998) 209, 220–1
celebrity persona 238
Century Schoolbook typeface 62
Chalamet, Timothée 6
Chaplin, Charlie 5, 126, 141, 143, 216–17
    'Billows Feeding Machine' 141
character 1, 5, 9, 12, 15, 22, 24–5, 29–30, 44–8, 51, 53, 67, 83, 96–102, 105–6, 110, 113, 120, 145, 152–3, 192–3, 205–6, 216, 234, 241 n.4. *See also specific characters*
    character-actor-star paradigm 152
    costume and 185
    development 172
    signs of 152, 156–7, 159, 175
    stars and 152–4, 163
chick flick genre 240 n.1
childhood memory 27, 86, 88, 102, 120, 195, 206
Chion, Michel 62, 71
    Words on Screen 62
choreography 209, 215, 217–18
chorus line 142
Cianfrance, Derek 230
Cimino, Michael 71
cinema of attractions 114–15, 128
CinemaScore 52
cinematic experience 20, 27–33, 70
cinematic memory 8, 33–6, 221
    as past/present register 35
cinematic valentine 48
cinephilia 20, 26
circulation and consumption 33
City Slickers (1991) 69, 71
CK, Louis 233
classical cinema 10, 14, 24, 29, 79, 128, 187 n.11. *See also* classical Hollywood
classical Hollywood 23, 79, 95, 103, 155, 192, 221. *See also* classical cinema

concealed artistry 79
class, representation of 3, 172, 221
Cleopatra (1963) 50
Close Encounters of the Third Kind (1978) 71
close-up shot 161, 171, 215
closing shot 30
clothing 46, 49, 152, 156–7, 163, 164 n.9, 169–70, 172–5, 177–8, 186 n.5, 187 n.9, 216, 220. *See also* costume; dress; fashion
the clown 216–17
Cobb, Shelley 240 n.1
Cocteau, Jean 172, 186
Coffin, Leslie 237
collective assemblage of enunciation 139
comedian comedy 178–9, 181
comedy film 26, 45, 52, 155, 160. *See also* romantic comedy
comedy of remarriage 45
comedy of the sexes 157
comic cynicism 12, 96–7
coming-of-age film 202
comi-tragedy 138–9. *See also* tragi-comedy
commercial cinema 40–1, 64, 156, 160
compulsory heteronormativity 15, 229, 238
Computer Opticals 62, 64
conscious uncoupling 228, 233
consumer culture 60
consumer medium and commodity 60, 74
"Contemporary Crisis in Western Man"! 134
'cool' media 14, 59–60
Cooper Black typeface 62
Coppola, Francis Ford 72–3
costume 10, 126, 156, 169–70, 173–5, 177–8, 184–5, 186 n.6, 216
Cowie, Peter 1–2
Crimes and Misdemeanors (1989) 70, 145
  Lester (fictional character) 145
Crist, Judith 48
Cuarón, Alfonso 73
cultural memory 8, 35–6
cultural stereotype 12, 114, 124–5

Curry, Renée R. 3, 222
The Curse of the Jade Scorpion (2001) 70

Daly, Ann 212
dance 15, 210–15, 218, 221, 223, 225
  hetero-choreography 215
  spectatorship 214
  theory 210, 213, 215
Dargis, Manohla 192
Davis, Johanna, *Life Signs* 40
Dawson, Nick 228
Days of Hope (1975) 21
dead time 201, 205
de Certeau, Michel 215
Deconstructing Harry (1997) 110 n.1, 140
Dederer, Claire 4
Deleuze, Gilles, *A Thousand Plateaus* 139–40
Deleyto, Celestino 113
Delpy, Julie 191, 193, 197, 199
de Man, Paul 116–17, 119
DeMille, Cecil B. 151
Denby, David 194
Der Witz 117, 128. *See also* Freud, Sigmund
Descartes, René 103
desire, representation of 13, 32–3, 100, 102, 116, 124, 133–4, 138–42, 144, 146, 157, 161, 163, 180–1, 185, 212–13, 225
Devroye, Luc 65
Diane-as-Annie spectrum 156
The Dick Cavett Show 115
diegesis 79, 97, 99, 100, 102, 106, 109, 119, 122, 235
disability
  representation of 7
  studies 7, 217
distraction 114, 125, 129, 143
Ditter, Christian 231
Doane, Mary Ann 123–4, 126–7
Doctor Zhivago (1965) 50
Donne, John, 'A Valediction: forbidding Mourning' 204
Don't Drink the Water (1969) 43
Dowse, Michael 231
dramatic role 39, 163

dress 10, 125, 135, 158, 164 n.9, 169–70, 173–5, 178. *See also* clothing; costume; fashion
Duane Hall (fictional character) 109
Duck Soup (1933) 141
Due, Reidar 11–12
Dunham, Lena 192, 233, 235, 242 n.5
Dutoit, Ulysse 116, 128
Duvall, Shelley 69
Dyer, Richard, *Stars* 152–4, 156. *See also* female star; male star; star
Dynasty (1981–9) 173–4

early cinema 113–14, 122, 128, 151
Edinburgh International Film Festival (EIFF77) 8, 19, 30
  Edinburgh Magazine 20–1
  'History/Production/Memory' event 19, 21–2
  little books 20
Educating Rita (1983) 134
Edwards, Gwynne 171
Ehrlich, David 237
Elkin, Lauren 215, 223
ellipsis 12, 201
Ellis, Jonathan 11, 13–15
Elsner+Flake 64
embodied form 10, 29
embodied spectatorship 8, 27–8
end credits 68, 183
Ermarth, Elizabeth 117
Escape to Witch Mountain (1975) 71
establishing shot 29
Esta noche/Tonight (1981–2) 184
Eternal Sunshine of the Spotless Mind (2004) 227
ethics 101–6, 118
ethics of speech 101–6
European art cinema 27, 29
Evanier, David 53 n.2
Evans, Peter William 177–8
Everything You Always Wanted to Know About Sex/But Were Afraid to Ask (1972) 42, 61–2, 142
extra-diegetic reception 122, 199

Fabe, Marilyn 25
Face to Face (1976) 81

failure 11, 24, 28, 45, 82, 90–1, 97, 137, 139, 196, 209–11, 216–19, 225
fake laughter 122–3. *See also* canned laughter
Falcon Crest (1982–90) 174
family drama 52
fan fiction 193
Farrow, Dylan 1–2, 4–6, 148 n.2, 164 n.1
Farrow, Mia 2, 5, 151
Farrow, Moses 5
Farrow, Ronan 6
fascism 117
fashion 9, 49, 73, 136, 152–3, 156, 169, 171, 173, 177–8. *See also* clothing; costume; dress
Fast & Furious 164 n.3
Faulkner, William, *The Reivers* 69
Feldstein, Richard 180
Fellini, Federico 58–9, 119
female
  audience 40, 48, 50
  desire 161, 184, 213, 225
  ensemble comedy 52
  flâneur 215
  friendship 181, 209–10
female star 40, 50–1, 53, 159. *See also* Dyer, Richard, *Stars*; male star; star)
feminine ignorance 133
feminine knowing 136
feminine not-knowing 12–13, 133, 136, 142–8
femininity 49, 135, 174, 175, 185, 187, 215, 224
feminism 165 n.14, 170, 175, 210. *See also* second wave feminism
feminist filmmaker 2–3
feminist film theory 174, 213
feminist icon 10
feminist lawyer 174, 177
fetishism 116, 119, 126–9
film(s). *See also specific films*
  appreciation 20, 25
  authorship (*see* authorship)
  canon 7, 27, 239–40
  criticism 3, 16, 19–20, 174, 180
  culture 16, 19–22, 50, 53, 102, 162, 230, 235, 239, 241 n.4
  cycle 230

gaze 15, 212, 214
genre 8, 10, 20, 22, 25–7, 52–3, 78, 155–7, 161, 181–3, 185, 192, 205, 237, 242 n.6
influence 2, 6–7, 10, 12, 14–16, 72, 77, 193, 209–10, 229
star 9, 35, 42–3, 49, 53, 98, 122, 137, 151–3, 159, 184, 233
studies 7, 19–21, 25, 27, 33, 95
theory 19–22, 28, 116, 174, 213
film history 7–8, 16, 20–1, 27, 33–6, 50, 162, 239–40
revisionist 8, 33
filmic space 28, 199
filmic wrappings 113
Filmmaker magazine 228
film narrative 8, 10, 20, 22–5, 83, 88, 97, 99, 113–14, 133, 144, 230. *See also* intra-diegetic narrative
plot and 23–5
The First Wives Club (1996) 161–2
Firth, Colin 6
Fitzgerald, Wayne 71, 73
5x2 (2004) 87
Flames (2017) 230
flâneuse 216, 223
flashback 15, 78, 80, 82, 86, 90, 92–3, 97, 115, 120, 125, 127, 205, 214, 228–9, 235–6, 238, 241–2 n.5
Flashdance (1983) 52
Fleabag (2016–19) 77
Fonda, Jane 40, 51
Font Review Journal 68
Footloose (1984) 71
Ford, Ford Madox 78–9, 86
formalist pleasure 139
Foucault, Michel 21
The 400 Blows/Les quatre cents coups (1959) 223
Four Films of Woody Allen (1982) 74 n.2
Fox, Julian 53 n.2
Frances Ha (2012) 11, 13, 15, 209–11, 213–25
Frances (fictional character) 15, 209–11, 213–24
Lev (fictional character) 209, 218–20, 224
self-critiquing process 214

Sophie (fictional character) 209–10, 215, 217–18
Freeman, Hadley 151
French cinema 10, 73, 230
The French Connection (1971) 51
Frere-Jones, Tobias 57
Freud, Sigmund 11–13, 25, 107, 114, 118, 122, 124, 133, 224
Der Witz 117, 128
narcissism, theory of 106–7
sexuality, theory of 107
Three Essays on the Theory of Sexuality 116
The Front (1976) 42, 54 n.8
Fujita, S. Neil 72–3
Fuller, Sam 20, 22
Funny Lady (1975) 71

gag film 26, 96, 99, 133, 139, 141
gangster film 25
Gatti, Juan 171
gaze theory 211–13. *See also* male gaze
Gehring, Wes 227
gender
gendered authority 105
performance 175
politics 170, 185, 194
representation of 3, 7, 121, 123–4, 126, 235, 237
Gerwig, Greta 6, 192, 209, 221–2, 225
Gill, Eric 70–1, 74
Gilliatt, Penelope 48
Gilman, Sander 124
Gilmore Girls (2000–2007) 192–3
gimmick theory 142
Girgus, Sam B. 4–5, 138, 184
Gittell, Noah 61
Glitre, Kathrina 165 n.13
The Godfather (1972) 1, 45–6, 51, 71, 115, 151, 158
cast of 72–4
opening titles of 73
The Godfather, Part II (1974) 45–6, 51, 151–2, 158
cast of 72–4
Goldberg, Rube 12, 133, 140–1, 144, 146
'The Inventions of Professor Lucifer G. Butts' 140

Gorbaty, Norman 62
Gothic typeface 72
Grandma's House (2010–12) 77
graphic design 61, 63
Grease (1978) 52
The Great Waldo Pepper (1975) 69
Grindon, Leger 26
Guadagnino, Luca 240 n.2
The Guardian newspaper 5, 64, 151, 203
Guattari, Félix, *A Thousand Plateaus* 139–40
Gunning, Tom 114, 128, 139

Habermas, Jürgen 104–5, 106, 108
   Theory of Communicative Action 104
Hachette Book Group 6
Haidegger, Ingrid 68
Halberstam, Jack 210, 211, 218
   The Queer Art of Failure 15, 210
Hale, Sonnie 35
Hall, Martin R., *Women in the Work of Woody Allen* 3
Hall, Sheldon 53 n.1
Hamad, Hannah 13, 15–16
Hamlisch, Marvin 61
Hample, Stuart, *Inside Woody Allen* 143
Hampstead (2017) 152, 158
   Donald Horner (fictional character) 158
   Emily Walters (fictional character) 158–9
Hannah and Her Sisters (1986) 3, 43, 65
   opening titles of 65
Hannington, Jessica 11, 13, 15
Hansen, Miriam 122
haptic visuality 27–8
Harrison, Rebecca 7
Harry and Walter Go to New York (1976) 45
Hassenger, Jesse 236
Haussegger, Virginia 165 n.15
Hawaii (1966) 50
Hawke, Ethan 191, 197, 203
Heath, Stephen 116, 128
Heaven's Gate (1980) 69, 71
Heck, Bethany 68–70
Hegel, Georg Wilhelm Friedrich 103
Heidegger, Martin, pragmatic philosophy 103

Hepburn, Katherine 159
Herman, Woody 63
hermeneutic reading 95
heteronormative storyline 211, 224
heteronormative time 219
heteronormativity 15, 210, 218–19, 229, 238
heterosexual break-up 185, 210
heterosexual love 157, 175, 209, 211, 223
Hill, George Roy 69
Hirsch, Foster 135, 194
historical drama 42, 52, 153
historical epic 49–50
Hitchcock, Alfred 61, 135
Hollywood 6, 20, 50–1, 53, 95, 151, 155, 157, 230, 240 n.1
   blacklist 42
   cinema 20–1, 40, 79, 95, 103, 221
   community 43
   ending 91, 178, 183, 205
   Foreign Press 151
   melodramas 175
   Renaissance 50
Hollywood Ending (2002) 65
Horton, Russell 59
'hot' media 14, 59–60, 68, 71, 74
How to Be Single (2016) 227, 231
humane typography 74
humour 58, 79–80, 82, 113, 124, 137, 177, 238
Hunt, Randy J 63
Husbands and Wives (1992) 192
Hutcheon, Linda 14, 114, 121
   A Theory of Adaptation 192

Ideal Ego 107–8
ingénue 82
Instituto de la Mujer (The Women's Institute) 177
intercultural romance 229, 232, 234, 237
Interiors (1978) 43, 49–50, 62
intermediality 122
International Typeface Corporation (ITC) 63
intertextuality 7, 27, 116
intertextual memory 89–91
In the Move for Love (2018) 230
intradiegetic narrative 87, 109. *See also* film narrative

irony 69, 79, 99, 116, 137, 147
iteration 9, 116, 118–19, 121, 128
I Wanna Hold Your Hand (1978) 71
I Will, I Will ... For Now (1976) 45

Jackie Brown (1997) 63
Jeffers McDonald, Tamar 155, 164 n.10
Jermyn, Deborah 155, 157
Jessup, Florence Redding 177
the Jewish American Princess (JAP) 124
Jewishness (Jewish)
  identificatory process 117, 128
  joke 113, 118
  representation of 117, 124, 220
  sexuality 124
  women, representation of 12, 124–5, 128, 147
The Johnny Carson Show 115
Johnston, Ruth D. 11–13
joke-work 11–12, 102, 113, 119, 123
  anaclisis 116
  central mechanisms 118
  as cinematic self-critical discourse 114
  dirty joke 124
  iterative process 121
  Jewish joke 113, 118
  parody and 117
  postmodernism 114–15, 128
  tendentious self-critical 118, 128
  uncertainty of truth 121
Julia (1977) 40, 51
Jungermann, Ingrid 228

Kael, Pauline 3
Kafer, Alison 217
Kang, Inkoo 237
Kant, Immanuel 103
Keaton, Buster 141, 143
Keaton, Diane 1–2, 5, 9–10, 13, 35, 39–40, 54 nn.10–13, 72, 115, 137, 145, 148, 148 n.2, 151–8, 162–3, 164 n.2, 164 nn.8–9, 165 n.14, 169, 181, 184–6, 187 n.9, 193, 238
  career 40, 44–9
  and New Hollywood 50–3
  performance traits 158
  rom-com career 159, 163
  Then Again 164 n.2, 165 n.16, 227
Kennedy, Sarah 12–13

kinaesthetic perception 28
King, Barry 153
King, Rob 145
Kinski, Klaus, *All I Need Is Love* 193
Kirkwood, William 65
Klapp, O. E. 154
Klein, Amanda Ann 230
Klevan, Andrew 158
Klinenberg, Eric 232
Knight, Christopher 81–2, 84, 87, 134–5, 194
Knightley, Keira 231
Kracauer, Seigfried 114
Krämer, Peter 9, 187 n.10
Kramer vs. Kramer (1979) 52
Kristeva, Julia 21
Krutnik, Frank 113, 157–8, 187 n.11
Kuhn, Annette 7–11

Lacan, Jacques 21, 113
Lacoue-Labarthe, Philippe 128
  'The Jewish People Don't Dream' 117
Lahr, John 146
Lambert-Beatty, Carrie 212, 214
Lanza, Joseph 140
L'Arroseur arrosé/The Waterer Watered/The Sprinkler Sprinkled (1895) 139
laughter 13, 26, 122–3, 125, 177, 179, 216
Lauren, Ralph 126
La voix humaine/The Human Voice (1930) 172, 175
La voz humana/The Human Voice (2020) 186
Lax, Eric 53 n.2
Lee, Jason 16 n.2
Lee, Sander 93
Let's Just Say It Wasn't Pretty (2014) 164 n.2
Lim, Dennis 191
Linklater, Richard 14–15, 192–205. See also Before trilogy
Li, Yiyun 196
Lloyd, Harold 141
Lobalzo Wright, Julie 9
logotype 63, 71–3
Lombard, Carole 159
long take 15, 29, 31, 57, 203
Looking for Mr. Goodbar (1977) 39, 46–7, 49, 163

Los Angeles 28, 83, 91–2, 101, 122, 164 n.12, 183, 204, 218, 231
Los Angeles Film Critics Association 41
The Los Angeles Times newspaper 4, 6
Love and Death (1975) 42, 45–6, 61–2
Lovers and Other Strangers (1970) 45
Lubitz, Rachel 236
Lumière brothers 139
Lyne, Adrian 71

machinic assemblage 139
machismo 177
MacLaine, Shirley 40
Magic in the Moonlight (2014) 151
male audience 239
male buddy films 51
male filmmaker 15, 234
male gaze 176, 211–13. *See also* gaze theory
male star 9, 40, 42–3, 50, 53. *See also* Dyer, Richard, *Stars*; female star; star
Malick, Terrence 200
Manguso, Sarah 15, 200, 202
  Ongoingness: The End of a Diary 200–1, 203
Manhattan (1979) 4, 42–3, 49–50, 52–3, 62, 68, 134, 135–6, 143, 147, 194, 209, 216, 220, 223
  Isaac (fictional character) 216, 223–4
  Mary (fictional character) 216, 224
  Tracy (fictional character) 4, 134, 223–4
Manhattan Murder Mystery (1993) 135, 145
Manic-Pixie-Dream-Girl 9, 154
mansplaining 135
Marchand, Philip, *Marshall McLuhan: The Medium and the Messenger* 74 n.1
Marghitu, Stefania 239
marital reciprocity 103
Marriage Story (2019) 227, 231
Marshall, Kelli 160
Martin, Chris 233
Marvin's Room (1996) 163
Marx Brothers 141, 143
Marx, Groucho 82, 90, 115, 125, 133
Marxist theory 137
Mary Poppins (1966) 50

masculine perspective 84, 211
masculinist film culture 239
Maslin, Janet 47–8
masquerade 126, 129, 175, 186, 186–7 n.8, 187 n.11
Master of None (2015–17) 228, 232, 240 n.2
masturbation 143
Matthews, Jessie 35
Maura, Carmen 172, 184–6
McBride, Eimear, *The Lesser Bohemians* 70
McDonald, Paul 152–3, 156
McLean, Adrienne L. 213
McLuhan, Marshall 13–14, 58, 68, 71, 74, 74 n.1, 81–2, 99, 101, 119, 141–3, 147
  fallacy 58–60
  The Gutenberg Galaxy: The Making of Typographic Man 60
  The Mechanical Bride 141
  Understanding Media 14, 59–60
  visual orientation 60
McNeil, Paul, *Visual History of Type* 65, 68
McQueen, Steve 69
Meade, Marion 53 n.2
mechanical bride
  married to machine 138–42
  not-knowing girl 142–8
  Pygmalion 133–8
media studies 59
media theory 13
the 'meet cute' 26, 134
Mehlman, Jeffrey 116
melancholia 230–1, 240 n.2
melodrama 165, 178–81, 183, 185, 196, 200
memory-film 11, 91
  act of looking back 78–80
  Annie 81–3
  impressionism 78–9
  intertextual memory 89–91
  (un)reliability 83–6, 88, 91
  time 86–8
memory-object 8–9, 77
memory studies 8
memory text 8–9, 25, 77
ménage à trois relationship 11
menstruation 219

metacinematic 92, 96, 99, 180, 185
#MeToo movement 6–7, 36
Metz, Christian 21
Midnight Cowboy (1969) 51
Midsummer Night's Sex Comedy (1982) 62
Mighty Aphrodite (1995) 136, 142
Millington, Roy 66
Minnelli, Liza 40
The Miseducation of Cameron Post (2018) 241 n.4
mise en scène 7, 25, 96, 156, 199, 213, 219
misfit-hero 113
misogyny 181, 219, 240
mockumentary 42
modernism 24, 67
Modern Love (2019) 228, 232–3, 240 n.3
modern romance 229, 232
Modern Times (1936) 141
Moi, Pierre Riviere/I, Pierre Riviere (1965) 21
Monaco, James 41, 51
   American Film Now 40
   'Looking for Diane Keaton' 39–40
monologue 77–9, 89–90, 93, 99, 114, 128, 134, 157–8, 176
montage 91–3, 96, 127–8, 160, 183, 198, 218, 224
Moor, Jonathan 54 n.10
moral education 95, 103
moral subjectivity 12, 95, 103–4
Moretti, Nanni 192
Morley, Ruth 156, 184
Mortimer, Claire 184
mourning 86, 196, 204, 229, 231–2
Movie Review Query Engine (MRQE) 240–1 n.4
movie star 43, 49
'Mrs. Uptight' ('The Good Woman') 154, 161
Mujeres al borde de un ataque de nervios/Women on the Verge of a Nervous Breakdown (1988) 11, 169–70, 173, 175, 177–8, 181, 184–5, 187 n.10
   Candela (fictional character) 173
   Carlos (fictional character) 175
   Iván (fictional character) 170, 172, 175–7, 183

Lucía (fictional character) 177
Marisa (fictional character) 176
Paulina Morales (fictional character) 173, 177
Pepa (fictional character) 169–74, 175–7, 181, 183–6, 186 n.1, 186 n.5
'Puro Teatro'/Pure Theatre song 181, 183
'Soy infeliz'/I am unhappy song 181
Mulvey, Laura 211–13. *See also* gaze theory
musical 50, 52, 195
Myers, Nancy 155
My Fair Lady (1964) 50–1, 134

Nancy, Jean-Luc 128
'The Jewish People Don't Dream' 117
Nannicelli, Ted 153, 156
narcissism 11–12, 95, 145
   as authority 107–8
   authority and assertion 108–10
   ethics of speech 101–6
   forms of authority 95–9
   hermeneutic method 95
   as narration 99–101
national cinema 10, 184
national identity 186 n.7
National Society of Film Critics 41, 49
Negra, Diane 240 n.1
neo-traditional romantic comedy 164 n.6, 164 n.10, 230–1
nervous romance 44–5, 133, 146, 148 n.1, 157–9, 181
Netflix, 'skip credits' feature 61
neurosis 11, 24, 139, 145, 161
New Cinema History 33
New Hollywood 50
   Allen, Keaton and 50–3
News from Home (1977) 8, 21, 30–1
   about New York 31
   mother-daughter relationship 32
   street shot 32
New York City 1, 3, 15, 28–32, 47, 90, 92, 102, 127, 155, 183, 222–4, 231, 235
   girls 82, 160
   Jew 96
   mandarin cultural establishment 98
   nostalgia 102, 209, 222, 225

New York Film Critics 41, 49
New York Magazine, 'Doomed Earth Catalog' 70
New York Times newspaper 4–6, 41, 48, 192, 232
    Dylan Farrow's open letter 4–6
    'The Hall-Mark of the Annie Look' 48–9
NexisUK 240–1 n.4
Ngai, Sianne 142
Nine to Five (1980) 52
Nine 1/2 Weeks (1986) 71
non-chronological 144
non-classical cinema 10, 24, 83. *See also* non-Classical Hollywood
non-Classical Hollywood 24. *See also* non-classical cinema
non-linear structure 235
Norman, Phill 61
nostalgia 11, 14–15, 68–70, 73, 79, 87–8, 102, 155–6, 158, 163, 164 n.6, 183, 199, 204–5

Oedipal complex 107, 223–4
O'Falt, Chris 236
An Officer and a Gentleman (1982) 52
O'Gieblyn, Meghan 143
Old Hollywood 73, 221. *See also* classical cinema; classical Hollywood
O'Malley, Sheila 236
One Flew Over the Cuckoo's Nest (1975) 51
ongoingness 15, 200–1, 203
On Golden Pond (1981) 52
Ong, Walter 60, 71
opening credits 57, 171, 179, 218
opening title 57–8, 60, 65, 72–3
Ophuls, Marcel 81, 90
Ordinary People (1980) 52
'outburst' scene 161
Out of Africa (1985) 52
Ozon, François 87

Pacino, Al 72
Paltrow, Gwyneth 233
parody 42, 45, 114, 146
    and joke-work 117
passing through, idea of 193–9
patriarchy 7, 13, 173–5, 177, 180, 185, 186 n.5, 210–13, 218–19

Patton (1970) 51
Paul, Kit 63–4
Pechey, Eleisha 64–7, 73
Pellegrini, Ann 124
People magazine 5, 46
performance cue 158
performance/performativity 9, 27, 43, 46, 48–9, 88, 95, 103, 106, 108, 113–15, 117–19, 121–3, 152–3, 156–63, 165 n.16, 169, 187 n.11, 216
Perri, Dan 71
Peterson, Lowell 5
Petulia (1968) 41
photography 8, 64, 87–8, 114, 119, 196, 214, 219–20
Photo-Lettering Inc (PLINC) 63
The Pink Panther (1963) 61
Planet of the Apes (1968) 63, 71
Platoon (1986) 71
Play It Again, Sam (1972) 42, 45, 54 n.8, 138, 151, 164 n.7
Polley, Sarah 231
Porter, Cole 61
post-apocalyptic comedy 137
Post-Classical Hollywood 155. *See also* non-classical cinema; non-Classical Hollywood
post-feminist 173, 177–80
postmodernism 114–15, 117–18, 128
post-Second World War era 124
pragmatic philosophy 103
Prell, Riv-Ellen 124
Previn, Soon-Yi 2, 4
problematic comedy 128, 178
proprioceptive perception 28
psychoanalysis 11, 21, 100, 107
psychoanalytical reading 11
The Purple Rose of Cairo (1985) 140
Puzo, Mario 72–3
Pygmalion 180, 194
Pygmalion (1913) 134
    Henry Higgins (fictional character) 134
    Pygmalion-syndrome 135
Pygmalion story 82, 133–8, 180, 194

Quart, Leonard 221
queer art 15, 210
queer intercultural relationship 228–9, 234, 238

queer minority 238
queerness 234
queer theory 239
queer women of colour 15, 222, 234, 238
'Quiero la Noche' song 61
Quigley Publications 43, 49, 51, 53, 54 n.6

race, representation of 3, 7, 124
Radio Days (1987) 79
Radio Times magazine 152
Rapf, Joanna E. 3, 181
realism 79, 171, 174, 179, 185, 198, 222
reception 2–3, 8, 12, 15, 25, 34, 41, 48–9, 53, 122–3, 126, 128, 229, 233–8
reception studies 33–5
Redford, Robert 69, 115
Redgrave, Vanessa 40
Reds (1981) 49
revisionist film history 8, 33
Ricoeur, Paul 11
  Freud and Philosophy 106–7
Riddles of the Sphinx (1977) 21
Riviere, Joan 175
Rob (fictional character) 29, 69, 79–80, 84, 120, 122, 191, 222
Robin (fictional character) 80, 82, 160
Rocky (1976) 52
Rogowsky, Scott 228
'A Rollercoaster Named Desire' 140
Rolling Stone magazine 69
romantic comedy 9–11, 16, 24–7, 42, 50, 52, 77, 152–3, 155–63, 164 n.6, 178, 181, 183, 192, 205, 236–7, 242 n.6
  revisionism 230
  and self-representation 9
romantic drama 52, 164 n.10, 230
romantic ending 81, 181
romantic innocence 12, 96
romantic love 48, 93, 174, 179, 181, 204, 209, 218, 240 n.2
romantic narrative 235
romantic nostalgia 11, 79
Rose, Margaret 117
Rosenblum, Ralph 87, 89, 91–2
  pieces of film 93
Rossner, Judith, *Looking for Mr. Goodbar* 39
Rowe, Kathleen 179
Rube-Goldberg machine 140–1

Running Late With Scott Rogowsky 228
Rydell, Mark 69

Sánchez-Arce, Ana María 10, 13, 187 n.10
San Filippo, Maria 228, 230–1
  destigmatizing of the breakup 233
Sarris, Andrew 48
Sartre, Jean-Paul, *Being and Nothingness* 109–10
Saturday Night Fever (1977) 52
Scannell, Paddy 58
Schatz, Thomas 79, 89
Schickel, Richard 47
schlemiel 92, 113, 124, 141, 179
Scott, A. O. 87, 192
screwball comedy 9, 159–60, 175, 181, 185
second-wave feminism 165 n.14, 173–4.
  See also feminism
Second World War 20
'Seems Like Old Times' 30, 68–70, 92, 183
Seinfeld, Jerry 233
self-consciousness 10, 26, 103
self-loathing 147, 235
'Self-Operating Napkin' machine 140
self-referentiality 138
sentimentality 53, 88, 204
sequence shot 29–30
sexual difference, representation of 116, 126, 133, 138–9
sexuality, representation of 3, 7, 107, 116, 121, 124, 187 n.11, 237
'Sexual Woman' 154
Shakespeare, William, *King Lear* 103
shared laughter 125
Shaw, George Bernard 134
shiksa 134, 147
Shingler, Martin 155
shot length 29
shot-reverse-shot 84
The Sicilian (1987) 71
sideways glance 15, 91, 198
sight gag 84
silent cinema 126, 216
Silver, Joan Micklin 21
Simon, John 54 n.13
Sinatra, Frank 85, 125
Sinyard, Neil 3
situation comedy 122
slapstick comedy 42, 141, 144

Sleeper (1973) 42, 45–6, 61–2, 136–7, 139, 141, 145, 147
   Luna Schlosser (fictional character) 137, 145, 147
   Miles Monroe (fictional character) 137
Sleepless in Seattle (1993) 155
Smith, Paul Julian 187 n.10
Snow, Michael 31
Snow White and the Seven Dwarfs (1937) 27
Something's Gotta Give (2003) 155
   Erica Berry (fictional character) 160–1, 164 n.11
   Harry (fictional character) 160–1, 164 n.11
Sontag, Susan 10, 171–4, 185
   'Notes on "Camp"' 174
   tube skirt 186 n.1
The Sorrow and the Pity (1969) 81, 90, 135, 222
Sorvino, Mira 142
The Sound of Music (1965) 51
Souvenir typeface 62–3
Spanish cinema 169–70, 182, 186
spectator 2, 8–9, 11, 13, 15, 33, 87, 99, 109, 114, 118, 121, 128, 179, 199, 205, 212, 214
speech cure 105
speech seduction 106
split screen 78, 120–1, 180, 221
stand-up comedy 42, 53 n.2, 89, 92, 108, 141
star 9–10, 35, 40, 42–3, 46, 49–51, 53, 98, 122, 137, 151–3, 159, 184. *See also* Dyer, Richard, *Stars*; female star; male star
   and characters 152–4, 163
   image 10, 152–3, 155, 184
   personification/impersonation 153
   studies 9
   vehicle 43, 155
Stardust Memories (1980) 43, 50, 53, 54 n.7, 143
A Star Is Born (1976) 52
Star Wars (1977) 34, 71
Stephenson Blake & Co. 57, 64–6, 68, 74
Stephenson, Henry 66–7
Stephenson, John 66

Stevenson, Adlai 124
Stewart Brand, *Whole Earth Catalog* 69
The Sting (1973) 51
Stone, Emma 151
Stone, Oliver 71
Stone, Rob 194–5
strange marriage 142
Streisand, Barbra 40, 51
Sturdevant, Andy 69
subjectivism 103
subtitles 12, 68, 87–8, 119, 138, 193, 196
Sundance Film Festival 241 n.4
Super Fly (1972) 63
surrealism 89
Swinton, Tilda 186
symbolic assertion 110

Take One journal 39, 51
Take the Money and Run (1969) 42, 61
Take This Waltz (2012) 227, 231
Talking as Fast as I Can (2016) 192
Tarantino, Quentin 63
Taxi Driver (1976) 71
Teachout, Terry 136
Terms of Endearment (1983) 52
therapeutic conversation 104
This Time 198
Thornham, Sue 171, 174, 185
thriller 25, 153
Thunderbolt and Lightfoot (1974) 71
Time magazine 39, 41
time travel 204–6
title card 44, 57, 62–5, 70–1
Tony Lacey (fictional character) 69, 83, 101–2, 155, 175
Tootsie (1982) 52
To Rome With Love (2012) 74 n.4
Tourneur, Jacques 20
tracking shot 29, 203, 218, 223
tragi-comedy 229. *See also* comi-tragedy
Trahair, Lisa 117
The Tree of Life (2011) 200
trompe l'oeil 113, 127
The Turning Point (1977) 40, 51
Turno de oficio/Public Defender (1986–7) 174
Twilight 203
2 Days in New York (2012) 193

2 Days in Paris (2007) 193
two-shot 29, 85, 204, 219
typeface 57, 60, 62–70, 72, 74. *See also* Windsor font/typeface
typography 14, 57, 60, 63, 68, 71, 74

uncoupling narrative 228, 230–1, 233, 235
Une femme est une Femme/A Woman is a Woman (1961) 96
uniform whiteness 15
United Artists 46, 49
universal whiteness 229, 238

Variety magazine 9, 41, 46, 49
Vaughn, Vince 230
Velikii put/The Great Way (1927) 21
Vertigo (1958) 135
Vice, Sue 8–9, 11, 13
Vietnam drama 52
visual monologue 89
voiceover 30–2, 44, 78–9, 127, 135, 185

walking-and-talking sequence 194, 203
Waller-Bridge, Phoebe 77
Walsh, Raoul 20
Waltz, Amanda 237
Warren Commission 125
WASP culture, representation of 90, 156, 221, 237
Waugh, Patricia 117
Weber, Samuel 128
the 'weepie' 25, 48
Weinstein, Harvey 2, 6
Welsch, J. T. 14
Western 25, 69, 103, 223
Whatever Works (2009) 72
What If (2013) 227, 231
What's New, Pussycat? (1965) 42–3, 61
What's Up, Tiger Lily? (1966) 53 n.3, 61–2
When Harry Met Sally (1989) 90, 155, 164 n.10, 191
whiteness, representation of 3, 15, 222, 229, 238
Williams, Richard 61
Willis, Gordon 1, 71–3

Wilson, Ruth 232
Windsor font/typeface 14, 57, 60, 62–3, 73
   abstract material features 70
   Benguiat's Caslon variant 63–4
   as 'EF Windsor' 64
   Elongated or Light Condensed styles 64–5
   history 63
   idiosyncrasies 68
   logotypes 71
   oblique axis 67
   Old Style series and 66–7
   parallel hybridity 74
   sense of nostalgia 68–70, 72
   signature 67, 73
   visual compositions 70–1, 74
Wittgenstein, Ludwig, philosophy of ordinary language 103
Wojcik, Pamela Robertson 154–5
women
   buddy films 40, 51
   filmmakers 2, 15–16, 47, 234, 240
   fragmentation and dehumanization of 171
   liberation 169–70
   lib movement 175
   misrepresentation 174
   picture 24, 49
   representations of 185, 186 n.7, 212–13
   sexuality 124
   womanhood/womanliness 136, 146, 175, 177, 186 n.8
The Women (1939) 181, 185
Women's Cinema 21
Wood, Robin, 'Rethinking Romantic Love' 197
Working Girl (1988) 173
Writers Guild of America 5, 41

You Will Meet a Tall Dark Stranger (2010) 70–1

Zemeckis, Robert 71
Zeuxis 113

www.ingramcontent.com/pod-product-compliance
Lightning Source LLC
Chambersburg PA
CBHW070025010526
44117CB00011B/1711